A history of gardening in Ireland

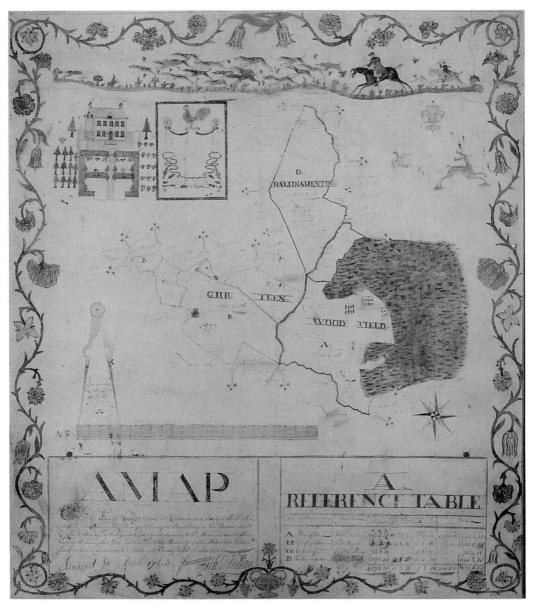

'A map of the lands of Woodfield ... Kings County ... surveyed in Aprill 1765'

A HISTORY OF GARDENING
IN IRELAND

Keith Lamb & Patrick Bowe

National Botanic Gardens
Glasnevin, Dublin
1995

The views expressed by the authors of *A history of gardening in Ireland*
do not necessarily reflect those of the National Botanic Gardens, Glasnevin.

The National Botanic Gardens, Glasnevin, gratefully acknowledges the
co-operation of
William Proby Esq., Elton Hall, Peterborough, in granting permission for the
reproduction of Gabriele Ricciardelli's *View of Stillorgan House* (cover).

Editor for the National Botanic Gardens, Glasnevin
Dr E. Charles Nelson.

ISBN 0-7076-1666-2

DUBLIN
PUBLISHED BY THE STATIONERY OFFICE
for the National Botanic Gardens, Glasnevin, Dublin

To be purchased through any Bookseller, or directly from the
GOVERNMENT PUBLICATIONS SALE OFFICE
SUN ALLIANCE HOUSE
MOLESWORTH STREET, DUBLIN 2

Printed by
Brunswick Press Ltd.,

Price: £10.00

CONTENTS

COLOUR PLATES

ACKNOWLEDGEMENTS

This book, being the first attempt at an account of the history of gardening in Ireland, owes much to the help of many friends. As well as the written word, ideas have come in conversation, so it is not possible to thank all who have contributed in one way or another. We are very grateful to Dr E. C. Nelson for reading the script and for much helpful advice, and the late Aidan Brady, Director, National Botanic Gardens, for providing essential facilities, as well as Donal Synnott, the present Director.

The many others we have to thank include The Duke of Abercorn, Mr and Mrs Allott, Mr and Mrs Grove Annesley, Dr T. C. Barnard, Peter Harold-Barry, Mr and Mrs David Hutton-Bury, John Cardigan, John Colleran, Patricia Cox, Allen Crosbie, The Dowager Countess of Dunraven, Patrick Dickson, Francis-Jane French, William Garner, Daniel Gillman, The Knight of Glin, Evelyn Goodbody, Brigadier and Mrs Hickie, Mark Bence Jones, Marian Keaney, Henry McDowell, Dr Brian Morley, Cynthia O'Connor, The O'Donovan, The Hon. Thomas Pakenham, Rosemary Porter, Sean Rafferty, Dr David Robinson, The Earl of Rosse, Maura Scannell, Kathleen Venderberghe, The late Viscount de Vesci, Jeremy Williams, and Ruth Brennan.

We thank Helen Lamb and Nicola Gordon Bowe for their patient forbearance during the disruptions of home life caused by the preparation of this book. Thanks are due also to Henry Lamb for correction of detail in Chapter 1.

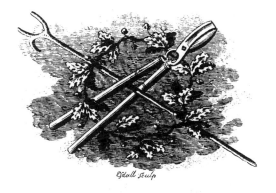

1. *Arbutus unedo*, strawberry tree; a portrait by Deborah Lambkin, commissioned to celebrate the bicentenary of the National Botanic Gardens, Glasnevin, 1995.

THE NATURAL SETTING AND THE EARLY YEARS OF IRISH GARDENING

In most of the mountains of Galway and Mayo grows an elegant sort of heath bearing large thyme-leaves, a spike of fair purple flowers like some Campanula, and viscous stalks.[1]

These words record one of the earliest references to an Irish wild flower well known to gardeners and botanists – St Dabeoc's heath (*Daboecia cantabrica*) (Plate 2). The finder, about 1700, was Edward Lhuyd.[2] The specimens he gathered so long ago are still preserved in The Natural History Museum in London.

There are several other flowers wild in Ireland which are valued in gardens. A brief discussion of some of these forms a useful introduction to the features of the Irish environment that are so favourable to the cultivation of species introduced from distant lands. St Dabeoc's heath itself is one of three heathers that are today found elsewhere only in south-west Europe, the others being Irish heath (*Erica erigena* formerly known as *E. mediterranea*) and Mackay's heath (*E. mackaiana*). Other native plants which have a southern distribution in Europe include the strawberry tree of Killarney (*Arbutus unedo*) (Plate 1), once carved into souvenirs for the Victorian tourist, the Irish spurge (*Euphorbia hyberna*), conspicuous enough to be seen from the train by travellers on the way to Cork, and a saxifrage (*Saxifraga spathularis*) rather like the London-pride of gardens. With these may be included two ferns which in the world context are temperate and tropical in their distribution. One of these, the Killarney fern (*Trichomanes speciosum*), suffered severely from plundering during the fashion for cultivating ferns in Victorian times. The other is the maidenhair fern (*Adiantum capillus-veneris*), more familiar as it is less exacting in its cultural requirements.

The occurrence of these plants underlines the mildness of the Irish climate, the coasts being washed by the North Atlantic Drift (in common parlance, the Gulf Stream) and the winds coming for much of the year from the south-west, moisture-laden and relatively warm. In contrast, there occurs a group of plants which elsewhere are regarded as alpine, or even arctic, such as moss campion (*Silene acaulis*), purple saxifrage (*Saxifraga oppositifolia*) and mountain avens (*Dryas octopetala*) which are familiar plants of the far north of Europe and in the Alps are accompanied by Spring gentian (*Gentiana verna*), so characteristic of The Burren region of County Clare.

There is a third group of plants, less important horticulturally, which grow on both sides of the Atlantic, but in Europe are found mainly in Ireland, a few extending to Scotland and beyond. Quite well known in gardens is the blue-eyed grass (*Sisyrinchium angustifolium*). The others include two orchids and two aquatic plants found in the western lakes.

Much more could be written of our native plants and their distribution, but these groups, containing several plants of interest to the gardener, show how varied in origin is our flora and how accommodating are conditions in Ireland for plants of diverse requirements. Many are survivors from times when the climate was more favourable to them; today they still live here, though often restricted to especially favourable locations. The Killarney fern, however, associated so much with the mild south-west, has or had outlying stations in Tipperary, Wicklow, Limerick and Donegal. So, correspondingly, gardens notable for their rare and often tender plants occur not only in the south-west (Fota and Ilnacullin (Fig. 1), County Cork; Rossdohan, County Kerry) but also in the east (Mount Usher, County Wicklow; Malahide, County Dublin; Rowallane, County Down) and in the north (Glenveagh and Mulroy, County Donegal).

These native plants of diverse origin indicate past changes in the landscape and climate of Ireland. The Ice Age did not end in an uninterrupted return to warmer conditions. The last ice sheet melted away about 14,000 years ago, although glacial climatic conditions returned in a shorter cold snap about 10,000 to 11,000 years ago. By studying plant remains preserved in peat and in lake sediments, scientists have been able to follow the corresponding changes in vegetation. The cold stages favoured an Arctic-alpine flora in unglaciated southernmost Ireland and on isolated mountain tops. Some of these plants still grow in Ireland today, but are rare and restricted to special localities, such as mountain cliffs or the stony country of The Burren. Their former widespread distribution is proved by the remains found in several lowland sites. In County Fermanagh, for example, evidence was found of the former occurrence of mountain avens, mountain willow (*Salix herbacea*) and purple saxifrage. Even in the south-west, now so mild and humid, plants typical of colder climates were once common.[3]

As milder conditions continued to develop over Europe the Arctic-alpine plants retreated northwards or towards the higher mountains. These plants were succeeded by a more grassy and herbaceous vegetation, followed by a

1: Ilnacullin, County Cork. Warm seas but shelter needed for garden plants. (Reproduced by permission of the Commissioners of Public Works in Ireland).

succession of shrubs and trees, culminating over much of the country in dense woodland. Some of these trees and shrubs, such as juniper, willow, alder, hazel, holly, yew, ash, elm and oak, remain. Others such as Scots pine (*Pinus sylvestris*), Norway spruce (*Picea abies*) and *Rhododendron ponticum* (Plate 3), present during inter-glacial warm periods, have died out as true natives though all grow well when planted in Ireland today. The rhododendron, in particular, has run wild since its re-introduction in the eighteenth century. Our moist climate is shared with the western parts of Britain, and is in contrast to the more continental-type extremes of temperature that characterise the midlands and south of England. The variability of the weather in Ireland is a main topic of conversation, and comment on it almost a standard form of greeting between acquaintances.

The coastal districts are the mildest areas of the island, although studies have shown that the coastal region, as far as temperatures are concerned, comprises a strip only twelve miles (20 kilometres) wide.[4] Castlewellan, Malahide Castle, Mount Usher, Mount Congreve, Fota (Fig. 2), Illnacullin, Rossdohan and Derreen, gardens noted for the tender plants that flourish in them, are all on this coastal strip. The National Botanic Gardens at Glasnevin, near Dublin, is less than two miles (three kilometres) from the nearest salt water, but as this is an estuary, and not the open sea, the gardens are not so favourable for the cultivation of tender plants. On 12 January 1982 the temperature at

2   *Daboecia cantabrica*, St Dabeoc's heath, a specimen gathered by A. B. Lambert in County Mayo; from J. Sowerby, *English botany* (1790), plate 35.

3   *Rhododendron ponticum*, an evergreen shrub from western Asia and southern Spain, now a pestilential weed in Ireland; from *Curtis's botanical magazine* (1803), plate 650.

Syd. Edwards del   Pub. by T. Curtis S.ᵗ Geo. Crescent May 1. 1803.   F. Sansom sculp

2: *Phoenix canariensis* beside the orangery at Fota, County Cork.

Glasnevin fell to –18.5°C, a record low for Ireland. Wind, however, is a problem in establishing gardens all over Ireland. In the east, Lord Talbot de Malahide has described how winds from both east and west were one reason why he specialised in growing *Olearia* (daisy bush), many of which are tolerant of such exposure.[5] Though the gardens on the south and west coasts are spared much of the harshness of the east winds of spring, they are exposed in extreme degree to the prevailing south-west winds. The winter on our west coast has been described as a succession of westerly gales with westerly winds in between. Thus the provision of shelter is a first necessity in planting a garden.

Besides its direct influence on living things, climate is also one of the factors involved in the formation of soil from its parent material, which can be weathered rock or a surface deposit such as those left by flood water or water action. Rainfall, for instance, can leach important constituents from the upper soil, and cool, moist conditions can encourage the formation of peat. The plant cover is another factor which can influence soil development, and as soon as man started to alter the native vegetation he, too, began to affect the processes of soil formation. By cutting down deciduous woodland on the better soils Neolithic man disturbed the development of the Brown Earth, a soil type enriched by the fall, decay and recycling of forest litter. The splendid growth of trees in the arboretum at Fota, County Cork, indicates a soil of this type, and

3: *Dacrydium cupressinum* at Ilnacullin, County Cork. (Reproduced by permission of the Commissioners of Public Works in Ireland).

similar soils in counties Kilkenny, Waterford, and Cork have been known from early times to be well adapted for the growing of orchard fruits. Mount Usher, County Wicklow, also on Brown Earth soil, is well favoured compared to Illnacullin, County Cork, where the heavy rainfall has leached the shallow soil to a grey sandy loam poor in plant nutrients. Glasnevin, County Dublin, Malahide, County Dublin, and Birr, County Offaly, are restricted in the range of plants grown by the alkaline nature of their soils. The good growth in Ireland of plants from such places as New Zealand (for example *Dacrydium cupressinum*, Fig. 3, and the cabbage palms, *Cordyline australis*, and tree fern, *Dicksonia antarctica*, Fig. 4) and Chile can be attributed, however, more to the climate than to favourable soils.

The earliest people to settle in Ireland, about 8,700 years ago, found a country clothed with forests of hazel, oak, elm and pine. These people of the Mesolithic or Middle Stone Age settled in the north-east and midlands, but as they did not know how to polish stone to make tools they could not clear large areas of the forest, the home of bears and wolves. They were hunters and fishers, and collected wild plants for food. From archaeological evidence it is known that the latter included hazel nuts and the seeds of the yellow water-lily (*Nuphar lutea*),[6] plants still common in the country today.

4: Tree fern (*Dicksonia antarctica*), cabbage palms (*Cordyline australis*) and Australian gum trees (*Eucalyptus*) in Rossdohan, County Kerry.

5: *Echium pininana*, a bugloss from the Canary Islands, flowering at Mount Stewart, County Down
(Photograph by R. J. Welch, May 1933).

The next people to come, about 5,500 years ago, have a link with all subsequent cultivators of the Irish soil, for they were familiar with the problem of weeds. They were people of the Neolithic Age, mainly livestock farmers, as is shown by the abundance of cattle bones found on the sites of their dwellings. Since such cultivation as they were able to undertake was carried out with digging sticks, primitive mattocks or spades, we may regard them as forerunners of gardeners. (The plough, the symbol of true agriculture, is likely not to have arrived in Ireland until about 2,700 years ago.) By examining pollen remains in the soil it has been shown that these laboriously cultivated plots became infested with weeds such as dock, nettle and ribwort plantain.[7] When these patches of cultivated ground became exhausted and were abandoned for fresh sites, the weeds must have flourished for a time.

The Celts arrived in Ireland about the beginning of the Iron Age. Among their records we find an indication of the importance to them of various native trees and shrubs and the uses to which they put them. In the Brehon Laws they divided woody plants into four categories, with a scale of fines for their unlawful felling or lopping that varied in severity according to their importance.[8] For example, the penalty for cutting the trunk of a chieftain tree was a cow, or a heifer for cutting the limbs. The seven Chieftain trees were: oak, valued for its size, handsomeness and its pig-fattening acorns; hazel, for its nuts and for the wattles made from its branches; crab apple, for its fruit and for its bark, suitable for tanning; yew, used for making household vessels and breastplates; holly, used for making chariot shafts; ash, valued for making royal thrones and weapon shafts, and Scots pine, used in the manufacture of casks.[9] Of less value were the Commoner trees, alder, willow, birch, hawthorn, mountain ash, elm and cherry. The Peasant trees were blackthorn, elder, whitebeam, aspen, spindle, strawberry tree and 'crann fir' (probably juniper). Least regarded were the bushy trees, bracken, bog myrtle, furze, bramble, heather, broom and wild rose.[10] Valuable trees were cared for, injuries to their limbs being treated with a composition of clay, cow-dung and new milk, thus anticipating by several centuries a somewhat similar compositon invented by William Forsyth, gardener to King George III.[11] Individual trees were chosen by the Celts for elevation beyond their merely economic and medicinal significance into a different realm of social and spiritual meaning. Although the traditional association of the druid and the oak has not yet been proven beyond reasonable doubt, the tree cult is well attested, there being even a special term, *bile*, for the sacred tree. Many such great trees are referred to in the literature of the time, such as the Tree of Tortu (an ash), the Oak of Mughna, the Yew of Ross, the Bough of Daithi (an ash) and the Ash of Uisneach. It seems each tribe had its own sacred tree which stood on the site where the kings of the tribe were inaugurated. One reads sometimes in the Irish annals of a raiding party entering hostile territory and felling its enemy's sacred tree.[12]

The arrival of an established art of gardening appears to have coincided with the arrival of Christianity, for the Roman-educated followers of St Patrick brought the knowledge and skills with them. The early fathers of the Irish church, in contrast to their late medieval successors, led simple ascetic lives. Their oratories were within enclosures that were often circular, the boundaries being delineated by a ditch and a bank with a palisade of timber posts on top. The enclosure around St Columba's foundation measured approximately 140 feet in diameter.[13] St Enda of Aran himself dug the ditch around his site in 500 A.D.[14] What was grown within these enclosures? There is evidence that peas, beans and leeks were grown alongside the staple agricultural crops of wheat, oats and barley. There were apple trees and beehives. The simple diet was supplemented by wild herbs and greens collected in the surrounding woods. The Rule of St Ailbhe, a contemporary of St Patrick, stipulated that when the monks sat down to dinner, they would get 'on clean dishes herbs or roots washed in water, likewise apples and mead from the hive to the depth of a thumb'.[15] We read of the day when Maedoc of Ferns planted trees – 'sweet, well-tasted apples and proper, ripe, edible nuts' – in his garden and one of the earliest Irish lyricists, Maolan, sings of the nuts, berries, and apple trees near to his hut, of the honeysuckle and that 'strawberries are good to taste in their plenty'.[16] The annals of the monastery of Clonmacnoise mention a man called Fiagha whom we may take to have been a good gardener, as he was surnamed Fionnscolaigh for 'the abundance of white flowers in his tyme'.[17] The luxuriant growth was favoured by the mildness of the Irish climate, of which the Venerable Bede (673–735) wrote:

Ireland is far more favoured than Britain by latitude and by its mild and healthy climate ... no need to store hay in summer ... snow rarely lies more than three days ... no reptiles, no snake can exit there ... milk and honey ... no lack of vines.[18]

The increasing importance of cultivated plants over those found in the wild is reflected in the appointment of a minor official of the monastery of St Columba on Iona to the position of gardener.[19] A little later increasing sophistication in the cultivation of plants is indicated by the fact that some monks who had been engaged in planting a hedge around a vineyard were rewarded with duck to eat.[20]

The Norman conquest of Ireland was followed by a further development in economic and ornamental gardening. Their military experience was reflected in the efficient organisation of their estates. Descriptions of the Earl of Norfolk's manor at Old Ross, County Wexford,[21] bear witness to this. The house, built of stone, its roof shingled with oak from the surrounding forest, gave on to a walled courtyard with a great entrance gate. Peacocks strutted here, doves flew from the dovecote and deer ran in their oak-paled park. The fishponds and warrens teemed with life and sporting tastes were also catered for by the walled falconry. Honey was obtained from the rows of beehives in the garden, which was sheltered by a boundary ditch, a palisade and a thorn hedge. The garden was entered from the court through an ornamental gate. In 1283 a gardener was paid for bedding out herbs and leeks, the orchard is recorded as producing nine bushels of apples, and, at another time a vineyard is also referred to briefly. The picture is one of a complex of enclosed gardens surrounding the great central court of the manor.

Following the introduction of the continental religious orders into Ireland the monastic communities of Celtic times were superseded by highly organised abbeys and priories. No complete description of a thirteenth century monastic garden survives, but by collecting together scattered references to monastic and secular manors, it is possible to build up a corporate picture of a foundation like the Augustinian Priory of Kells, County Kilkenny, much of which still remains, sited on the banks of the King's River. From its carefully maintained eel weirs and pools the river would have provided fish for the monastic table and also, when diverted into a watercourse, it drove the mill that ground the wheat, barley and corn from the monastery's granges and farms. The priory garden would have produced roots and fruits in separate enclosures which were usually ditched and palisaded, but sometimes walled. Each enclosure was entered through a carefully guarded timber gate. We know that root rather than green vegetables were commonly grown. There are frequent references in the literature to leeks, onions, garlic and artichokes (cardoons). Early Irish poetry refers to apples and to vegetables, as in the 'Vision of Mac Conglinne':

A row of fragrant apple trees
An orchard in its pink-tipped bloom
Between it and the hill
A forest tall of real leeks
Of onions and of carrots stood
Behind the house.[22]

In addition to the vegetables there were herbs, the range and variety of which can be judged from the Irish herbals produced in the Middle Ages.[23] Of flowers the documents refer only to the rose. 'A rose on the Feast of the Nativity of John the Baptist' (24 June)[24] is frequently stipulated as the annual rent for a small piece of land. Occasionally a red rose is specified.[25] For larger acreages a chaplet of such roses was requested,[26] for until the Reformation the clergy wore chaplets and garlands on festive days.

In contemporary records a dovecote is often mentioned in association with the garden. Its size and design can be seen in the one which survives at the ruined abbey of Ballybeg, County Cork.[27] Close to this dovecote lie three circular fish stews or ponds. A further adjunct to the garden we may assume to be the straw hives in which the bees were kept. As in Celtic times the apple continued to be an important article in the Irish diet and would have been grown in ditched enclosures, like that provided for in the lease of the manor of Turvey, County Dublin, by the Earl of Ormonde to William Caussan and William Thomkyn.[28]

> Also the Earl has granted to the said William and William all the commodities and profits of his orchard there, for which they shall ditch the said orchard and clear it and make a palisaded fence at their own cost and charges ... May 16, 1404.

The size and value of such orchards is indicated in the writ issued against Theobald de Verdun by Simon de Feyo on account of the former's waste of the houses, woods and gardens of the manor of Santry in 1303.[29] Among those things which were destroyed are listed two hundred apple trees valued at twenty livres each.

There is a reference to a scribe's garden, of which the function would have been to provide plants from which some of the colours for the illuminated manuscripts were obtained, such as woad, which gave a blue colour.[30] In some abbeys gardens were set aside for the abbot's exclusive use. The Abbot of St John in Kilkenny appears to have had a Bon Chretien pear in his garden.[31] The Abbot of Newry had a yew tree as well as some pears in his.[32] Of the planting of the cloister garth, the place traditionally associated with monastic gardens, there is little evidence. The traditional layout around on ornamental central well was found at Grey Abbey, County Down,[33] while at Muckross, County Kerry, a yew tree appears to have occupied the centre, for when Arthur Young visited the ruins in 1777 it was then 'the most prodigious yew tree I have beheld, in one great stem two feet in diameter and fourteen feet high from whence a vast head of branches spreads on every side, so as to form a perfect canopy to the whole

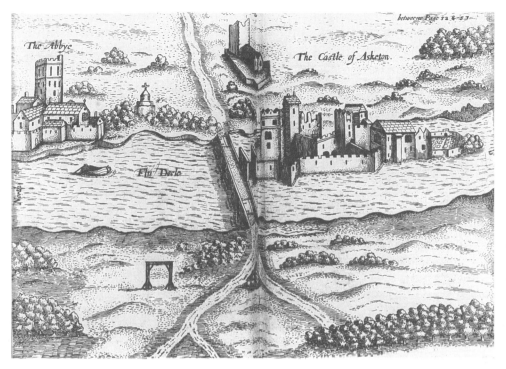

6: Askeaton Castle, County Limerick; note the garden within the walls. (Reproduced by permission of the National Library of Ireland).

space ...'.[34] The Irish monastic garden at its most extensive, therefore, would have comprised a complex series of separate enclosures: the cloister garth, the private garden of the abbot, the specialist garden of the scribes, the general garden of the abbey, its hives and fishponds dominated by a dovecote, and an orchard of apple and pear trees.

One important feature of the medieval monastic demesne which should be noted is the deer-park, which can be regarded as a forerunner of the eighteenth century ornamental landscape park. The hunting of wild deer in the forest had been a favourite sport for centuries. At the beginning of the thirteen century began the enclosure, at first with wooden palisades, of areas of woodland as private hunting pleasaunces and the introduction to them of fallow deer. In 1213 King John granted a mandate to the Keeper of the See of Coventry 'to cause Henry the Archbishop of Dublin to have thirty fallow deer of the King's gift in the park of Brewood and to lend aid in taking them'.[35] His park was at Shankill, County Dublin. In it we can imagine the archbishop and his guests hunting to hounds like any seventeenth century squire.[36]

The Norman families settled down in the fifteenth and sixteenth centuries to become 'more Irish than the Irish themselves'. Accounts of their castle gardens are few during the troubled periods of Reformation and Plantation. In 1583 the castle of the Fitzgeralds, earls of Desmond, at Newcastle West, County Limerick, boasted a fishpond, orchards and a three-acre garden within its curtain walls.[37] Another of their castles, at Askeaton nearby (Fig. 6), is described in a survey two years later as 'having a garden triangular in plan, in which a fishpond lies to the south ... all of which is enclosed in a stone wall'.[38] Cahir Castle, County Tipperary, a seat of a branch of the Butler family, possessed an orchard big enough, it was said, to hold within it, 300 men.[39] As late as 1639, old Irish families like the O'Briens who had reached an accommodation with the new reformers and planters, still possessed gardens of this type. The O'Brien castle at Leamanagh, County Clare, then had walled gardens which were graced with a pair of summerhouses and a brick turret, and had a fish pond fed by a stream.[40]

Though the monastery gardens grew herbs and simples, the Irish chiefs had long been served by families of hereditary physicians who took a keen interest in botany and horticulture as a source of their cures. This knowledge was transmitted from generation to generation by means of manuscript herbals. One of the most widely known was *The treatise of medicine and botany* written in 1432 by Donal Og O'Herlihy.[41] Another family, the O'Shiels, were physicians to the Macmahons of Oriel. Murtough O'Shiel, who died in 1548, was reckoned to be the best physician of his time. Their book of medicine, *The book of the O'Shiels*, survives. It contains the aphorisms of Hippocrates, commentaries on Galen, Avicenna and Vesalius (all early authors on medicine), as well as a dissertation on the therapeutic use of Ireland's flora.[42] An indication of the kinds of herbs grown for such use is given in a list prepared about 1620 by Philip O'Sullivan Beare, a scion of one of the old Irish families. It includes camomile, parsley, tamarisk, fennel, mint, tansy, hyssop, wormwood, rue, mustard, rosemary and sage. To this he added a list of other kinds of plants grown. Among vegetables he notes cabbage, lettuce, parsnip, pumpkin and radish; among the flowers the sunflower and the lily; among trees the apple, pear, arbutus, chestnut, walnut, mulberry and pine.[43]

About the year 1600, Dr Peter Lombard, member of a Waterford family, reported to the Pope that 'the Irish climate is favourable to many plants which, though neglected, do better in Ireland than the countries from which they are imported'.[44] He listed globe artichokes, cabbages and various kinds of roots as well as hops, and stated that vines, when carefully cultivated in the south and west, produced grapes not inferior to those of France and Germany.

The old order was swept away on the dissolution of the monasteries and the rapid progress of the Reformation. The new settlers in Ireland, many of them merchant venturers, were keenly interested in the exchange of new economic and ornamental plants then taking place between Britain, the Continent and the New World. An Irishman, Richard Harris, was fruiterer to Henry VIII and imported scions of new apples, pears and cherries into England from France and the Low Countries.[45] About 1586 an unknown official sent the strawberry tree to England, as recorded in the State Papers of Ireland:

7: Myrtle Grove, Sir Walter Raleigh's house at Youghal.

You shall receive herewith a bundle of trees called the woolaghan tree, whereof my Lord of Leicester and Mr Secretary Walsingham are both very desirous to have some, as well for the fruit as the rareness of the manner of bearing, which is after the kind of the orange to have blossoms and fruit green or ripe all the year long, and the same of a very pleasant taste, and growing nowhere else but in one part of Munster, from whence I have caused them to be transported immediately unto you, praying you to see them safely delivered and divided between them my said Lord and Mr Secretary, directing that they may be planted near some ponds or with a great deal of black moory earth, which kind of soil I take will best suit them, for that they grow best in Munster about loughs and prove to the bigness of cherry trees or more and continue long.[46]

The strawberry tree was to become a prized rarity in the English garden of the following century.

The potato was supposedly introduced to Ireland by Sir Walter Raleigh, who was for a time Mayor of Youghal, County Cork. It is related that the gardener at his house there, Myrtle Grove (Fig. 7), thought the plant was grown for its green and bitter berry. When he dug over the earth for the next crop he was surprised to find the potato tubers in the soil. In recent times some authorities have thrown doubt on the story, doubt which would seem to be well supported by the claim of Sir Robert Southwell, President of the Royal Society, that his grandfather brought the potato into Ireland in 1593, having obtained it from Sir Walter after the latter's return from Virginia. Salaman, however, in his monumental work on the potato,[47] investigated the question thoroughly. He concluded, in the light of contemporary evidence, that Sir Walter himself introduced the potato into Ireland and that Southwell's grandfather obtained his tubers from Sir Walter's Irish garden. Raleigh is also credited with the introduction of the myrtle, from which his house was to take its name, and the cherry, which he grew on that part of his estate at Affane, County Waterford.[48] The cherry trees flourished for many years afterwards. It was in a fall from one of Raleigh's cherry trees that his neighbour, the old Countess of Desmond (who was alleged to have lived to the age of 120), met her death. At Myrtle Grove, Raleigh also grew the American tobacco plant and a sweet-smelling wallflower he had brought from the Azores.[49]

In 1591 the College of the Holy and Undivided Trinity was founded by Queen Elizabeth I on the eastern boundary of medieval Dublin. The college soon acquired lands elsewhere and was able to lease plots to the citizens of Dublin. On 1 October 1594, the college let two plots of land and the lessee was required to 'make three fair gardens planted with good and profitable herbs and fruit trees'. The fellows of Trinity College had the right, however, to walk in the gardens 'for their recreation'.[50] A decade later in 1605, Harry Hollander signed a deed allowing him 'the use and possession of the College's five gardens and the great orchard (except the little garden without the brick wall ...)'. He was permitted, under the terms agreed, to take 'half of all the herbs that grow, lavender, roses, fruit of the trees' and in return he was required to 'dig dung, prune, set and plant the garden with some herbs, especially the garden known as Dr Challenors which [was] already half under herbs, the remainder [was] to have only herbs and under the brick wall such roots as shall be thought fit'. The complicated lease further stipulated that Hollander was to cultivate 'in the rest of the garden reserved to his charge ... turnip, parsnip, carrot, artichoke, onions, leeks', and in the 'low garden outside the wall and great orchard ... cabbages, turnips and other things as they shall need for 30 persons or 8 messes as the cook shall think good'.[51] While the Provost and Fellows got the other half of the herbs, lavender, roses, fruit and vegetables, the College agreed that Hollander should have 'a chamber' for keeping his seeds in.

While these leases give us some notion of what was grown in the garden, an indication of its design is offered in the bird's eye view of the Master's Garden and orchard in 1600. It is divided into a number of compartments of different designs; one is a knot-garden apparently planted with flowers, a second boasts a heraldic design and another has parallel rows of beds.[52] Edmund Spenser, a friend and neighbour of Raleigh in County Cork, wrote a love poem (his 64th sonnet) in 1593 in which he lists some of the flowers grown in these Elizabethan gardens.[53]

8: Richard Boyle, first Earl of Cork. (Reproduced by permission
of the National Library of Ireland).

Comming to kisse her lyps, (such grace I found)
Me seemd, I smelt a gardin of sweet flowres,
That dainty odours from them throw around,
For damzels fit to decke their lovers bowres.
Her lips did smell lyke unto Gillyflowers;
Her ruddy cheekes, lyke unto Roses red;
Her snowy browes, lyke budded Bellamoures;
Her lovely eyes, lyke Pincks but newly spred;
Her goodly bosome, lyke a Strawberry bed;
Her neck, lyke to a bounch of Cullambynes;
Her brest, lyke lillyes, ere they leaves be shed;
Her nipples, lyke young blossomd Jessemynes.
    Such fragrant flowres doe give most odorous smell;
    But her sweet odour did them all excell.

At this time there occurred an important development in garden design in
Ireland. The Italian Renaissance had revived the idea of the garden as a place for
cultivated pleasure. Their gardens were designed as an extension of the house
and so followed the architectural rules of ordered symmetry in the lay-out of

terraces, flights of steps, parterres and fountains. This approach to gardening appeared in England in that period called the Elizabethan Renaissance, whence it was introduced into Ireland.

The earliest recorded example is that of the Great Earl of Cork (Fig. 8) at The College, Youghal, County Cork.[54] The property had been a medieval college, which was dissolved in the reign of Henry VIII and made over to Sir Walter Raleigh, from whom it was acquired by the Great Earl, and converted into a house for his own use. It was surrounded by walled courts, one of which had a fountain in it. Behind the house was a simple parterre of rectangular beds along the lines of those which appeared on the frontispiece to Gerard's *Herbal* of 1597. It was for these beds, presumably, that the Great Earl acquired a consignment of rose trees from Bristol in 1613.[55] Six years later, he recorded in his diary the arrival of 100 apple trees, prunes and quinces for the adjoining orchard. From the parterre flights of steps rose to a formal terrace, whence a series of paths ascended through a wilderness to what was known as the Earl's Walk. Thomas Dinely described the garden in 1681:

> The garden is extremely pleasant, being on the side of the mountain overlooking the whole town, College and Harbour, with Walks, one above another, which Nature itself hath contributed much to and stone steps of Ascent to each, the uppermost walk had also a spring at the end thereof, which it is said the Earle of Cork intended to supply fountains with belowe, to form delightful throws of water.[56]

But one of the earl's sons was accidentally drowned in the spring and the project was never carried out. The Earl moved to Lismore Castle in 1620.

Sir Arthur Chichester, a contemporary of the Earl, was the fortunate possessor of three gardens. One, Chichester House in Dublin, stood on the site of the present Bank of Ireland opposite Trinity College.[57] Like the college in Youghal it was entered through a walled court and the principal feature of the garden was a terrace, 20 feet wide, with a banqueting house, all looking over riverside plantations. Another was at Belfast Castle. It comprised a network of walled courts, gardens and orchards, all within a great defensive dyke and rampart. The only detailed account states:

> The Great Roll of 1666 abounds with allusions to the gardens, to the bowling green, to the cherry garden and the apple garden, and to the arbours and walks which were the cool shades, the favoured retired retreats of the castle inmates and guests of rank who were frequent visitors ... There were also payments of wages for rolling, cleaning, weeding, wheeling in ashes and cinders for the improvement of the walks referred to.

While strawberries, currants and gooseberries are mentioned, no notice is taken of flowers, except this: 'Paid for making boarders at the Rampier and for women gathering Violatts in ye fields to sett in the Gardens'.[58]

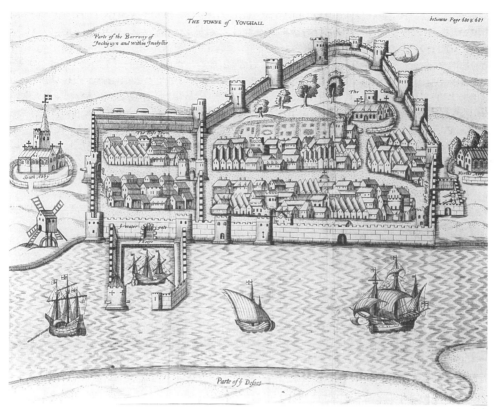

9: Gardens of the Earl of Cork, Youghal. (Reproduced by permission of the National Library of Ireland).

The introduction of the Renaissance garden into Ireland during Elizabeth's reign was succeeded by a period of development in the reign of James I. This more peaceable time was reflected in the abandonment by the Jacobean aristocracy of their fortified castles and their replacement by a series of splendid new mansion houses.

The first was Joymount, erected in 1618 by Sir Arthur Chichester at Carrickfergus, County Antrim. It is described in a contemporary account:

> a stately house, a stately gate house, and a graceful terrace; and a walk before the house as is at Denton, my Lord Fairfax's house. A fine garden and mighty spacious orchards and they say they have a goodly store of fruit. I observed on either side of this garden and twixt the garden and the orchard, a dove house placed one opposite the other, a most convenient place for apricockes but this is not made use of ... .[59]

In the same year the Earl of Clanrickarde began his great house at Portumna, which was burned down in 1826 but is now being restored. His wife had been prominent at the court of Queen Elizabeth and was abreast of the latest developments in garden design. The mansion was approached through a series of walled courts, the gates to which were embellished with typical Jacobean Renaissance architectural detail.[60] No plan of the layout of these courts has been found but the extant plan of the garden of Monaghan Castle[61] and the view of Charlemont Fort, County Armagh,[62] the seat of Sir Toby Caulefield, suggest what it might have been.

As already mentioned, the Great Earl of Cork moved to Lismore in 1620. Here is the only Jacobean garden to survive in anything like its original form. Helped by his gardener, John, he built a high surrounding wall and a raised terrace terminated at either end by turrets or summer houses. His diaiy of 1626 recorded payments by his mother 'for compassing my orchard and garden at Lismore with a wall of two and a half feet thick and fourteen feet high of lyme and stone and two turrets at each corner'.[63] Ten years later he constructed the terrace: 'I paid Turlough and William May for digging, mowing and laying my terras at Lismore with paved, hewn stones in all one hundred and six feet'.[64] The adjoining orchard had by 1641, as well as the traditional apples, named varieties of peach, pear, nectarine, apricot and cherry.[65] Nearby, lay a suite of nine fishponds stored with carp and tench sent from the Low Countries.[66] In his hunting park some miles away, he had a brick-built lodge to which he would retire occasionally in the company of his friends. The nearby garden was also constructed of brick which may have been the first time that this material, whose ability to retain heat is favourable to the growing of tender fruit, was used for garden walling in Ireland.[67]

In the towns there were gardens belonging to the wealthy and cultured merchants. These were attached to houses of which Rothe House in the city of Kilkenny is a good surviving example. A map of 1651[68] shows that many of the principal houses within and without the walls of the city of Galway had gardens, such as the 'great mansion of the Blakes', the Chapel of St Brigid, the Abbey of St Francis, the Plague House and the Leper Hospital. These gardens are shown, perhaps conventionally, as laid out in rectangular plots, usually with a tree standing in the middle in a raised bed. Dovecotes are marked and outside the walls an orchard is shown.

The year 1649 marked the end of the period which we have called that of the Irish Renaissance garden. In that year began the rule of Oliver Cromwell. It was to be a very troubled period for Irishmen of every political persuasion and virtually no gardening of any consequence took place, but on the restoration of the monarchy in 1660 a new and elaborate approach to gardening was taken under French influence. During Cromwell's ascendancy Charles II had lived in exile at the court of Louis XIV in Versailles. At that time the great gardens in the baroque style which we have now come to know as the French style, were being laid out by Le Nôtre, and his colleagues of the Mollet family. With Charles in exile was the Duke of Ormonde, who was appointed Lord Lieutenant of Ireland on the Restoration. On his return to Kilkenny Castle, his ancestral Irish seat, he laid out new gardens in the French style to which he had become accustomed during his exile. On account of his close connections with the new king's court, he was able to employ the court architects and engineers to advise on this work.

One of his initial undertakings appears to have involved the employment of a French fontainier by the name of Carrie to construct a fountain with a jet of 24 feet in the castle courtyard.[69] It was not until perhaps 15 years later, in 1679, however that work appears to have begun in earnest. In that year a banqueting house to the design of the court architect, Hugh May, was begun. Circular in plan and rising through two stories, it was crowned with a cupola and gallery. The lower room was conceived as a grotto the walls of which were ornamented with marble piers, with the design of which the Duke was not happy. On the resolution of this problem he consulted Sir Christopher Wren.[70] When finished the floor was paved with black and white marble tiles, the ceiling was frescoed with angels and the centre occupied by a fountain of black Kilkenny marble in the shape of a cup out of which a jet of water rose into the hollow of a ducal crown which had been suspended above it, all in celebration of Ormonde's elevation to a dukedom in 1661.[71] The fountain was, perhaps devised by another fontainier from France, du Keizar, with whose work the Duke expressed himself well satisfied in 1689.[72] There were difficulties in finding water at sufficient pressure to work the fountains as it had to be raised many feet from the river below. A number of engineers were employed to no avail. Finally, Sir Samuel Morland, who had succeeded in lifting water from the Thames up to Windsor Castle for the king, was consulted and he devised a hydraulic machine for the purpose.[73]

The influence of France is also discernible in the use of lead as a material from which to fashion architectural and sculptural ornaments. The terraces above the fountain garden were dressed in lead, and in 1689 a contract was placed with a London statuary maker, John Bonnier, to copy in lead four pieces – Diana, the Sabine women, Hercules, and Commodus and Antoninus – which stood in the King's Privy Garden in London. An indication that the duke and his duchess did not entirely approve of the frivolity of the Restoration court is provided in a clause of their contract stating that they would reserve the right to require Bonnier to provide draperies over the privy parts of the copies if they should so desire. They ordered, in addition, the figures of 16 cupids, emblems of the four seasons and the twelve signs of the zodiac, all to be cast in lead. Whether these were intended for the garden or the grotto is not clear but Hugh May, the architect, was set down as the arbiter of the quality of Bonnier's work.[74] The famous woodcarver, Grinling Gibbons, gave a design for the gates to the great courtyard but in the end a local ironmaster was employed.

A wilderness cut through with avenues and vistas was planted outside the bowling green. It can be seen clearly in Francis Place's drawing. The principal vista is lined with fir (i.e. Scots pine) trees, which are, perhaps, those mentioned in a letter to the duchess from her agent written in 1689: 'Lord Granard's servant came here with seven score firr trees'.[75]

Ormonde's successor as Chief Governor of Ireland, the Duke of Tyrconnell, laid out an even more sophisticated garden at Carton, County Kildare, the design for which was closely based on a plate from *Le jardin de plaisir* by André Mollet,[76] Le Nôtre's colleague.[77] The approach to the house was by way of three avenues of trees in a crow's-feet pattern and the formal pleasure garden was surrounded by a raised terrace wall, with orchards, flower and kitchen gardens adjoining. The gardens of the viceroys were the most important but there were many others of note during this period of advancement, Kilruddery, County Wicklow, being one which has come down to us in an almost complete state. It appears to have been started about 1682, for in that year the agent wrote that 'Captain Brabazon has and will make new great improvements there, the park for his coults is long since finished and he is making also a deer park and decoy ... the pond is already made'.[78] Two years later, Sir William Petty was complaining that Bonnet, his French gardener, who had been in his service for twelve years, had gone to live with the Earl of Meath.[79] The design of the garden, with its twin canals leading to a circular fountain is similar to the garden at Courances, near Paris, which is attributed to Le Nôtre. The first detailed description of Kilruddery, which appeared in 1711,[80] referred to its separate parts as 'a Pleasure Garden, Cherry Garden, Kitchen Garden, New Garden, Wilderness, Gravel Walks and Bowling Green, all wall'd about, and well planted with fruit trees, with several canals or Fish-ponds'.

Other important features of the Restoration garden included the development, as an extension of the garden, of ornamental woodland planting, cut through with avenue and vistas. This practice, also, was derived from the French style, as was the introduction of parterres with embroidered designs. Such features were seen at Doneraile Castle, County Cork, seat of the St Leger family.[81] It was entered through a courtyard at the centre of which stood a figure of a classical gladiator, probably copied, as many were, from the figure then at Hampton Court Palace. The embroidered parterres between the castle and the river were probably made with box hedging, like those at the king's house at Chapelizod, near Dublin, which were described by the Countess of Clarendon in a letter to John Evelyn, the author of *Sylva*, in 1682.[82]

A parterre with embroidered designs was also laid out by Lord Sidney when he was Chief Governor at Dublin Castle. This was flanked by lime walks and overlooked by terraces whose walls were studded with pots of flowers and evergreens. The more modest gardens continued to use old-fashioned geometric designs in their parterres rather than the newer embroidered ones. 'A plat of the Skinners buildings at Dungiven' and 'A plat of Sir Thomas Phillip's buildings' at Limavady, both in County Londonderry, exhibit geometric designs of a pre-Cromwellian type.[83]

Trees were planted not only as adjuncts to the garden area but also in deerparks designed for the sport of hunting. These may be regarded as the precursors of the eighteenth century demesnes. Similarly the bowling green, with its fine smooth turf can be claimed as the form in which the lawn first became a garden feature. In the Restoration period almost every Irish town and mansion had one. It is recorded in 1665 that the bowling green at Oxmantown Green, Dublin, was a 'most notable place, and every evening my Lord Deputy bowls there, and the ladies at Kettlepins'.[84]

The Royal Hospital for retired soldiers at Kilmainham, near Dublin, was completed in 1684. In the minute books of the Board of Govenors we have reference to early efforts to lay out the gardens there.[85] In 1685 it was resolved that the 'Committee do consider whatsoever trees are to be bought and what sorts for planting for the gardens' and, in 1693, £20 was paid to Mr. Miller, gardener, for planting 200 lime trees.[86] Such plantings of limes were characteristic of the times, as, for example, those carried out at Hampton Court, London, in 1662.[87] Later entries in the minutes refer to the Earl of Meath being asked to prepare plans for the garden and the walls to be arranged 'so that the garden may lye all open to the North part ... for the greater grace for the House.' In 1695 Dr Dun, first physician to the Royal Hospital and a celebrated medical figure of his day, asked that part of the garden be set aside for herbs and plants. In 1698 it was decided that the garden 'be layed into the grass plots and walks with dwarf trees.'

Nevertheless, by 1717 little appears to have been done to keep the garden in order, for when General Palmes took up his appointment as Master of the Hospital he found it necessary to take drastic measures without waiting for authority from the governors. In October of that year the minutes state:

> Wheras the said Lt. Gen. Palmes upon his entrance into that employment found the Garden of the Hospital extremely neglected and in no manner of order, and being informed that several plans for ye beautifying it had been formerly laid before the Board in order but to no effect, and judging it impossible to make any calculation of the emprovement which could be laid before the Board in order to receive their commands on it, did employ several workmen the last two years for the laying out the said garden, planting, and improving it to what it now is, which work of the labourers and carpenters as well as the plants and fruit trees amounted to the sum of £168–16–1 ... your memorialist hopes and desires may be allowed by his Grace and ye Honble Board. He also humbly proposes then for the farther beautifying the said garden, iron rails may be sett at the bottom of ye garden the whole breath of the great walke in order to open the prospect of ye river from ye garden and the terraces, and the fields adjacent may be planted with Elm trees ... .

The Master's initiative may have caused some consternation among the Governors, for Captain Burgh, Engineer and Surveyor General, was asked to inspect the work. He duly reported:

> The work I observed to be done in the said garden are the enclosing two distinct quarters with posts and rails and planting fruit trees against them in order to form espaliers, the making eight boarded screens (intended I presume for sheltering the fruit trees on the south wall from the injuries of blasting wind).
> The making of a terrace at the stair foot, digging borders for fruit hedges and the quarters for kitchen stuff and the planting several trees against the walls and in the borders.

Three bills were adjudged reasonable:–

Carpenter's work and stuff	£ 36–5–0
Painting work	£ 12–15–0
Gardeners tools, trees, dung, seeds and plants, and labourers employed	£ 132–10–5

The proposal for iron rails at the bottom of the garden and planting of elms in the landscape was not accepted. 'The Govenors do not think fitt at present to allow of any ornaments that may bring an unnecessary charge upon the House.'

With the rapid development of demesnes came the first important plant collections. In 1682 Lord Granard of Castle Forbes, County Longford, was praised for the improvements effected in his demesne:

> Lord Viscount Granard hath improved it to a very great degree by reducing much of red bog into firm and good land, and planting orchards, groves and hopyards etc., and hath by such industry managed the soyles, that it beareth all sorts of plants and flowers, that are set out and sowed there. There is now growing there in great verdure, large groves of fir of all sorts, with Pine, Juniper, Cedar, Lime Trees, Beech, Elm, Oak, Ash, Asp and the famous Platanus tree, I suppose not growing anywhere else in this kingdom. He hath built a fayre and spacious house, with lovely gardens of pleasure, enclosed by high stone walls against which plenty of fruit of all sorts grows, and in the said gardens, are all sorts of flowers and many more with Philarea hedges, lawrel, etc., and the Tubirose which beareth there, which is not to be raised but with the assistance of glasses.[88]

At this time the first pineapples in Ireland were grown by Lord Granard and by Lord Massereene of Antrim Castle. These landowners, with Austin Cooper of Blessington House, County Wicklow and Sir Arthur Rawdon[89] of Moira, County Down, were among the first to use glass for raising tender plants.

Sir Arthur Rawdon (1662-1695) had an extensive garden at Moira, County Down, with walks, vistas, a labyrinth, canals, ponds and groves. His interest in plants was stimulated by his friendship with Sir Hans Sloane, the famous naturalist whose collections became the nucleus of the British Museum. Sloane, himself born in County Down, had been physician to the Governor of Jamaica and this no doubt influenced Rawdon in sending a gardener, James Harlow, there to bring back trees and plants for the garden at Moira. Harlow's achievement in bringing back alive from the tropics about one thousand living trees and shrubs was a remarkable one in the circumstances of the time. Little is known of how the plants were grown at Moira, though there was a conservatory there as early as 1690, one of the earliest in Ireland. Rawdon received many plants from the Chelsea Physic Garden, of which Sir Hans Sloane was a benefactor, but he, in turn, gave generously to 'the garden of the Bishop of London at Fulham, Dr Uvedale's at Enfield; the Chelsea Garden and especially into that of her Grace the Duchess of Beaufort at Badminton' as well as to the botanic gardens at Amsterdam, Leiden, Leipzig and Uppsala. The collection at Moira, one of the most remarkable collections of living plants ever held in

Ireland, did not long survive him, despite efforts by the family to keep the plants alive. In 1744 Walter Harris listed the trees and plants that still survived:

> The Locust of Virginia, a Tree thirty feet high, the Ucca or Adam's Needle, the Indian Honeysuckle spired like a rocket, with a Crimson-coloured flower, which it emits but once in three or four years, the Parsley-leaved Elder, the Pinaster, Calamus aromaticus, the Gooseberry-leaved Currant, the Gooseberry Thorn, the double-blossomed whitethorn.[90]

The Restoration period of gardening in Ireland may be said to end with the ascent of William and Mary to the throne in 1689. During the Williamite wars many of the great mansions of the Stuart period, such as Kilkenny Castle and Burton Park, County Cork, were fired by the retreating Jacobites and their great gardens thereafter abandoned.

It is sometimes assumed that William III brought the Dutch style of gardening to Ireland, but the Dutch influence had already been present for some time. The gardens at Lisburn Castle, County Antrim, for example, were begun in 1656 when Lord Conway brought over a Dutch gardener who had been working with Mr Kames of Kensington.[91] The garden took the form of terraces falling from the foot of the castle to the bank of the River Lagan below. They were surrounded by stone walls coped with brick. It was the practice to decorate such walls with rows of pots containing alternately colourful flowers and sober evergreens, so it is likely that the twelve dozen flower pots and the 'greens' imported from Ostend by Lord Conway in 1667 were for such use.[92] The terraces were broken by broad gravel paths, one ending in a mount on top of which was a 'Dutch tent'[93], evidently a summerhouse in the Dutch style. In 1667 some seven thousand painted tiles were ordered from Holland to decorate the interior.[94] As they were badly packed only 3000 of them survived the journey by sea and his agent felt obliged to write to Lord Conway in a reproachful tone: 'a very dear commodity they prove and in these scare times I think your Lordship may better lay out or keep your money'.[95] On one of the lower terraces was an orchard for which 'golden pippins, base sweetings and red strakes' were imported from Bordeaux in 1689.[96] According to a letter from the agent these were planted at a distance of 32 feet apart.[97] A bowling green and a walled wilderness with a turret in each corner completed the ensemble of this mainly Dutch-inspired garden.[98]

The Dutch influence would seem to have continued into the late eighteenth century, especially in the gardens of the smaller estates, judging by a map of such an estate, Woodfield (Frontispiece & fig. 10), near Clara, County Offaly, drawn in 1765. This shows a formal garden with topiary.

French expertise in practical horticulture was brought by the regiments of Huguenot refugees who fought in the Williamite armies. After the war it is related that they 'exchanged the sword for the plumb-rule, the pruning-hook and the plough-share'. The register of the French church at Portarlington starts in 1694. In that town the Huguenots made gardens, planted the Jargonelle pear and grew vegetables. A bill for seeds and plants bought from The Hague by a

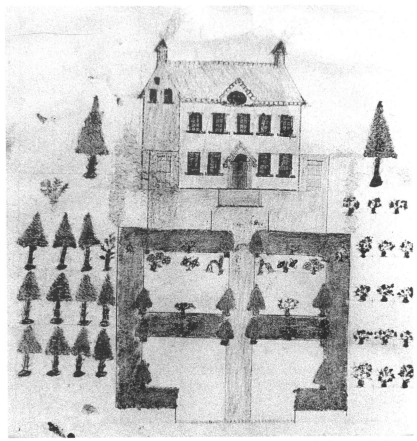

10: Detail of the 1765 map of Woodfield, King's County (see Frontispiece), showing the house and a small formal garden with topiary. The map also shows an orchard and hop yard.

Huguenot in 1722 lists among others 'asparagus, radishes, tomatoes, sensitive plants, several sorts of lettuces and about 60 sorts of flower seed, lemon or citrus trees, mhirtle balls in pots and turnip seed'.[99] The Dublin Philosophical Society sent to Holland in 1694 for several market gardeners to teach its members new techniques of growing fruit and vegetables. Some years later, Captain Theophilus Desbrisay, agent for the Huguenot regiments, was active in founding the Dublin Florists' Club.[100] The florists were more interested in beautiful flowers for their own sakes than for the contribution they might make to the overall design of a garden. Glasshouses, frames and cloches, then called bell-glasses, were used to protect tender plants and seedlings. To the flowers were added a variety of new shrubs, including variegated types, two of which were charmingly called gilt box and gilt holly.[101]

William's arrival, then, did not bring an increase of interest in the Dutch approach to garden design as William had already adopted the French baroque style before he left Holland. The first real change came with Queen Anne and, as in other applied arts such as furniture and silver, it was a simplified style. The embroidered patterns of box, coloured gravels and flowers were discarded in favour of a simpler parterre of panels and slopes of mown grass outlined by gravel. Queen Anne removed the elaborate parterres from the garden of her palace at Hampton Court[102] and a similar fate befell flowers and box hedging in front of Irish houses. In 1709 Samuel Molyneux wrote that the gardens at Burton Hall, County Carlow, were 'of the new manner, Grass and Gravel' and that those at Belan, County Kildare were 'Handsome improved gardens of Greens, Grass and Gravel'.[103]

These changes in fashion originated in the gardens of Marly, the retreat of Louis XIV near the Palace of Versailles. There the embroidered parterre of box, coloured gravels and flowers of the Le Nôtre period was discarded in favour of simpler parterres and mown grass. It is ironic that at the very moment when horticulture was reaching a new peak flowers should be banished by designers from the immediate setting of the house, to remain so condemned for almost a century.

It was said that the decision to do without parterres at Marly had been influenced by the need to save money, but this cannot have been generally the case in Ireland for any savings that resulted were more than counterbalanced by the costs of the new fashion for extending gardens far beyond their hitherto carefully delineated boundaries into the surrounding countryside. The century of the settled landed estate had begun and the face of the countryside was being transformed by the agricultural improvements of drainage, enclosure, road-making and fertilisation which were to become the principal economic achievements of the eighteenth century. It was in the light of this transformation and the desire to make the countryside beautiful as well as useful that the landscape gardener turned his back on the garden, as we know it, to use his talents on the countryside at large. For the rest of the century he was to be concerned not simply with the design of gardens but of landscape scenery. Since the Restoration period long avenues had spread out from the gardens around great houses into the countryside, but they were never seen as more than mere avenues, whereas the new movement saw them as landscape features capable of considerable improvement and ornamentation. They might be adorned by canals running down the middle. They might be entered by triumphal arches or the vista might be terminated by an obelisk. There was not much point in using architecture or sculptural ornament like a piece of statuary or a sun-dial of a scale suitable for the smaller garden, when it came to embellishing large landscape designs. Only ornament on a grand architectural scale would be appropriate.

The first essays in the new art of landscape design were in the simplified baroque style of 'Grass, Greens and Gravel' elaborated with formal pools or canals of water. Lord Molesworth, whose park at Brackenstown, County

Dublin, was one of the principal achievements of the Queen Anne style in Ireland, consulted Alessandro Galilei, the great Italian architect and Stephen Switzer, the English landscape gardener and contriver of water works.[104] The design of the park was not unlike that at Carton, County Kildare. On the south front was an enclosed parterre of four panels leading into a series of allées radiating through woodland and then out across open countryside towards the sea. On the east side a long canal was conducted through lines of embanked trees leading the eye to the round tower of the church of Swords. Lord Molesworth, following the example of the Queen's gardeners, London and Wise,[105] from whose nursery he had bought plants, designed circular basins to mark the crossings of his avenue. In 1712 he was planning a complex suite of waterworks on the rise to the north of the house. Water from a canal emptied into a fishpond over a stepped cascade. It was then raised by a hydraulic machine to the level of the canal again. A high-level storage cistern was cleverly disguised as a summerhouse raised on pillars.

No garden of the Queen Anne style, however, surpassed that conceived for Dromoland, County Clare, by Lucius O'Brien, who had in 1701, married a cousin of the Queen, Catherine Keightly. To provide a suitable background for the life of his well-connected bride, he embarked on an exhaustive reconstruction of his house and garden. His enthusiasm for gardening was such that while he was waiting for the new work at Dromoland to be completed and was living at what was normally a tenant's house nearby,[106] his father was obliged to write to his daughter-in-law that her husband was mistaken:

> to continue the expense of an unnecessary improvement, and charge for walkes and gardens at a place that will never make any suitable returnes for it and where my posterity cannot be presumed to make it their residence, nor that any tenant will pay ... for the land ... and not for walkes and gardens.[107]

A complete set of plans for the gardens at Dromoland survives.[108] It shows a complex scheme in the later baroque style ordered by three principal radiating avenues. Similar straight avenues cut through the surrounding woods and fields. Some of them stretch far into the landscape to enclose and ornament the fields of the estate in what was called 'Extended or Forest Gardening' by Stephen Switzer in his book *Iconographia rustica*.[109] The influence of Switzer is confirmed in the labelling of the principal drawing as 'Iconographia Dromolan'. It would appear however that the plan may have been by one Browne, a 'contriver' who was paid a fee in 1720 for his work there. He was presumably the same Browne who was recommended to the Earl of Kenmare by his aunt, Mrs Da Cunha in a letter of 1720:

> one Browne, who has for several years been employed by most of the people of quality of Ireland and who has a greater genius for laying on new ground than anybody of his time, and I find my brother Aylmer thinks you can't have a better contriver.[110]

The early Georgian landscapes at Kenmare House and at Lyons House, County Kildare, the seat of Mr Aylmer, are, disappointingly, quite simple arrangements of avenues radiating from the house into the landscape. Mrs Da Cunha's assertion of Browne's superiority would appear to be contradicted by Joseph Cooper Walker in his essay on the 'Rise and progress of gardening in Ireland' (1791) for he wrote that the nurserymen Rowe and Bullein were the principal rural artists at the beginning of the century. As he contrived to spell the names of both partners incorrectly – they should be Roe and Bullen –perhaps his contention is not to be relied upon. Although it is known that Walter Roe commenced a nursery business at New Street in Dublin in 1711[111] and that he was later joined by Daniel Bullen, there is no concrete evidence that they laid out ground. A payment to Roe of £66 in 1722 by the Earl of Meath[112] could have been for the supply of trees to Kilruddery rather than for designing an extension to the garden.

The influence of Marly on the early Georgian gardens of Ireland in the 1720s can be observed in the widespread use of the cascade or water-staircase. Mrs Delany wrote of the 'artificial cascades in the Marly style with statues[113] and urns on either side 'which were made at Templeogue House, County Dublin. The Restoration garden at Kilruddery was extended beyond its walls about the year 1725. Down the centre of one of the new vistas ran a similar cascade which originated in an octagonal basin at the top of the hill and ended in one at the bottom called The Ace of Clubs after its shape. Many more stepped cascades are referred to in the literature of the time but the most spectacular must have been that built at Saunders Grove, County Wicklow,[114] in about 1725. Another example of the influence of Marly was in the copying of its serpentine paths, an innovation from the usual straight lines of the baroque style, in the landscape garden at Dromoland which we have already described, although the influence may have reached Ireland through the drawings of Stephen Switzer.

The obelisk, being tall and needle-like, seemed the architectural feature most appropriate in shape to terminate these long vistas. At Dromoland an obelisk, a triumphal arch and a domed rotunda were all used for this purpose. In the landscape garden at Stillorgan, County Dublin, an obelisk based on that by Bernini in the Piazza Navona in Rome was erected to the designs of Sir Edward Lovett Pearce, the Surveyor General for Ireland.[115] Pearce is also assumed to be responsible for the design of the arch with obelisks terminating a vista at Gloster, County Offaly.[116] The finest of these obelisks was the one built to close the vista at the back of Castletown, County Kildare, as late as 1740 and now known as The Connolly Folly. It was built by Mrs Connolly, widow of Speaker Connolly who had built the house. Mary Jones wrote:

> My sister is building an obleix to answer a vistow from the bake of Castletown House; it will cost her three or four hundred pounds at least, but I believe more. I really wonder how she can do so much, and live as she does.[117]

Her purse was not yet dry, however, for three years later she closed another vista of the park's baroque layout by erecting a building known as The Wonderful Barn.[118]

The spirit of general improvement was now widespread and was beginning to result in an agricultural landscape of which its makers were proud. There was a growing impatience with a situation in which these improvements were shut out from the view of the house by the walls of the old-fashioned garden or the closed vistas of the more recent landscape gardens. With this impatience came a new movement to incorporate extensive view of the surrounding countryside from the house and garden. It was this desire which was to be one of the principal determinations of landscape design for the next century. The development is seen at one of its most telling moments in the view of Howth Castle, County Dublin, painted in about 1740.[119] Surrounding the castle are walled Restoration gardens which have been extended behind by a baroque scheme of vistas but the wall enclosing the garden in front of the castle has been taken down and replaced by a sheet of water so that the surrounding countryside is laid open to view. The landscape as a whole was truly displacing the garden as the centre of interest.

LANDSCAPING IN IRELAND
THE EARLY FLORISTS

During the seventeenth century, the great houses and gardens of Ireland had been constructed by the viceroys and other officers of the king. By the beginning of the eighteenth century, the king's power as the central authority in the land had been replaced by that of a landed aristocracy and gentry exercised through the House of Lords and the House of Commons, the two chambers of the Irish Parliament seated in Dublin. The attendance at parliament which was required over a long period of each year led to the erection of a splendid series of town houses in the squares and streets which are now recognised as a valued part of Ireland's heritage. The base of the parliament's power, however, and the wealth of its members lay in their landed estates, both great and small, which were distributed throughout the countryside. To the development and ornamentation of these, even greater attention was paid than to the Dublin houses. The agricultural revolution, which was brought about by field enclosure, drainage and planting on a wide scale, was altering the traditional face of the countryside by superimposing on it a rectilinear geometry which many came to believe was at variance with the natural beauties of unenclosed countryside. The enlightened landowner came to see that the transformation could not continue to be seen simply in terms of agricultural advancement and financial gain but should also take into account the indigenous beauties and character of the landscape. With this in mind, he began to employ men who were not only expert in the practical exigencies of land drainage and planting for shelter but who were also sensitive to the landscape's character and to the idea of ornamenting the countryside. Such men were the landscape gardeners of the Georgian period and the rural landscape of Ireland to-day, with its hedgerows, trees, woods and lakes, reflects their work.

The reaction against the geometricisation of the countryside did not, at first, come from the landowner but from a small and close-knit group of *literati* in England and Ireland. The aesthetic appreciation of the landscape had been given literary expression since the days of the poet Milton and had been elevated to an intellectual plane by the seventeenth century philosopher Lord Shaftesbury. The full implications of their attitude to nature for the landscape gardener did not become explicit until the publication in 1711 and 1712 of Joseph Addison's essays which criticised the unnatural character of the formal gardens then in vogue. Addison lived in Dublin Castle[1] while secretary to the Viceroy and his friend, the poet Alexander Pope, was the first to translate the idea of a natural gardening style into reality at his garden in Twickenham, near London.[2] Its design, as it has disappeared, is only known to us through contemporary plans, had vistas lined with trees grown in a natural manner rather than in the clipped dress of the formal baroque garden. Its subsidiary vistas were in the form of meanders or angles. The mingling of baroque order and formality with nature-sentiment which was characteristic of Pope's garden is what is called in the world of art history, the rococo style.

This style of gardening emerged in Ireland in the work of Jonathan Swift, Dean of St Patrick's Cathedral, Dublin and author of *Gulliver's Travels*. He was a good friend of Pope whom he had first met in 1713. His interest in landscape gardening is first recorded in the following year when he was advising his friend, Knightly Chetwode, on the ornamentation of his demesne at Woodbrook, County Laois.[3] Some years later there is a letter written by him from Gaulstown, County Westmeath, in which he describes himself as being 'deep among the Workmen' improving the demesne. Both of these developments were carried out in the old formal manner. It is not until 1721, two years after Pope had begun his rococo garden at Twickenham, that we learn of Swift beginning his own garden near The Deanery of St Patrick's Cathedral. Being in an urban situation it is not surprising that it was a smaller garden than that of Pope, which was located in the suburbs of London. Nevertheless, he was able to recount with pride, in 1725, of his winding walks in the new natural style and his trees, shrubs and roses. Although there exists no documentary evidence of its layout, his reference to the line of the walks allows us to assume that it was in the new rococo style. Pope often entertained Swift at Twickenham and brought him in 1726 to inspect the various gardens on which he was advising.[4] Although Swift's continued interest in the new style of gardening in England is borne out in his later letters, he did not return after that visit, contenting himself with visiting his friends in Ireland. Among these were Sir Arthur and Lady Acheson at Market Hill, County Armagh, and the Earl and Countess of Howth of Howth Castle, County Dublin, in the ornamentation of whose demesnes he took a practical interest.[5]

His friend, Dr. Patrick Delany, Dean of Down, was another of the select band of savants responsible for the introduction of the new manner. He bought the suburban demesne of Delville at Glasnevin near Dublin in 1724. It was more akin in size and location to Pope's garden than was that of Swift, and Delany was likewise imbued with the ideas of Addison and Pope. Thomas Tickell, Addison's friend and literary executor, lived at Glasnevin,[6] and we know that he and Delany, despite the complaints of their friends, absented themselves from Dublin society for long intervals while they worked in the garden at Delville.[7] Delany accompanied Swift to stay with Pope at Twickenham in 1726 and therefore had an opportunity of familiarising himself with Pope's approach. Fortunately there still exists a comprehensive series of views of Delville which were drawn by Mrs Delany in 1745 and which show it to have been in the intricate, whimsical and natural rococo style.[8]

The word rococo is used in describing the intricate shell work with which ornamental grottoes in European gardens had been decorated since the Renaissance. It is fitting, therefore, that though there were earlier grottoes in the gardens of Howth Castle and of Stillorgan Park (the latter designed by Sir Edward Lovett Pearce), Mrs Delany was the first in Ireland to decorate them extensively with shell work in the authentic manner. Her diaries record these creations at Killala, County Mayo, in 1731, at the palace of the Bishop of Clogher, County Cavan, and at Delville. The gardens of the two deans, together with those on which they advised (Dean Delany gave suggestions for improvement of the demesnes at Belleisle, and perhaps Manor Waterhouse, County Fermanagh[9]) make up a modest complement of Irish gardens in the rococo style.

Their pioneering if wayward efforts were cemented by the subsequent work of the professional landscape gardeners. Evidence of the latters' adoption of a more natural style can be found in their increasing use of the serpentine rather than the straight line for the laying out of woodlands, walks and ornamental ponds. The serpentine line was soon to be elevated to an important aesthetic plane through its identification by the painter Hogarth as the 'Line of Beauty'. Batty Langley's influential plans, which were published in *The principles of gardening* (1728), are examples of the traditional approach in which the serpentine and straight lines are frequently combined in the same design. Although Loudon, the early nineteenth century writer, stated that Langley came to Ireland, no evidence of his work has yet been found. Robert Stevenson, however, who was employed in the 1740s, seems to have been a close follower of his style. Stevenson's drawings for the garden at Headfort House, County Meath,[10] exhibit a blend of straight and serpentine walks from Langley's designs. His plan for the Dublin Rotunda Gardens[11] pleasure grounds like the better known Vauxhall Gardens in London, laid out for the enjoyment of a paying public, and a near contemporary plan of a garden at Trinity College, Dublin,[12] repeat the blend. The serpentine was used to more dramatic effect in the creation of ornamental sheets of water. The Earl of Shannon, when he undertook the improvement of the river between his estate and the village of Castlemartyr, County Cork,[13] canalised its banks into a sweeping serpentine line. A more lively serpentine is exhibited in the painting by Thomas Roberts of 'The Sheet of Water' at Carton, County Kildare.[14] These extensive and expensive effects were admired by the connoisseurs of the new natural landscape style, but they were soon found wanting in that the hand of man was still too visible in their design. The serpentine was a geometrical figure, albeit a curvilinear rather than a rectilinear one, and therefore could be but a transitional answer on the road to a landscape that was truly natural in style.

The eventual breakthrough had its source in the experience of the Italian landscape gained by those gentlemen who travelled through it on that journey through Europe known as 'The Grand Tour', then *de rigueur* for any man of cultural aspiration. This countryside appeared as if it had been unchanged for centuries; its rivers went unchannelled, its pastures unenclosed and its woods and trees untouched by the geometricising hand of man. Their appreciation was augmented by the sight of the many ruined classical structures with which it was still adorned. It began to seem to them the ideal landscape, one which might be used as a model with the assistance of which their own countryside at home might be rescued from the hitherto untrammelled progress of agricultural revolution and the drawing board designs of baroque landscape gardening. On their return, often armed with pictorial representations of this landscape by the great and prolific painter Claude Lorraine, they examined their estates with a critical eye and considered whether they could not be made to resemble what they had seen.

Their approach to landscape gardening was a rarefied one, appreciated fully only by those who had the benefit of classical learning and the most refined connoisseurship. The leader of the group was Lord Burlington, a great-grandson of the Great Earl of Cork and a frequent visitor to Ireland where he had inherited large estates. He patronised the publication of Ireland's first architectural book compiled by John Aheron in 1745. It contains designs for the kind of classical garden temple with which the newly landscaped demesnes might be decorated. More important for the history of gardening in general was the earl's patronage of William Kent, an English painter who had been with him in Italy. Kent took up the practice of landscape gardening in 1730 and was employed to create the first English parks designed in the manner promoted by this group. His most important work was in the great park of Lord Cobham at Stowe, Buckinghamshire. The influence of Kent's work there was first brought to Ireland by Matthew Peters, who advertised thus in *Faulkiner's Dublin journal* in 1746:

> Matthew Peters, nurseryman ... likewise designs lawns and improvements for gentlemen in the most natural and rural taste, in which business he was bred under his uncle who was chief gardener to Lord Cobham at Stowe. He can give sufficient proof of this particular and that he may be relied upon for the good of his seeds etc by the testimony of a gentleman of credit in this kingdom, who brought him from England and whose improvements (with several others) he designed and executed to their satisfaction and is now employed by a noble Earl and others.[15]

The 'noble Earl' may have been the Earl of Charlemont, for whom we know he was working soon afterwards at the demesne of Marino, County Dublin,[16] which is now better known for its principal ornament, the Casino, designed by

Sir William Chambers. Marino was among the first of the Irish demesnes to be developed in simulation of the Arcadian landscape of Italy. The interior was left unfenced, trees flourished in natural groups and flocks of sheep wandered without restriction through its groves and pastures. From the Casino, which had been designed as a neo-classical temple, there were views of the watery crescent of Dublin Bay with a background of receding ranges of mountains which were often bathed in the golden light of evening. The entire scene was reminiscent of the landscape of Italy as it was painted by Claude Lorraine, and in such a manner it was painted by William Ashford. In 1785 Ashford painted another ideal landscape – that created by the Ward family around their house at Castle Ward, County Down. The painted view is framed by the portico of a temple, the design of which was copied from the one erected by William Kent for Lord Burlington at Chiswick near London. In this picture can be observed the close resemblance, albeit in reverse, between the park and an ideal one painted by Claude in his 'The Expulsion of Hagan'. The closest such correlation occurred between the setting of the Mussenden Temple, erected by Lord Bristol in his demesne at Downhill, County Londonderry, and the painting by Claude known as Parnassus.[17] In each a domed and circular temple is perched on the edge of a precipitous cliff at the base of which extends an apparently limitless sea. Our northern skies could not be relied upon to reproduce the golden light which suffused Claude's canvases but this shortcoming was remedied, at least for the connoisseur, with the invention of the 'Claude glass', a tinted panel hung in a carriage window, through which one might survey the passing landscape in its proper light.

One of the most curious results of the new concentration on the landscape was the decline of the part played by the flower in ornamental gardening. The scale of landscape design required rather the impact of large forest trees which were sometimes augmented by an underwood of flowering shrubs. A small group of enthusiasts kept an interest in botany and horticulture alive however. Flowers continued to be grown in the old-fashioned parterres or the formal gardens of conservatives like Nicholas Halfpenny who in 1727 was described as the best gardener for a hundred miles around Rostellan, County Cork, where he was employed. As late as 1760, he is known to have staked out an old-fashioned parterre at Castlemartyr[18] not far away. Knightly Chetwode, though a friend of Swift, formed a labyrinth in 1729 which was an imitation of one at Versailles[19] and the father of Maria Edgeworth, the novelist, copied the plan for his garden[20] from the frontispiece to the famous *Gardener's dictionary* of Philip Miller, which was in the Dutch taste. Miller's *Dictionary*, first published in 1732, had many Irish subscribers. A Dublin edition was published and it continued to be the most widely used handbook for practical gardening until the publication of Loudon's *Encyclopaedia* in the early part of the nineteenth century. His advice was frequently sought on matters horticultural, although it did not in every case lead to satisfactory results. Though Sir William Fownes of Woodstock, County Kilkenny, bought fruit trees from a nursery in France recommended by Miller in 1736[21], Lady Kildare some twenty years later was writing about the appointment of a head gardener: 'Everyone says those recommended by Miller ... never turn out well'.[22]

Miller, who was Curator of the Chelsea Physic Garden, corresponded for many years with Linnaeus, the great Swedish botanist who revolutionised the classification and nomenclature of plants. An Irishman, Patrick Browne, also corresponded with Linnaeus over a period of some twenty years. Though Browne was primarily a botanist he is of interest to gardeners, not only through his connection with Linnaeus but also because the genus *Brownea* is called after him. At the end of the nineteenth century two Irish gardens were noted for their culture of *Brownea*. In his later years Browne seems to have been out of touch with the scientific world, for it was with surprise that Aylmer Lambert, on a visit to Westport, County Mayo, at the end of the eighteenth century, heard the country people speak of an old man living in retirement at Rushbrook near Claremorris, who was interested in botany. This old man turned out to be Dr Patrick Browne, the writer of a celebrated book about Jamaica and a connection of the Marquis of Sligo, whose family had estates in the West Indies. Lambert's curiosity must have been aroused further when he heard that Dr Browne had been a friend of Linnaeus, for he himself was a member of the Linnean Society of London, and here, in this place so remote from Sweden, was a link with the great naturalist.

Lambert determined to make the acquaintance of Dr Browne. He sent a message to say he would call on him, but perhaps he was abashed to find the old man bed-ridden, for he made a point of recording that he was received with much cordiality. Browne was delighted to have a visitor with whom he could discuss botany, and confirmed that he had indeed corresponded with Linnaeus for 20 years and had sent him many specimens. Browne graduated at Rheims as M. D. and afterwards lived in the Caribbean.[23] While there he compiled his *The civil and natural history of Jamaica*, published in London during 1756 and illustrated by George Ehret, the famous botanical artist.

Lambert and Browne became good friends over these reminiscences during the course of several meetings, so much so that Lambert was entrusted with several valuable manuscripts. One was the beginning of a *Flora Indiae Occidentalis*; another was material towards an Irish Flora entitled *Fasciculus Plantarum Hiberniæ*.[24] He also gave him a small herbarium of plants collected in Galway and Mayo, and a collection of mosses.

Browne was an all-round naturalist. As well as studying flowering plants he made a list of the toadstool fungi of County Mayo and published a catalogue of birds and fishes of Ireland in the *Gentleman's and London magazine* (1774).[25] He urged the publication of an Irish flora with both English and Irish names: 'I wrote them as much to the pronunciation of the Irish as I could, but not according to the Irish orthography, which I could not find in any book'.[26]

In view of Browne's wide interests, Lambert was surprised at the absence of a large library at Rushbrook. This was a sorrow to the old man, for on his last voyage he had entrusted several hundred books to the care of a friend in Dublin only to find on his return that they had all been lost. Browne was indeed dogged by ill-luck, for the copper plates of his great work on Jamaica were all burnt in a fire at Cornhill in 1765.

Jacquin, the Austrian botanist, dedicated the genus *Brownea* to Browne, a small genus of about eight evergreen trees from tropical America, belonging to the bean family.

Floriculture was widely undertaken for the purpose of providing material for the posies, nosegays, garlands and other fabrications of the florist which had become an integral part of eighteenth century social life. Of the florist's flowers, the most popular was undoubtedly the auricula. The Earl of Meath, for example, in 1746 listed no fewer than 74 Irish, 23 English and 690 other seedlings in his collection.[27] Mrs Delany wrote of the houses in which she forced auriculas. Next in popularity was the carnation, of which Lord Meath had about a hundred in 1732. To his collection he subsequently added many varieties of ranunculus, tulip and hyacinth.[28] The meetings of urban florists' club were occasions for much jollification. A minute book survives of one such club, the Dublin Florists' Society, covering the years 1747 to 1766.[29] The members, limited to thirty in number, were noblemen, clergy, army officers and gentry, who met together each month to dine in a tavern. The minute book is mainly a list of members present at these meetings, with records for the innkeeper's account of the number of bottles of wine they drank. The wine was to be provided as specified, for we read 'March 1st 1748. Ordered that it is the resolution of the club to remove to another house because the order of the club was not complied with to give the wine which was directed to be procured'. The club then patronised the Phoenix Tavern, Werburgh Street, one of the most fashionable and frequented houses in Dublin.

As was the fashion of the time, dinner was served in the afternoon. 'Resolved that the dinner shall not be called for until half an hour after three, and that four shall be the latest hour to bring it to the table'. Every member was to bring to the meeting some flower, otherwise he had to pay the penalty of half a crown, later changed to the forfeiture of a bottle of wine. Toasts were drunk to carnations from July to January and to auriculas for the rest of the year. These flowers were displayed on a mahogany stand, and after the names had been approved as correct and entered in the records, the members drank toasts to them.

Occasionally the club met in the garden of a member, Captain Desbrisay, where a cold dinner was laid on by Mr Hoey of the Phoenix Tavern. Another diversion was a party on the water, arranged for 16 May 1760, the members to meet at The George, George's Quay, 'at farthest by seven o'clock', when a boat was to be ready. Though the friends no doubt enjoyed their drinks, their dinners and the flowers that were the excuses for further toasts, they were not unmindful of gardening in general. On 3 May 1751 Captain Desbrisay was appointed chairman of a committee to award premiums to gardeners who raised the best flowers. The Society offered prizes to the person who shall raise the best polyanthus from seeds, 16s 6d, for the second best 8s: to the person who shall raise the best auricula £1 10s, for the second best ditto 15s.

Every summer, in June, the club was dissolved and every member had to notify his intention to re-join for the following year.

It was in the form of nosegays gathered up with coloured ribbons that Samuel Dixon chose to illustrate his florists' flowers. These were advertised in *Faulkiner's Dublin journal* on 26 April 1748:

> Samuel Dixon at his Picture-shop in Capel Street ... Said Dixon, having now completed his Set of Flower Pieces, in Basso Relievo, takes this opportunity to acquaint such of the Nobility and Gentry as have not yet subscribed and are pleased to have sets of the same, to favour him with their directions in order to their being served in their Turn. These Flower Pieces, which are a new invention, are not only ornamental to Lady's Chambers, but useful to paint and draw after, or imitate in Shell or Needle Work.

These were pictures embossed in low relief on coarse grey paper, and coloured afterwards in gouache. A set consisted of twelve pictures, each about nine by eight inches, depicting carnations, ranunculus, columbines, tuberoses and narcissi. It is interesting to see also included *Fritillaria pyrenaica* and *Lilium chalcedonicum* as familiar flowers of the period, though they were not recent introductions to cultivation, the latter being the 'Red martagon of Constantinople' of John Parkinson.[30]

Dixon also issued a 'Sett of Curious Foreign Bird Pieces', but these were not wholly original, being taken from the *Natural history of uncommon birds* (1743-51) by George Edwards. Such 'borrowing' was a common practice at the time and indeed Dixon was a victim in his turn as he had to complain about 'Imitation of my foreign Bird Pieces in Basso Relievo, put into Auctions, in order to deceive the unwary'.

Samuel Dixon was the third son of Thomas Dixon, a hosier of Cork Hill, Dublin. He set up a linen printing industry at Leixlip, County Kildare, but this was not a financial success and he had to sell out. After an attempt to run a picture shop in London, a project lasting only three years, he returned to Dublin and started again at Capel Street, but died the following year, 1769.[31]

Further encouragement to the growing momentum of the landscape movement was given by the discovery that the Chinese had been making gardens in the natural style for many years. Sir William Temple, who lived at Staplestown, County Carlow, for some years and to whom Swift was secretary later, wrote of these in his book *The gardens of Epicurus* (1685).[32] *Chinoiserie* features were not incorporated into gardening designs until the 1740s, however. There were Chinese bridges in the park at Belan, County Kildare,[33] and Rathkenny, County Cavan,[34] but none remains. One of the books most influential in the introduction of *Chinoiserie* was the description of the gardens of the Emperor of China at Peking by a French Jesuit missionary, Père Attiret, which was translated into English by Joseph Spence of Byfleet. Spence, the biographer of Pope, was also a landscape gardener of some repute and was asked to provide suggestions for Irish gardens. In 1765, he drew a plan for Dean Paul's garden at The Glebe, Cootehill, County Cavan, in which the outline of the rectangular plot was concealed by irregular groves and serpentining walks. Spence had advised the Dean to develop a network of ornamental walks and drives through his farmland.[35] In this use of the idea of the ornamental farm, or as it was then called, the *ferme ornee*, Spence was following the notions developed by Philip Southcote at Wooburn Farm, near Surrey. Southcote when travelling from Rome to Venice, had become enamoured, like William Kent, of the Italian countryside, but he appreciated rather more than Kent that it was not simply an ideal Arcadian landscape but one which was the result of a subtle combination of beauty with agricultural utility. On his return he improved his own farm at Wooburn in such a pastoral manner; his herds of sheep and cattle grazed freely through pasture apparently unrestricted by bank or hedgerow, his poultry house was disguised as a temple and his meadows and cornfields were encircled with flowering shrubs and groves of trees. It was to demonstrate to his many visitors that a landscape ornamented in a natural style need not be the prerogative of a small coterie of connoisseurs who had returned from 'The Grand Tour', but might also become a practical proposition for the smaller landowner whose circumstances forced him to keep a watchful eye on his pocket as well as his pleasure.

As we have come to know it, the landscape park was primarily the invention of one of the great geniuses of the history of gardening, Lancelot 'Capability' Brown (1716–1783),[36] of whom it was said, when he commenced his practice as a landscape gardener, that he had 'set up on a few ideas of Kent and Mr Southcote'. His designs were not for gardens as they are understood to-day, but for a gentleman's demesne, whose house, farmland, woodland gardens and the respective buildings of each were all conceived by him as being capable of formation into a single aesthetic unity. It was his practice, following Southcote, to begin by enclosing an entire demesne with a belt of woodland wide enough to contain a drive which would not only prove easy access through the demesne for farm traffic but also provide an entertaining carriage ride for the owner and his guests. With the latter purpose in mind it was often diverted, from what would have been its shortest course, to take in interesting panoramas of the demesne and the surrounding countryside. Inside the belt all hedgerows and rows of trees, whose straight lines offended the eye of this new taste, were grubbed out. Any shortcomings in the natural contours of the ground were corrected by what was often considerable earthmoving – inclines which were too steep were rendered gentle, rock protrusions were covered over. Low-lying wetlands were drained, often with the aid of an artificial lake created by the damming of a river or stream flowing through the demesne. Those areas of land which could not be so improved without intolerable expense were concealed beneath thick woodland plantings. What remained was developed as open, rolling parkland in which herds of deer, cattle, or flocks of sheep might freely and safely graze. Shelter in winter and shade in summer were provided by the groves and clumps of trees scattered through the interior. 'Beauty with utility' being a watchword of eighteenth century aesthetics, the design of all of these factors was conducted with one eye on their beauty but the other on their value as agricultural improvements. Other carriage drives threaded discreetly through the demesne, serpentining vigorously to give the occupants of the carriages views from the side windows which in the time of the straight, formal approach to the country house, had been the sole prerogative of the coachman up front. The gentle roll of the pasture allowed carriages of the newly-introduced sprung-type to leave the drive and wander without restriction through the grazing herds. When Edmund Burke, the Irish philosopher and aesthete, wished to illustrate by example his theory of beauty, he did not choose a piece of classical statuary, an inspiring ode, nor even a beautiful woman, but one of the experiences of a Brownian park:

Most people must have observed the sort of sense they have had of being swiftly drawn in an easy coach on a smooth turf, with gradual descents and acclivities. This will give a better idea of the Beautiful than almost anything else.

Large areas of the countryside were thus rescued from the geometricicising hand of the merely agricultural improver and given to the landscape gardener to develop in a way which would combine a sensitivity to the natural character of the landscape with the requirements of agricultural progress.

Between 1751 and 1783 Brown laid out no fewer than 200 such places in England. The Duke of Leinster wished him to come to Ireland. The Duke's wife, then Lady Kildare, recorded how she pleaded with him:

I saw Mr Brown the day before yesterday at his house at Hammersmith; he returned the night before from some place he has work going on. He says he will certainly come if he can possibly and will let me know a month before; he said he was very ambitious of coming and would certainly if his health would permit him; he was indeed very ill.[37]

On another occasion, he refused the Duke's offer of £1000 on landing if he would come to Ireland, excusing himself lightheartedly on the grounds that 'he had not finished England yet'.[38] He did, however, apparently send over designs to Lord Conyngham for alterations to outbuildings at Slane Castle, County Meath[39] and the influence of his assistants and followers is predominant in the Irish landscape to this day, as is the beech that trademark of their planting, which is still a conspicuous tree.

Humphrey Repton, Brown's best-known follower, was in Ireland in 1783 when he was acting as secretary to his friend William Windham,[40] but it is not known if he took part in any landscaping projects. Brown's son-in-law Henry Holland designed a gate lodge for Westport House, County Mayo,[41] and John Webb, one of his assistants who was also a designer of many remarkable parks in England, came to Ireland to create settings for John Nash's castle at Shanbally, County Tipperary,[42] and at Mitchelstown, County Cork.[43] He is also credited with the layout of parks at Ballyfin and other places in the county of Laois.[44]

The greater number of these improvements, however, were laid out by landscape gardeners living and working in Ireland. Among the most prolific were Thomas Leggatt, W. King and Peter Shanley, though little is known of their activities to-day. Thomas Leggatt was buried at Fort Hill, near Galway as we are informed by Hely Dutton:

Thomas Leggett [sic], a very celebrated landscape gardener, who after beautifying almost every demesne in the county, is most ungratefully suffered to lie here neglected, without even a *Hic Jacet*. I proposed, some years since, to receive subscriptions, to enable me to raise a humble monument to his memory, but alas I felt a freezing indifference except from the gentleman, who would give twenty guineas, provided it was erected in his own demesne.[45]

Further evidence of his contemporary reputation is provided by the knowledge that when an Irish landscape gardener, Denis McClear (1762–1840) called 'Mikler' in Poland, arrived in that country under the patronage of Isabella Czartoyrska, he declared that he had learnt to design gardens 'under the famous Legat'. (It was Isabella who introduced the landscape park to her native country, writing the standard textbook in Polish on the subject.).[46]

Although it is known that Leggatt was resident in Dublin at one time, surprisingly little else is known of his life and work. Three designs of his are however recorded: Mount Bellew, County Galway,[47] Marlay Park[48] and Stillorgan Park[49] in County Dublin. From contemporary maps it can be seen that the style of these parks was Brownian in that they were enclosed by curving belts of trees and their interiors formed of correctly undulating parkland varied with clumps and groves of trees. All three were, however, subsequently altered, Mount Bellew and Marlay Park being worked over by Hely Dutton in the later picturesque style of landscaping and Stillorgan Park built over in the mid-nineteenth century. Leggatt's work, like that of Browne, did not escape the critical blast of the subsequent generation of picturesque landscapers, one of whom wrote in 1818 of:

how much the gentlemen of this country have been led astray by the pompous and dictatorial manner of Leggett [sic], who I frequently met in my younger days and whom I admired with the herd, he was quite the fashion.[50]

The tussle for ascendancy between the rival schools of landscapers unfortunately descended to bitter personal invective.

Among Leggatt's colleagues in the early days of the movement in Ireland was W. King. Though the eccentric Lord Bristol was a great patron of 'Capability' Brown in England, he did King the honour of consulting him on the layout of his demesne at Downhill, County Londonderry, and his proposals were received with enthusiasm by the Bishop's architect, Michael Shanahan, in a letter to his patron:

On receipt of your Lordship's favour of the 5th June I wrote to Mr King at Lord Enniskillen to procure in time an ample store of Tamarisk, Laburnum, Myrtles, roses of every kind, sweet briars etc, etc, as your Lordship ordered; this is the only scheme I approve of that has as yet been proposed for adorning Downhill, the walks around the demesne will be very delightful and soon come to perfection without any degree of suffering by storms.

His scheme may have fallen victim to the severe exposure of the site on the north-west coast of Londonderry, for his client was writing to Lord Abercorn some years later asking permission for his gardener, Mr Hudson, to come to Downhill: 'Mr Hudson has given proof of his ability ... far beyond what Mr Shanley or King or any of the common manufacturers of lawns and plantations can rise to'.[51]

Such were the vicissitudes of the landscape gardener. The correspondence is of interest also in that it demonstrates that contrary to the popular belief that gardeners in the Brownian style planted only large trees and neglected the planting of flowers or flowering shrubs, some like King did carry out large-scale shrub plantings. The fact that these tended to be shorter-lived than the trees may have given rise to the more popular notion.

Shanahan's letter also discloses that King was being consulted at Florence Court, County Fermanagh, the seat of the Earl of Enniskillen, which had been recently completed.[52] The park was conceived in the classical mode of 'Capability' Brown, being entirely ringed with a belt of trees, through which ran a belt drive. The interior was then divided by three long fingers of wood into separate reaches of parkland, the largest, 140 acres in extent, forming the immediate setting of the house. Nearby, at Castle Coole, the seat of the Earls of Belmore, there is a bill for repairs to a greenhouse and the purchase of a stone roller which is attested by him in 1780.[53] At about this time the old formal garden in the baroque style was altered so that it seems reasonable to attribute the new design to King. The modelling of the ground into artistic swellings and curves was an effect much prized by the Brownian school. It was especially so when the undulating line was allowed to sweep under the clumps and groves of trees and on across the park until it reached the encircling belt of trees. The groves were therefore left unfenced so that cattle and deer might graze freely through them and thus discourage the growth of a shrubby underwood which would have the effect of breaking the continuous line of the ground. This practice was severely criticised by the next generation of landscape gardeners, one of whom James Fraser, when consulted by Belmore in 1846, advised that the plantations left open by King should be fenced to encourage the growth of a luxuriant underwood considered by him to be more 'natural'.[54]

Of Peter Shanley little more is known. Samuel Hayes of Avondale, County Wicklow, in his *A practical treatise on planting* (1794) refers to the late Mr Shanley whose skill and natural taste in ornamental gardening had early attracted his notice. That Shanley had an eye for the picturesque is shown by Hayes' account of his favourite trees at Avondale. These included a particularly fine specimen of the 'long-coned Cornish fir' (a form of Norway spruce) with cones nearly a foot long and drooping branches. This he had pruned in a manner suggested to him by Shanley, removing all the branches for the first seven feet and above this every second tier of branches:

> by which as the lateral shoots of branches encrease [*sic*] in weight they fall into the space formerly occupied by the branches immediately below them; this, in a vigorous tree, adds much to the picturesque appearance ... such was the state of this beautiful tree ... that the lower branches which covered a considerable space on every side, nearly touched the ground at their extremities, though they grew from a height of 7 feet.[55]

We have already seen that though Lord Bristol did Shanley the honour of consulting him at Downhill his proposals were ultimately rejected. More successful were his designs for the park and the remarkable greenhouses at Bellevue, County Wicklow, for David La Touche, the Dublin banker. When John Ferrar wrote his *A view of ancient and modern Dublin* (1795) he considered that 'so many circumstances lend their aid to embellish Bellevue and its vicinity, that we scruple not to pronounce it one of the best excursions from the capital.' The conservatory was 264 feet in length:

> The apparatus of glasswork cost three thousand pounds. This amazing work was commenced about the year 1785, and the outline nearly finished by a Mr Shanley, a native of Ireland, and an ingenious honest man, deservedly esteemed for his natural talents, whose death was a public loss.[56]

Another contemporary figure was Jacob Smith who was described by Hely Dutton in one of his books as 'long-time planter to the Duke of Leinster and his father'.[57] The Duchess wrote in 1762 of his enthusiasm:

> I had the great pleasure in seeing ten men thickening that part of the plantation between the Dublin and Nine Mile Stone Gate with good, tall shewy-looking trees-elm and ash; but there are still quantities of holes not fill'd and I suspect that to satisfy our impatience last autumn Jacob Smith dug more than he will get trees to fill this winter.[58]

When the widowed Duchess remarried, Smith came from Carton to her new house at Frascati in Blackrock near Dublin and devised the garden there.[59] Eventually Smith established himself as a professional landscape gardener and was employed to make improvements at Russborough, County Wicklow, and many other places throughout the country.[60]

The most celebrated of them all was undoubtedly John Sutherland (c. 1745–1826). His practice was immense, his character, during a long and active life, a model of probity and diligence, and his correct and elegant taste widely commented upon and much used. His earliest known design was for the summer cottages and park of the Lord Chancellor, Isaac Corry, at Derrymore, County Armagh, which was applauded by Sir Charles Coote in 1803:

The very fine improvements at Derrymore (built 1776) show the correct and elegant taste of Mr Sutherland, who planned them and supervised their execution. The young plantations already display a fine appearance of wood, the approaches are extremely well planned and the cottage, which is as yet the only residence is without exception the most elegant summer lodge I have ever seen.[61]

A small park, it is still enclosed by the belt of trees he designed. The open undulating lawn of the interior is dotted with solitary trees and only interrupted twice by larger clumps, the first to conceal the home farm and the second the walls of the kitchen garden. His practice was soon fashionable, as not long afterwards he was reshaping the park at Slane Castle, County Meath, after the castle itself had been altered to the Gothic designs of 'Capability' Brown.[62] The scale of the earthmoving and planting required to carry out his designs is indicated by the news in *Faulkiner's Dublin journal* for 1787 that 'last winter 350 to 450 men were engaged in making improvements' there.[63] His woods still hang down from the heights above the castle to the banks of the River Boyne below.

Towards the end of the century, he was advising at three parks, Killester, Peafield and Annesley Lodge, all of modest size and among the northern suburbs of Dublin. To the owner of the latter, the Hon. Richard Annesley, he recommended a gardener, Kelly, who took up residence with his wife in the gate-lodge. One day when Mr Annesley was being visited by his brother, the second Earl Annesley, the gates were opened by Sophie Kelly, the gardener's wife. She and the earl fell in love at this first sight. On his way out after visiting his brother, the earl persuaded Sophie to elope with him and they drove north together to his house in County Down, where they were married a few days later by the local clergyman. It was not until after Sophie had borne him two children that he discovered that she had neglected to tell him that she already had a husband. Their bigamous state and its resolution became one of the *causes celebres* of late eighteenth century Ireland. Sutherland played a diplomatic part in calming inflamed tempers and assisted in effecting the eventual solution by which the offending lady was sent off to Paris with her children, where they were established by Lord Annesley in some style, and Sutherland recommended Kelly, who had previously threatened to crush Annesley for absconding, albeit unwittingly, with his wife, for another position.[64]

The Annesley connection was to prove a fruitful one. He laid out the park of Mountainstown, County Meath, for John Pollock, who was the Annesley lawyer, and the brothers, whose town houses were in Mountjoy Square, Dublin, recommended him to the Commissioners of the Square as a suitable person to lay out the gardens at its centre.[65] The design he provided comprised all of the essential features of a rural park save that their disposition was modified to suit an urban setting. A serpentine walk wound its way through a perimeter belt or shrubbery which enclosed a circular lawn the centre of which was marked by a single weeping ash. James Mahony's watercolour of the area (1851)[66] shows the effectiveness of this device of a circle within a square.

11: John Sutherland, landscape architect. (Reproduced by permission of the Ulster Museum, Belfast).

The early nineteenth century brought Sutherland larger and more prestigious commissions. Among other works at Caledon, County Tyrone, he was responsible for the erection of hot houses costing over £2000 which must thus have been on a scale approaching those designed by Shanley for Bellevue.[67] Caledon was the first of five country houses designed by the renowned architect, John Nash, for which Sutherland was to design the garden and park.[68] The next was at Rockingham, County Roscommon, an enormous park created for the first Lord Lorton on a remote promontory jutting out into Lough Key.[69] Lorton had expended £60,000 on the erection of his house and was then about to expend a similar amount on the park and ancillary buildings. The entire commission for this second stage of the work was given to Sutherland. It eventually comprised digging a service tunnel from the stable block to the house so that the supply of goods and services might take place without disturbing the peace of the lawns, erecting a series of follies, castles and lodges as focal points on the islands and promontories of the lough, and developing the entire demesne as a Brownian landscape park. Caledon and Rockingham were in Nash's classical style, but Shane's Castle, County Antrim,[70] and Lough Cutra Castle, County Galway were in his more familiar gothic mode. Both stood romantically on terraces overlooking the spreading waters of a lough and in each park long screens of woodland framed distant view of the waters. Shane's Castle was unfortunately burned to the ground in 1818 but there is a portrait of the elderly Sutherland by Martin Cregan at Shane's Castle to-day (Fig. 11). It depicts him, cravat undone as benefits a working gardener, with the park and ruins of the burnt-out castle behind him. At Lough Cutra only the outline of Sutherland's planting survives. It was eulogised in its day by Hely Dutton:

> I do not know of any part of this country that will so repay the picturesque traveller than a day's stay at Gort ... when a view of Lord Gort's highly picturesque demesne of Lough Coutra [*sic*] is included. A view of a magnificent castle placed on the brink of an extensive lake surrounded with wood, will add to the pleasure. The recent improvements, including a front and back approach, do infinite credit to the long established taste and skill of Mr Sutherland, the celebrated landscape gardener.[71]

The fifth and last of the Nash houses around which he worked was Gracefield Lodge, County Laois, which was in the cottage style just then becoming fashionable. Neale's description of the alterations to the old formal park shows how Sutherland made clever use of the old avenue trees to give an impression of maturity to his new layout:

> The grounds have undergone an extensive and decisive change under the superintendence of Mr Sutherland whose sound judgement, fine, practical taste is universally acknowledged. Many formal rows of trees have been broken, numerous fences levelled, and the ground occupied by artificial pieces of water restored to its natural state.[72]

Sutherland's conservative approach to the old-fashioned lines of timber was in contrast to the more ruthless policy of 'Capability' Brown who insisted on clear felling them in many places. J. N. Brewer emphasised this in his description of Gracefield:

> The straight avenues of oak, beech and lime no longer offend the eye of taste. Mr Sutherland has here displayed great judgement, and achieved a very difficult task, in altering and embellishing the grounds without injuriously divesting them of timber.[73]

From a modern perspective it is difficult to appreciate how mature avenues of oak, beech and lime could possibly offend the eye of anyone's taste, but the feeling against the geometricisation of the landscape, which these lines of trees represented, was very strong. Brewer's account also shows how Sutherland departed from the Brownian rule of attempting to discourage the growth of underwood in plantations, for the West Wood was:

> intersected in various directions by spacious avenues and winding walks. It is thickly interspersed with holly of a large size, and an underwood consisting of laurel, hazel, acacia, syringa, whitethorn and honeysuckles, a profusion of hyacinths, primroses and violets.

The account ends with an encomium for Sutherland:

> and it must be observed in justice to that gentleman, that some of the most splendid places in the kingdom acknowledge him for their founder and reformer.[74]

About 1818 Sutherland became involved in a family quarrel over the park at Mitchelstown, County Cork. When the first Earl of Kingston built a new house there the village still lay under its walls, so that it was impossible to create a landscape park around it. It was decided to erect a new village some distance away to which the inhabitants would be moved. With its houses almshouses and church laid out in a series of squares and vistas, it is one of the most interesting examples of eighteenth-century town planning in Ireland. Cut-stone houses with slated roofs replaced the thatched cabins of the older village. The earl then commissioned the celebrated English landscape gardener, John Webb, to prepare designs for the layout of the park. In order to provide the appearance of maturity it was decided to retain some of the old lines of hedgerow timber until the new plantations got up. When this time came the earl had died, and his widow wished to complete his good work by grubbing out the old lines of timber and thinning the plantations in accordance with good forestry practice. She was accused by her son, the second earl, of wasting the estate timber, a charge which substantiated the constant complaint of all the professional pundits and knowledgeable visitors of the time, that the Irish gentleman invariably neglected the thinning of his plantations.

The Dowager Countess decided to employ the advice of a man whose authority and expertise it would be difficult to question. Sutherland was called in, and his subsequent report exonerated the old lady, recommending even further felling. Lord Kingston, notwithstanding this report and the fact that he himself had employed Sutherland to design his 'house, offices, gardens and outhouses' at Oakport, County Roscommon, put the whole matter in the hands of his lawyers. The complex legal dispositions which resulted are among the principal sources for Sutherland's life and work. He also succeeded Webb as a landscape gardener in the development of the park at Ballyfin, County Laois, when that place was bought by Sir Charles Coote in 1812.[75]

Sutherland's life and career were so long that before he finally succumbed through old age, it was often mistakenly assumed that he was dead. An article in the *Journal of Irish agriculture and practical horticulture* did so in 1819, and the journal was forced to print a denial in a later issue: 'Mr Sutherland is alive and in good health and in very general practice'.[76] It was not until seven years later, and two months before his death, that he felt it necessary to announce in the same journal that he was handing over his practice to his assistant:

> To the Noblemen and Gentlemen of Ireland: As I have had the honour of being employed by the most respectable of the Nobility and Gentry of this Kingdom, and now from the decline of old age, I find that I cannot fulfil any more of my engagements, I recommend Mr Arthur Snow as a fit and proper person. We have been concerned together upwards of thirty years in making approaches, Ornamental planting and all other Ornamental improvements.[77]

It is unexpected to see Sutherland described in the Dublin directories between 1819 and 1826 as an architect rather than a landscape gardener, but drawings for two of his architectural projects survive, a bridge over the River Inny at New Castle, County Longford,[78] for the Earl of Rosse, and a stable block for Donard, County Wicklow.[79] Sutherland died in 1826 at his house, 24 Great Brunswick (now Pearse) Street, Dublin, leaving property in more than two countries. He left uncompleted one of his designs, that of the approach to Mount Shannon, County Limerick, for the Earl of Clare.[80]

Sutherland's work, however did not escape the sometimes virulent criticism of a younger generation. One of these, James Fraser, complained in 1827 that he had failed to harmonise his scheme for the park at Slane Castle with the character of the surrounding countryside. He wrote:

> [It] exhibits many of the beauties and defects peculiar to his style. Prejudging of effects and harmonising of the outlines with the surrounding scenery seem matters too often lost sight of by him in some of his happiest designs.[81]

Edmund Murphy, another of the younger generation of landscape gardeners, also attacked him in a description of the park at Ely Lodge, County Fermanagh, now a seat of the Duke of Westminster:

Exclusive of a great extent of natural wood, there are many plantations designed about twenty years ago by Mr Sutherland. These afforded until recently a perfect example of the serpentine lines so much admired by him but which harmonised indifferently with the bold projections and deep irregular lines of the natural woods.[82]

To the early eighteenth century eye, accustomed as it was to the strict geometry of the formal garden, the parks designed by 'Capability' Brown and his followers seemed to represent the epitome of natural gardening. However, those who by the end of the century had become familiar with this style over many years were struck more by what they came to see as its artificiality and ultimate disharmony with the native landscape. Its serpentine lines were too smooth, its lawns too shaven, its plantations too primly disposed and the surface of its lakes too suave ever to be truly natural.

Their criticisms were, in part, a response to the growing appreciation of the natural beauties of these islands, in preference to the gentler landscape of the Italian *campagna* which was the inspiration of the earlier landscape movement. Since 1782, the Rev. William Gilpin had written a series of highly popular books extolling the picturesque virtues of the River Wye, south Wales, the Lake District of England and the Highlands of Scotland. It was his designation of these areas as 'picturesque' that led to the landscape movement which followed being known as 'picturesque' movement. This movement originated in a series of essays by two English gentlemen, Uvedale Price and Richard Payne Knight, who themselves lived along the valley of the Wye, one of the areas whose beauties Gilpin acclaimed. They advocated that the belt of trees which so characteristically surrounded a Brownian park separating its ideal world from that outside, should be broken to let in glimpses of that native landscape, the attractions of which were now seen in a new light. The outlines of new plantations were to be made more intricate, varied and so more natural than the smooth serpentines and soft lines of Brown's school. Their boundaries were to be fenced to keep out grazing animals and so the growth of a wild and picturesque underwood would be encouraged. A greater variety of tree species, including conifers, would give a rugged and varied outline to new woodlands, which might also be enhanced by the variety of their different foliage tints. The smooth contours which were the result of elaborate earthmoving in the formation of the earlier parks were henceforward to be despised as having altogether too tame an effect. More natural, broken and rocky ground was to be preferred, despite the fact that it would not be suitable for pasturing herds. The eighteenth century ideal of marrying beauty to utility was being ushered out by what was merely an aesthetic desire for the natural. The rushing water of a naturally designed cascade was preferred to the mirror-like surface of a Brownian lake, areas of rough woodland to those of tailored parkland, a picturesque cottage or a gothic folly to a temple in what came to be seen as a 'foreign' style. The movement was seen as a welcome return to commonsense and realism, and was tinted not a little with nationalism.

The criticism of the Brownian style in England was mirrored by the criticism in Ireland of the work of Sutherland which has already been recounted. The work of Shanley and Leggatt was also deprecated. Hely Dutton, one of the most vociferous of the new generation, wrote disclaiming any connection with them in 1819: 'My pretensions to the title of landscape gardener are based on foundations materially different from Shanley, Leggatt or any other deceased professor, except the late Mr Roach.'[83] The exception of Mr Roach is intriguing as nothing is known of him except that he was still in practice in 1808, when Dutton recommended him to the readers of his statistical survey of County Clare: 'I beg leave to advise gentlemen before they begin to improve to procure the very tasteful superintendence of Mr Roach and not pursue their own whims, which they dignify with the name of taste.'[84]

Dutton, a farmer's son, from Malahide, near Dublin seems to have first established himself as a seedsman at 19 Dorset Street, Dublin. He was later to relate of a nurseryman who had established a business in County Clare:

> He already begins to complain of a want of punctuality in payments. It is a well-founded complaint of every nurseryman in Ireland. I have had a severe trial of it myself formerly.[85]

This may present us with a clue as to why he abandoned his first pursuit in favour of agricultural improvement and landscape gardening.

At the end of the eighteenth century, the Dublin Society, which had been founded in 1731 to promote the progress of industry, agriculture and the arts, undertook the publication of a series of statistical studies of the counties of Ireland. The first to be published, in 1801, was that of Dublin. Dutton was dissatisfied with it to the extent that he was able to persuade the Society to publish his critical observations on it the following year. In these he remarked on the improvements he had undertaken on behalf of David La Touche in the demesne of Marlay, County Dublin, and also took the liberty of offering suggestions for the improvement of certain other demesnes with those whose development he had not been concerned, a liberty which appears not to have endeared him to the owner of the demesnes for he was soon writing: 'To find fault with a gentleman's demesne is to me an unpleasant task, and AS I HAVE FOUND LATELY a dangerous task for a professional man'.[86] The society, however, asked him to compile the survey for County Clare which was published in 1808. In this he was more diplomatic in avoiding reference to the demesnes on the improvement of which he had advised. On the other hand, he was not averse to dropping broad hints as to which some of them were. He reported, for example, his frequent visits to, and irrigation of, the demesne of Bindon Blood at Riverston.[87] He particularly noted a new plantation of 80 acres there, which contained, as was dictated by the new picturesque taste, a wide variety of tree species: 'oak, elm, beech, birch, Scotch and spruce fir, alder, sycamore, pinaster but chiefly larch or ash'. He also took the trouble to laud the planting of Sir Edward O'Brien at Dromoland, a property, he wrote, which he had 'often experienced'.[88]

In 1813 he was thinning the plantations at Russborough, County Wicklow, the seat of the Earl of Milltown.[89] Work was by no means continuous, however, for he was forced to advertise in the *Irish farmer's journal* during 1818:

HELY DUTTON

LANDSCAPE GARDENER

Mr Dutton informs his friends and those of the late celebrated Mr Roche (sic) that he will be disengaged for a short period at the end of May. His designs for producing Picturesque effect will be found very different from the tame imitations formerly introduced from England, that with some few exceptions, have continued to the present time a reproach to the taste of Picturesque Ireland.[90]

(The familiarity of his approach to his clients (his 'friends') is in contrast to that of Sutherland who always addressed himself in his advertisements to 'The Nobility and Gentry of Ireland'.)

In 1819, the Dublin Society published Dutton's statistical survey of County Galway in the introduction to which he announced that he was to eschew any detailed accounts of the country's demesnes 'as in very many of them I have been concerned in the embellishment and improvement'.[91] We must remain content with some oblique references to his working at Netterville Lodge,[92] the demesne of the Misses Netterville, Portumna Castle, the seat of the Marquis of Clanrickarde,[93] and Marble Hill, that of Sir Thomas Burke.[94] In County Galway also, he thinned the growing plantations of Mr Lawrence of Belview,[95] but the work by which he wished to be remembered was the embellishment of the park at Mount Bellew, the seat of Christopher Bellew in the eastern part of the county.[96] On the making of the lake, the centrepiece of the whole design, he was employed for three years, from 1816 to 1819. Prince Puckler-Muskau, the maker of the remarkable German garden which still survives at Muskau and author of the standard German text on the subject of natural landscape gardening, wrote that the lake 'afforded a perfect study for the judicious distribution of water, to which it is to difficult to give the character of grandeur and simplicity that always ought to belong to them'.[97]

After this Dutton appears to have found it difficult to obtain another commission. He was forced to advertise:

From many years' experience in a very extensive and varied practice, and an attentive study of the higher branches of landscape gardening. Mr Dutton presumes he may, with some degree of confidence, claim the notice of his countrymen. In sketching designs for water, and its necessary Accompaniments (the most difficult part of his profession) he trusts his ideas are more natural than many of those hitherto executed.

His aim in Thinning and Pruning Plantations (so ruinously and obstinately neglected in Ireland, and also it seems in England) is the union of Profit with Picturesque effect.

A considerable practice in draining and irrigating enable him, in many cases, to lessen the Expense by making each contribute to the benefit of the other: a practice unknown to the mere drainer. Mr Dutton will superintend a few demesnes by the year; but a decided preference would be given to a permanent engagement in one extensive place, where a considerable knowledge of, and fondness for, improvement and experimental Agriculture may be desirable:

He will contract to find everything for Designs sufficiently extensive, or enter into a partnership on adequate terms. Letters directed to Galway will be forwarded to him.[98]

Perhaps the outspokenness of his surveys led to a certain unpopularity. In that which he wrote on County Clare, for example, he accused the gentry and clergy of general indolence in the improvements of the lands in their ownership, and further diverted from the main purposes of the survey to note for his readers that the ladies of the county 'go in shoes without stockings'. As he tended to irascibility, his long residence at a place he was improving may have been trying for his clients.

Although at one time he wrote: 'Emolument with me is a secondary consideration. I have no pecuniary interest. I have no person to provide for but myself',[99] it did not prevent him at another time complaining that 'a drawing master of eminence will receive three or four guineas a day with pleasure, whilst an improver of land shall with a grudge be paid half a guinea.'[100] His advertisements indicate that he expected 30 guineas for superintending a demesne, three or four of which he would take on per year. (Mr Snow, Sutherland's assistant, advertised in 1818 for work on his terms of £1–2–9d. per day exclusive of expenses, indicating an expectancy considerably higher than that of Dutton.)

Dutton seems to have felt himself beset with unscrupulous rivals and impostors, for in his survey of County Galway, he wrote of a Mr Hill, a drainer from Britain, who had criticised his work:

I shall never imitate the illiberal remarks Mr Hill has thought proper to make on my works; I feel myself, from the partiality of my friends, high enough to look down on them. One of these itinerant gentlemen, I understand, has done me the honour to assume my name in many places where I am not known and has arrogated to himself the designing of the lake at Mount Bellew, etc., A letter to Mr Bellew will immediately detect the impostor. I never pay a professional visit without a previous invitation.[101]

Although it is known that he carried out another commission, the planning of a new approach to Sir Thomas Lighton's house at Merville, Stillorgan, County Dublin,[102] he eventually retired to a small bogland holding of 60 acres near Ballinasloe, County Galway, where it was his intention, under the patronage of the Earl of Clancarty, to build a cottage and model farm with the purpose of proving that with proper management and agricultural improvement, such an unpromising holding, of a size and type on which many unfortunate Irish families then lived, could be made viable.[103] Here in his retirement he planned also to revive his earlier interest in flowers. In June 1828 he wrote to Loudon's *Gardeners' magazine* for advice. 'My present avocations have engrossed my attentions for so many years that my favourite pursuit had lain dormant until your magazine awakened it, and I wish to amuse my latter days with that greatest solace, next to religion, a flower garden.'[104] He wished to obtain polyanthuses, pinks, dahlias and chrysanthemums, expecting to get them at trade prices, and had ambitions to raise improved kinds, for he was 'once very high in the fancy' (i.e. in the hobby). The date of his death has not been traced but it is presumed to have occurred while he was carrying out his improvements on his bogland holding. Although in many ways an erratic personality, he was an original and gifted improver of demesnes.

Edmund Murphy, like Dutton, was accounted by Loudon in his *Encyclopaedia of gardening* as one of the principal 'rural artists' in the Ireland of the day. He was for a time the Irish correspondent of *The gardeners' magazine*, a periodical published by Loudon, and also conducted a number of short-lived agricultural and gardening periodicals in Dublin. Only one of his landscaping works is known for certain – the deer park around the great waterfall at Powerscourt, County Wicklow,[105] but he was at Baronscourt, County Tyrone, the seat of the Duke of Abercorn,[106] for some time during 1823 which strongly suggests that he may have been acting professionally there.

It was considerably more expensive for an Irish landowner to employ one of the eminent English or Scottish landscape gardeners. William Sawrey Gilpin, grandson of that William Gilpin in whose topographical writings lay the origins of the Picturesque movement, was a landscape gardener of considerable importance. His charges of five guineas a day were four times that of Mr Snow and his expenses were certainly higher. Nevertheless his reputation was such that he was brought to Ireland to plan the landscape of island, lough and wood around the new castle of the Earl of Erne at Crom, County Fermanagh.[107] Nearby, and in a similar setting, he carried out one of his principal achievements, the landscape around Lough Muckno at Castleblayney, County Monaghan. Although Gilpin was a landscape gardener in the Picturesque tradition, his approach did not prevent him from introducing a formal terrace on occasion to act as a foreground to the distant view. He laid out such a terrace at Caledon, County Tyrone.[108]

Lewis Kennedy, a landscape gardener who prepared books of exquisite watercolours to show the effect of his suggested improvements when completed, was asked to come over to alter Sutherland's park at Slane Castle so that it might conform with the more romantic taste of the Picturesque movement.[109] The predominance of this movement, however, was already giving way before the rising popularity of the Gardenesque style of J. C. Loudon, for the pre-eminence of the large landowner on the political and social system of the eighteenth century was now being challenged by the increasing wealth and importance of the cities. It was to a different clientele that Loudon, who had already come to Ireland in 1811 to carry out some commissions, was to address himself.

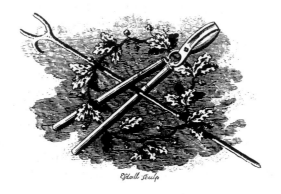

THE RISE OF PLANTSMANSHIP
ARBORETA AND PINETA

The late eighteenth and early nineteenth century was a period of transition in gardening style, encouraged by the increasing number of plants introduced from abroad and associated also with the rise of the middle classes. One of the most prolific of British garden writers was John Claudius Loudon (1783-1843). His great book, *An encyclopaedia of gardening*, about one and a half thousand pages long, ran into several editions between 1822 and 1850, reflecting the demands of changing society. Until this time all the great gardening texts, even one as recent as Humphrey Repton's *The principles of landscape gardening* (1816) assumed that gardening was the prerogative of the aristocratic demesne. Loudon, however, laid down guidelines for three classes of garden, the cottage garden, the suburban villa garden and the demesne garden, thus providing for the needs of the wider class structure of the nineteenth and present centuries. His basic thesis was 'gardens are to display the art of the gardener', and stated that:

> One of the greatest of all sources of enjoyment resulting from the possession of a garden is the endless variety which it produces, either by the perpetual progress of vegetation which is going forward in it to maturity, dormancy or decay, or by the almost innumerable kinds of plants which may be raised in the smallest garden.[1]

This attitude to gardening, familiar though it is today, was in contrast to that of the previous century, when the garden had been taken over by the painter, the architect, the stage designer and the landscaper in turn as a medium by which to display their arts. Loudon himself referred to an Irish example of such usage when he mentioned that at Thomastown, County Tipperary, there were the remains of a hanging garden (i.e. one formed on the side of a hill) in one corner of which was 'a verdant amphitheatre, once the scene of occasional dramatic exhibitions'.[2] The gardener's art being best displayed in the cultivation of plants, there began an increasing emphasis on them for their own sake rather than for the contribution they might make to a pre-judged design. No longer were areas of the garden laid out for their association with classical idylls, as in the Nymphaeum of Drenagh, County Londonderry,[3] or with famous heroines (e.g. Rosamund's Bower at Marino, County Dublin,[4] dedicated to the ill-fated mistress of Henry II, and the temple at Castletown, County Kildare, in honour of the actress Mrs Siddons[5]), but rather with the intention of showing off the beauties of one particular type of plant. Thus at this period we find areas of the garden designated for specific plants – the arboretum for trees, the pinetum for conifers, the rosarium for roses and the American garden for *Rhododendron* species (including azaleas) and *Kalmia*.

The earliest known arboreta in Ireland were those at Oriel Temple, County Louth, and at Tollymore Park, County Down, both begun in the year 1768.[6] The first was the creation of John Foster (1740–1828), last Speaker of the Irish House of Commons and later Lord Oriel. He was son of Anthony Foster of Collon, County Louth, Chief Baron of the Exchequer of Ireland, who was praised by Arthur Young for his great work in reclaiming 5000 acres at Collon, and for planting trees.[7] In 1763 he built glasshouses for grapes and pineapples.[8] His son followed his example in extending the plantations and developed a great interest in exotic trees. Young noted that John had introduced 1700 sorts of European and American plants. For 50 years he continued to plant for ornament and profit at Collon, assembling his magnificent collection of trees and shrubs in the setting of over 600 acres of plantations, his ambition being 'to have every tree and shrub in plenty that will stand our climate'. [9]

Foster's guide to plants was the celebrated *Gardener's dictionary* of Philip Miller, Curator of the Chelsea Physic Garden, London, which first appeared in 1724 and went through many editions, including at least one Dublin printing. Foster was a remarkably progressive collector, mainly of trees and shrubs from Europe and from the east coast of North America, for the expeditions of David Douglas had not yet transformed our ornamental and forest landscapes with trees from the Pacific coast; nor had Asia, Australia and South America yielded the many species that were to thrive so well in Irish gardens. One of Anthony Foster's official appointments was that of a trustee of the Linen Manufacture in Ireland and we find John writing to the Linen Board's agent in London, John Ellis, a noted naturalist of his day, to ask if he would procure for him a sensitive plant[10] (Venus's flytrap, *Dionaea muscipula*) and 'also to buy for me from some of your correspondents in America 10 or 12 guineas worth of such forest trees as will thrive here'.[11] This was but a beginning, and his eagerness for new plants is shown further by his planting of *Rhododendron ponticum* about 1778, probably some of the first in Ireland, since it arrived at Kew fifteen years previously and its commercial distribution by Loddiges of London only took place after 1770.[12]

This plant, once native, is now often regarded as an alien pest in many of our scenic regions. In 1778 Foster planted the Lucombe oak, only 15 years after it was raised by the Exeter nurseryman, Lucombe.[13] He had the purple beech in 1783, six years after it was first listed by Loddiges,[14] and added the fern-leafed beech 14 years after it was listed by Loddiges in 1804.[15] He sowed seed of cedar of Goa (*Cupressus lusitanica*, actually a Mexican species), which his son had collected in Portugal in 1809.[16] He had a mudan (moutan peony) which probably came from the original introduction to Kew from China by Sir Joseph Banks, since by 1824 it was twelve feet tall, about the same size as Sir Joseph's own plant at Isleworth, near London.[17] In planting the pin oak (*Quercus palustris*), a native of eastern North America, about 1788,[18] Foster was well ahead of his fellow collectors, since its first introduction to England was not, according to W. J. Bean, until 1800.[19]

Loddiges' nursery, and its Hammersmith rival, Kennedy and Lee, were noted at that time for their introduction of new species. Other landowners in Ireland bought plants from them, including the Pakenhams of Tullynally (p. 57). Foster was one of the chief initiators of the Botanic Gardens at Glasnevin and when he placed the order for the foundation collection for the new garden three quarters of the expenditure was incurred with Kennedy and Lee.[20] No wonder Wakefield recounts of him 'that nurserymen in the neighbourhood of London have often assured me that he was by far the best arborist of a gentleman of fortune they ever knew'.[21]

Foster's collection at Collon was described as second only to Kew.[22] The rhododendrons struck everyone with astonishment, and the novelist Maria Edgeworth was the grateful recipient of twelve plants for which she thanked him profusely in a letter of 1826. Foster himself was regarded as possessing 'more knowledge of trees as to their propagation, growth, connection to the soil and value when timber than any person I ever met with'.[23] It was sad, therefore, that so much labour and knowledge were wasted when the demesne was clear felled after the last world war.

Lord Clanbrassil (1730–1798) began collecting exotic trees at the same time. Although Loudon lists many of the trees planted by him in his demesne, Cypress Grove, near Dublin (the name reflecting the preponderance of coniferous trees), his more lasting contribution was his idea of the re-afforestation of the more remote mountains and hills of Ireland with commercial coniferous woodland, an idea which was to become the basis of commercial forestry in Ireland up to and including the present day. The Duke of Atholl had been planting conifers on a large scale at Dunkeld in Scotland and developed quite advanced techniques of commercial planting and propagation. To introduce these techniques to Ireland Lord Clanbrassil published in 1783 his *Account of the method of raising Scotch fir as practised in Scotland*. From 1775 onwards he planted great quantities of larch and silver fir round his demesne of Tollymore Park, County Down, on the lower ridges of the Mourne Mountains. The larch and spruce grew best on the shady side of the mountains, as they do in their native Switzerland, so that their position and their sombre colouring must have given the landscape a shadowy gothic character, not unlike that which was to become fashionable through the efforts of William Beckford at his gothic folly of Fonthill Abbey in Wiltshire. In keeping with the character of the landscape Clanbrassil built a series of gothic follies around the demesne of Tollymore – gateways, a barn with a steeple, a bridge and a grotto recording his friendship with the Marquis de Monthermer, son of George, Duke of Montagu.[24]

In 1775 he began to plant clumps of *Rhododendron ponticum* through the woods, lightening the sobriety.[25] Although this plant was to become a feature of many Irish demesnes, at that time it was an advanced idea, since rhododendrons were then usually planted within the confines of the formal American garden. Following the introduction of *Rhododendron, Kalmia* and similar plants from the eastern parts of North America it was realised that these species needed special conditions for their culture, especially in the provision of lime-free peaty soil. It was usual for them to be planted by themselves in beds of such soil, laid out formally in parterres. There was such a garden, for example, at Pakenham Hall (now Tullynally), County Westmeath, made by the second Countess of Longford,[26] whose gardening activities were admired by Maria Edgeworth in 1834:

> I never saw in England or Ireland such beautiful gardens or shrubbery walks as she has made. In a place where there was formerly only a swamp and an osiery she has made the most beautiful American garden my eyes ever beheld ... and even now when the rhododendron bank was not in blow and all American plants out of bloom it was scarlet-gray with Lobelia fulgens and double dahlias of all colours in the green grass their flower knots looking most beautiful.[27]

This American garden, later replaced by a pond, is shown on an estate map of 1834 as a semi-circular layout divided into two matching beds.

The demesne at Tollymore has remained in a good state of preservation and is now open to the public as a forest park. The original tree of the slow-growing form of spruce, *Picea abies* 'Clanbrassiliana', discovered by Lord Clanbrassil still grows there.[28]

The plant hunting expeditions of David Douglas, and in particular his introduction of new conifers from the Pacific coast of America, led to the creation of a number of specialised arboreta called pineta. These were designed to include collections of pines, firs and spruces, all of which at that time were known under the name of pine. The growing importance of the botanic gardens at Glasnevin and Trinity College, Dublin, is evident from the fact that by the year 1838 their pineta each contained several more species than did that of Kew. The only private pinetum begun at this time in Ireland was that at Tittour, Newtownmountkennedy, County Wicklow.[29] There John Nuttall had growing over 20 species in 1834, including *Pinus ponderosa* and one listed by him as *Pinus serotina Duglassii* which had been introduced by Douglas just seven years previously.[30] Nuttall contributed an article to Loudon's *Gardener's magazine* describing how his pines grew so fast that they were inclined to become top heavy and to lean over when planted in exposed positions in stony soil. He overcame this problem by a method he devised of disbudding the trees in spring before they started into growth to check their upward progress and to increase the bulk of the stems. New buds formed the same season, and by the following year the trees had recovered their healthy aspect.[31]

A northern garden which was the forerunner of things to come was that at Cranmore, the suburban villa of John Templeton (1766–1825), a wealthy Belfast wholesale merchant. A remarkable amateur naturalist and botanical illustrator, he corresponded with Sir Joseph Banks who tried unsuccessfully to persuade him to abandon his business and go plant hunting in Australia.[32] He was the first in Ireland to make a consistent attempt to acclimatise a range of half-hardy trees and shrubs in the open air, a pursuit which, on account of the mild nature of our climate, has since been an important part of Irish garden history. Templeton began his experimental garden in 1793. His practice was to start the new plants in his hothouse and then to transfer them to a cool greenhouse. Finally he planted them in a carefully prepared site outside, having closely observed each stage of the process. He prepared appropriate soils for each plant; a light soil for alders and willows, a gravelly soil for pines and *Cistus* and a fine peaty one for heathers and rhododendrons.[33] His collection was the first to contain a substantial proportion of Far Eastern importations in addition to those from America.[34]

Such pursuits led Templeton and many of his contemporaries to neglect, in the layout of their gardens, the classical compositional devices of symmetry, asymmetry and the serpentine line in favour of a layout evolved from the cultural requirements of the plants. This subordination of the overall design to the beauty of individual species came to be called by Loudon the Gardenesque style. From the design point of view it led to an odd, rather whimsical style of no particular pattern. The return to fancy from the strict rule of taste was encouraged by the introduction of an enormous range of plants from the regions of the world now coming under the influence of the European empires. These new riches were augmented by the fruits of a movement to improve plants by careful selection and hybridisation. These combined developments led Loudon to pronounce with confidence that 'no residence in the modern style can claim to be considered as laid out in good taste in which all the trees and shrubs employed are not either foreign ones or improved varieties of indigenous ones.' This must have shocked his more conservative contemporaries brought up on the Picturesque idea that landscape design should harmonise with the surrounding countryside to such an extent as to appear almost indistinguishable from it.

Though many of the landowners of the eighteenth century had their own tree nurseries there were a few commercial nurserymen in the country districts, such as John Hares of Otway, County Tipperary, and Fennessy of Waterford. The latter introduced a curious form of the common oak (*Quercus robur* 'Fennessii') with very variable leaves.[35] Edward Hodgins of Dunganstown, County Wicklow, had a sharp eye for variation in native trees and shrubs. Today he is remembered as the raiser of two hollies which were extensively planted in Victorian times. These, *Ilex* x *altaclerensis* 'Hodginsii' and 'Hendersonii', are still well known.[36]

An indication of the wide range of plants already available for cultivation can be obtained from the catalogue of Edward Bray, nurseryman and seedsman of Merchants Quay, Dublin, issued in the 1780s.[37] The forest and ornamental trees are European, except for cedar of Lebanon and five species from North America. Though flowering shrubs and evergreens are offered, the main feature of the list is the great number and variety of vegetables. For examples there are 19 kinds of pea, twelve of bean and ten sorts of French bean. 'Salad seeds' include seven varieties of radish and eleven of lettuce. An intriguing item is the 'True Cork asparagus'. Flower seeds are very numerous also, and, though mainly annuals and biennials, include auriculas and carnations. Bulbs that could be purchased include anemones, *Ranunculus*, crown imperials, lilies, jonquils, tulips and hyacinths. No less than 52 different kinds of peach and nectarine are named, along with figs, apricots, pears and cherries. Of 32 apples in this catalogue only three are of Irish origin, though many more existed around this time (p. 95). The culture of melons was regarded as a subject for rivalry. In *The Dublin chronicle*, 21 August 1787, it is recorded that an annual melon feast was held at Blackrock, County Dublin, in Conway's Tavern. The first prize, a gold medal, was won by the Right Hon. John Beresford, and a silver one by Dr Robert Fowler, Archbishop of Dublin.

The wealthy businessman in his suburban villa was from this time to play an important part in the horticultural patronage which had previously been the preserve of the landed interest. Frederick Bourne of Terenure House, County Dublin, was a pioneer of the natural style of gardening and made an interesting collection, not of forest or park trees, but of smaller flowering and berrying kinds more appropriate to the scale of his surroundings. Beginning about 1808, he planted varieties of thorn, nettle tree (*Celtis*), pear and service tree, and other small flowering trees which might still find a place in the smaller gardens of today.[38] His head gardener was James Fraser (p. 107), who was to become one of the principal garden designers in Ireland during the mid-Victorian period.

Bourne also had conservatories and grew the popular florist's flowers of the day: 'the beautiful flower plots – such beds of roses, such amaranthine odours, as neither Damascus itself, nor these Sabean vales that gave the Arabian prophet an idea of his sensual paradise – can surpass!' No wonder a correspondent of the *Dublin penny journal* was grateful to Mr Bourne for opening his garden to the public despite the risk of light-fingered visitors, who might, it was suggested, even use a lady's muff to conceal stolen plants.[39]

Terenure House still stands, now part of Terenure College.

Not all imported plants were hardy, so the old eighteenth century orangeries soon became hothouses of increasing elaboration in order to provide suitable environments for them. So glamorous were many of these plants that a desire soon arose to bring the hothouse out of the kitchen garden where it was first located and to attach it to the house, thereby contributing to the luxury of its surroundings. Called the conservatory, it became one of the unique features

To Peter La Touche Esq.
County of Leitrim this Plate is

S.Closedel, et Sculpt

Knight of the Shire for the
Inscribed by his obliged Friend

12: Bellevue, County Wicklow. A landscape in the Brownian style by Peter Shanley.

"In one bright Point admiring nature eyes, Such Pleasures here we may at once enjoy.
The Fruits and Foliage of discordant Skies! Pleasures which never cease, yet never cloy."

13: Hothouse and greenhouse at Bellevue, County Wicklow, designed by Peter Shanley.
(Reproduced by permission of the National Library of Ireland).

of the nineteenth century garden. The first one in Ireland was conceived by the landscape gardener Peter Shanley (p. 50)[40] for Mr La Touche at Bellevue, County Wicklow, in 1785. From the house one stepped directly into a range of glasshouses 264 feet long, which cost Mr La Touche the sum of £3000 (Figs 12 & 13). The centrepiece was a large oval conservatory which, although constructed of wood, was curvilinear and therefore an anticipation of the curvilinear iron conservatories of the mid-nineteenth century. On either side stood matching vineries flanked in turn by a pair of peach houses, the left hand range ending in a tall cherry house, which matched a similarly tall and square orangery on the right. Among the exotic fruits grown were passionfruit, pineapples, cherries, grapes, oranges, figs and peaches. The culinary plants included ginger, Arabian coffee, cayenne pepper and tomato. So rich was the variety that Edmund Burke, the statesman and philosopher, was moved to pronounce after a visit to the houses that 'the fruit grows in such perfection that I envy not the nabobs of India, nor the rich merchants at the Cape of Good Hope'.

Rare and tender plants were grown in pots which stood on the flues which warmed the house. Planted among the fruit were ornamental climbers and tender shrubs, many of them from the Cape, and Mr Pennick the gardener had mignonette, sweet peas and lupins in flower in March, a remarkable achievement so early in the year.

Loudon himself came to Ireland between 1809 and 1812. He 'made the general tour of Ireland and had been engaged professionally in three or four counties'.[41] In 1811 he laid out an arboretum at Charleville Castle, County Offaly,[42] but of his other works we know nothing, but an indication of his visits perhaps can be gained from the fact that the only demesnes on which he made original comments were Bellevue, County Wicklow, Moira, County Down, and Baronscourt, County Tyrone. All the other descriptions in his *Encyclopaedia* are taken from Fraser's *A traveller's guide to Ireland*. Of Bellevue he wrote 'A romantic residence, with extensive gardens and hot-houses, on which no expense is spared to preserve their reputation of being the first in Ireland.'[43] He indicated the antiquity of Moira by noting that it 'contains some old trees and also some young plantations; gardening in all its branches having been here attended to by the present owner's father, when neglected in almost every other part of Ireland'. Baronscourt was criticised as having 'no park scenery or gardens deserving notice. Extensive plantations, however, have been made in various parts of the demesne'.[44]

In his *Encyclopaedia* Loudon was disparaging in his remarks on the state of landscaping in Ireland. 'We are not aware that any English artist of eminence has been employed as a landscape gardener in Ireland, the more common practice being to engage a good kitchen gardener from England, and leave everything to him.'[45] He did, however, acknowledge Sutherland, saying that he 'was, in 1810, the native artist of greatest repute'. Loudon anticipated an improvement in Ireland, for he stated that 'A. M'Leish has since settled in this country and from what we know of this artist, we have little doubt he will contribute in an eminent degree to establish and extend a better taste than has yet appeared there'.[46]

Alexander M'Leish, who came to Ireland in 1813, was in fact one of Loudon's own pupils. He was described in 1818 as having been 'regularly bred to landscape gardening under the celebrated Loudon of London and to architecture under the famous Nicholson, author of the *Architectural Dictionary*.'[47] He brought the Gardenesque style to Ireland and from the early Ordnance Survey maps we can deduce that his gardens at Lisnabin, Reynella, and St. Lucy's,[48] all in County Westmeath, were in this style, being a mixture of informal shrubberies combined with the tentative introduction of formal designs at a distance from the house, often in association with the kitchen garden. His designs for the grander gardens at Knockdrin, County Westmeath, and Headfort, County Meath, were rather simple formal layouts placed with more confidence in front of the house itself. That at Headfort had a circular feature at the centre flanked by matching scroll designs, and at Knockdrin there was a planned sequence of formal designs – an English parterre, a Dutch parterre and a rosarium; these were an early anticipation of the elaborate Victorian formal garden.[49] M' Leish's architectural style was similarly varied; his designs for Lisnabin was in a castellated style with polygonal turrets, but for Reynella and St Lucy's he used simple classical forms. His combined talents were useful in his design for a gardener's house at Trinity College Botanic Gardens[50] and in the erection of the first iron and glass hot houses in Ireland at Clonmannon, County Wicklow,[51] followed in 1816 by a pair at Merville, County Dublin. The latter, one a greenhouse and the other a stove, were at the focal point of a flower garden surrounded by a semi-circular canal situated at some distance from the house. Detached from the garden proper was a small American garden described by James Fraser (p. 107) as 'the best private collection of bog plants we know in the vicinity of Dublin.'[52] Fraser praised Merville as a delightful, well kept villa. He acknowledged that the parterre in front of the glasshouse was remarkably pretty, containing the best collection of spring flowers in the kingdom, but he criticised its formality, and hoped that stiff geometrical figures would be banished from flower gardens. Such gardens as these foreshadowed the revival of the flower garden as an ornamental feature in its own right, after a century of relegation to the kitchen garden, where it was merely a utilitarian reservoir for florist's flowers grown for bouquets and posies.

Of the rest of M'Leish's busy life we know that he was employed on the west coast, in County Sligo and in County Galway where he met James Fraser, his future critic and successor who was employed as head gardener at Dartfield, near Loughrea. He was the author of the Irish section of the entry under landscape gardening in Loudon's *Encyclopaedia* and ran a nursery at Harold's Cross, Dublin, in conjunction with his practice. He was the prime mover in the regeneration of interest in ornamental gardening that took place in the early nineteenth century. By the time of his death in 1829 he had more than fulfilled the hopes expressed by Loudon on his arrival in Ireland. Nevertheless his widow was left in poor circumstances, the nursery having run into debt. His children had predeceased him, so friends set up a fund for her relief.[53]

Right Hon.ble John Foster

BOTANIC GARDENS IN IRELAND
IN THE EIGHTEENTH & NINETEENTH CENTURIES

The increasing interest in growing plants for their own sakes stimulated the development of botanic gardens; no less than four were founded in Ireland during the 33 years from 1795. Botanic gardens are of ancient lineage, for their origin can be traced back to the monastery gardens where herbs were grown for medicinal purposes. With the establishment of universities, medicine and botany were generally taught by the same professor, who needed a garden to grow the herbs and botanical specimens he required. The short lived Dublin Philosophical Society owned 'a fair garden' in 1684.[1] Very soon after its foundation in 1591 Trinity College had let out plots for growing herbs and other plants, but in 1687 the College board took a more direct interest, resolving that the kitchen garden should be made a physic garden at the charge of the College.[2] In 1712 Dr Nicholson, the first lecturer in botany, published in connection with this garden a pamphlet *Methodus plantarum in horto medico Collegii Dublinensis iamiam disponendarum*. In 1722 this physic garden was moved to a new site under the control of Dr William Stephens, whose catalogue of the plants include, besides medicinal herbs, such garden plants as auricula, tulip, narcissus and primula.[3] For a time the College's botanic garden was at Harold's Cross under the direction and part ownership of Professor Edward Hill, who had a salary of £130 a year, out of which he paid two permanent gardeners and two temporary helpers in the summer. This garden lasted only a few years.[4]

National Botanic Gardens, Glasnevin

The establishment of the National Botanic Gardens at Glasnevin can be traced back to the efforts of that remarkable society of amateurs of science and art, the

Dublin Society. In 1732 a minute records the appointment of a committee to 'look out a piece of ground, about an acre, suitable for a nursery'. These first efforts met with a number of setbacks. A piece of ground near Ballybough Bridge was taken, rent free for three years, and then at £6 per acre. Although members took a deep interest in the garden, a Mr Ross for example, sending 500 poles for hops from Rostrevor, the garden does not seem to have lasted long. In 1737 four acres were taken near Martin's Lane (now Waterford Street). The garden seems to have been biased towards the growing of economic plants, for in addition to Mr Ross's gift there are references to cider trees and to a house for laying up flax. By 1740 these experiments had come to an end, the gardeners dismissed and the site condemned as being on unsuitable soil.

Another 50 years were to pass before further attempts were made. In 1790 a petition was drawn up by Dr Walter Wade, botanist and surgeon, which was presented to the Dublin Parliament. It had the sympathy of the Speaker, John Foster, himself, as we have seen, a keen plantsman with a notable collection of trees and shrubs at Collon, County Louth. Following this petition a grant of £5000 was made to the Dublin Society out of which £300 was to be reserved for starting a botanic garden.

A committee was formed to advise the Society. In addition to Wade the members were Dr Robert Percival, Secretary to the Royal Irish Academy and Dr Edward Hill, Professor of Botany in Trinity College. Wade was primarily a botanist, author of papers on grasses, oaks and willows, and of an essay on *Buddleja globosa*[5] as a plant for bees. He was the first Irish botanist to use in a publication the Linnaean system of naming plants in his list of plants native to County Dublin, *Catalogus systematicus plantarum indigenarum in comitatu Dublinensi inventarum*, published in 1794.[6] This little book of 275 pages so pleased the Society that they printed and distributed 500 copies at their own expense.[7] Although Wade identified some of the plants erroneously, he was meticulous in seeing for himself every species he recorded and not, as he might have done, compiling his list from other people's findings. He added 130 new species to the county flora, including 32 grasses. He was the first to find the bee orchid in County Dublin, near St Doulough's Church, Balgriffin, where the species persisted until destroyed by dumping in 1977.

When the site at Glasnevin was finally acquired in 1795 Wade threw himself into the project with enthusiasm. He gave public lectures on botany, waiving in favour of the Society the fees to which he was entitled.[8] The first account of the garden was attributed to him – 'A short description of the Dublin Society's Botanical and Agricultural Garden at Glasnevin' (1800). This merely sets out the divisions of the garden and their functions without descriptive detail, and was bound up with his *Catalogue of plants in the Dublin Society's Botanic Garden at Glasnevin*. The accompanying map by Thomas Sherrard shows the layout of the garden as it was in 1800. With the Society's strong interest in agriculture it is not unexpected that a large part of the Botanic Gardens was concerned with farming. Plots were laid down to 'sheep herbage, wholesome, [and] injurious. Goat herbage, wholesome, [and] injurious' and similarly for horned cattle, horses and swine. These plots were known as the Hortus Ovinus, the Hortus Caprinus, the Hortus Bovinus, the Hortus Equinus and the Hortus Suinus, the whole being the Pecudarium or Cattle Garden. Wade's interest in grasses was no doubt responsible for the Foenarium or Hay Garden, 'one of the most interesting divisions of the establishment'. Seeds of the more valuable grasses were distributed to landowners wishing to try them on their own farms.

The western boundary of the garden was sheltered by a plantation screen. Within this was the Arboretum and the Fruticetum or collection of trees and shrubs. There was a large esculent garden, the object of which was 'to point out, with scientific accuracy and precision, the several kinds, species and varieties of plants immediately subservient to the use of man.' This was divided into separate portions for root vegetables, stem and leaf vegetables and those of which the flowers were used, as well as plots for plants giving edible seeds and those of which the pods were eaten. Other features of the garden were the dyer's garden, the rock garden (p. 196), the collection of climbing plants, the garden of native plants, the medicinal garden, and provision for water and bog plants. Furthermore,

> to render the establishment still more complete, a plan is under consideration for erecting a suitable apparatus for Marine or Sea Plants. ... To add to the beauty and dignity of the whole, a green-house has been erected, at present furnished with a very curious and valuable collection of plants, particularly the Ericae, or beautiful heaths of the Cape, amounting to above 150 species.

The early efforts at providing glasshouses at Glasnevin were not entirely successful. Sherrard's map shows, situated near the entrance to the gardens, five parallel glasshouses 60 feet long, connected by a passage running along the north end. The centre house was a conservatory 23 feet high and broad; the other houses were 20 feet high and 16 feet broad. This range of houses were found to be unsatisfactory on the grounds of aspect, ventilation and the difficulty of heating them efficiently. By 1818 they had been demolished and replaced by two others. One, a conservatory with wings, was on rising ground near the centre of the garden and was 153 feet long. The other, near the entrance, was similar but smaller. These glasshouses did not please the authors of a contemporary description!

> These conservatories are built without any attention to architectural ornament. They are obtruded into the most conspicuous parts of the garden, where they are coarse and formal objects, destroying that picturesque effect which was so particularly attended to in every other arrangement.[9]

Wade's catalogue of the Society's garden was not complete. 'The Escarium, Foenarium, Hortus Medicus, Creepers and climbers, Pecudarium etc will be given in our next Publication, as the Catalogues could not be made out in time for this volume'. A glance through the catalogue shows how extensive were the collections listed. The trees included many species and varieties of elm, oak,

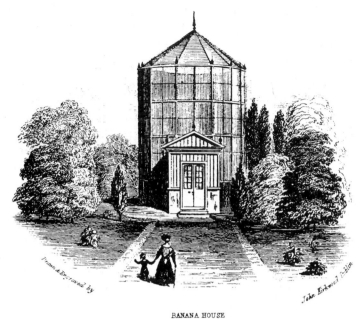

BANANA HOUSE

14: The Octagon House, as illustrated in Ninian Niven's *A companion to the Botanic Gardens*.

willow, birch, poplar and ash. Gold and silver blotched forms of some of these and of apricot, plum, hornbeam and maple aroused much interest, and many variegated shrubs were included also. Though the great influx of decorative species from Asia and America were still to come, the list already included azaleas, a few dull magnolias, the mayflower (*Epigaea repens*), a *Ceanothus* and a few other shrubs still highly valued today. Naturally there were good collections of well-known European genera such as hollies, hawthorns and roses. The herbaceous and bulbous plants were well represented – *Iris*, European primroses, daffodils, *Allium*, *Scilla*, peonies, anemones, as well as numerous plants of more botanical than horticultural interest. There were alpines (p. 196) and even terrestrial orchids. Thus in five years a good garden had been developed under the direction of Dr Wade.

The first head gardener was John Underwood, who had been brought over from Scotland in 1798 by Speaker Foster on the recommendation of William Curtis, editor and publisher of *The botanical magazine*. Underwood compiled the Gardens' second catalogue, published in 1804.[10] This was not a guide to the Gardens, but a list of plants arranged on the Linnaean system, and not according to their location in Glasnevin. No complete catalogue of the collections has been published since then, over 190 years ago.

Underwood worked at Glasnevin for 30 years. He was the first to find whitebeam and wild radish in County Dublin.[11] At first all went well at Glasnevin and the Society's Committee of Botany reported favourably on the condition of the plants at Glasnevin, but in 1819 the train of events started that led to the row between the Society and the head gardener. One of the treasures of the Glasnevin Gardens was a splendid Norfolk Island pine, *Araucaria excelsa*, commonly seen today as a pot plant but then, in the words of the Committee, 'a beautiful and rare botanical specimen'. In June 1819 the Committee reported on the condition of the Botanic Gardens. In particular they were concerned about the overcrowded state of the pine, which had outgrown its glasshouse. They thought that 'the state of the Norfolk Island pine is really reproachful.'

James Carpenter was given a contract to build a new house round the pine. This was the remarkable Octagon House, long to be a landmark in the Gardens (Fig. 14). In November 1819 Carpenter was duly paid £150 'on account of building round the Norfolk Island pine' and the following January received the balance of £165–7–2.[12] Soon there were disturbing accounts of the condition of the tree, and in April the Society resolved that the Committee of Botany 'be requested to view the Norfolk Island pine, to inquire whether it has sustained any and what injury, and if so that they be requested to inquire and report by what means and by whose mismanagement or neglect such injury has been occasioned'.

Thus a menacing tone was adopted from the beginning. The Committee lost no time in presenting their report. Only four days later they stated that

> they considered the present state of the plant very bad indeed; its health and beauty are very much impaired and its recovery very doubtful. ... it appears to your Committee that the injury which the plant has sustained has arisen from the non-performance of the contract entered into with the Society, for erecting a building round the plant, by James Carpenter ... to have been completed ... on the 24th of September 1819, but which was not effected until Saturday the 4th of December; that in consequence the plant was left exposed to the open air until that time and from the unfortunate circumstances of an unusually severe and early frost having taken place in November, more particularly on the night of the 24th and 25th of that month, during which the thermometer stood at only 20 (twelve degrees below the freezing point) having ... fallen ten degrees in the night, the plant became injured by its unaccustomed exposure to the severity of the weather and to a degree of cold not usual so early in the season.[13]

John Underwood and Mackie, the under-gardener, were summoned before the Committee. Despite written pleas from both of them that the tree, though very sickly, would recover, the roots and top being perfectly safe and young buds already appearing, the Committee blamed Underwood. They said that in their opinion some neglect or mismanagement is immutable to the head gardener ... that he did not report ... the improbability of the enclosure being completed previous to the time when cold and harsh weather might naturally have been expected in this climate; and further, as it does not appear to your Committee, that any efforts were made by him to shelter or protect the plant when the harsh weather had set in.

The tension mounted. On 4 May 1820 notice was given to the Committee that a motion would be introduced to dismiss Underwood. On hearing of this, Underwood submitted a 'memorial' stating that he had discovered, with the utmost concern, that he had incurred the displeasure of the Society in consequence of the injury sustained by the Norfolk Island pine and pleading that he had never been told that the builder was bound by contract to finish by 24 September. He believed that the Society's architect had full oversight and responsibility, and he had repeatedly remonstrated both with him and the contractor over the delay. He pointed out how sudden and exceptional was the frost, and how the pine could normally have been uninjured even as late as December. Furthermore, he said he was 'afflicted with a severe illness, so that your Memoralist's life would have been endangered by removing from his bed' on that critical night. He reminded the Society that he had served them for more than 22 years and that he had a wife and seven children to support.

The following week a special committee reported that John Underwood's memorial was justified. Nevertheless the proposal for his dismissal was put forward, but an amendment reduced this to a fine of £5. This in turn was not passed; instead Underwood was severely censured and warned that he would be dismissed on the first well founded complaint against him.

This censure by the Society seems to have demoralised Underwood, for from then on the garden declined. The apprentices, for whose instruction he had received payment, became undisciplined. Underwood himself was rude to visitors, let the lake run dry so that the aquatics died, and was generally uncooperative with the Committee. By the time he retired in 1833 the garden was a mass of weeds, with plots of cabbages and potatoes grown by the staff for their own use, and it was alleged, laundry was dried in the glasshouses. Underwood was allowed to retire to the model cottage that had been built in the Mill Field, but died a few months later. His widow lived on there for another 28 years.[14]

TRINITY COLLEGE BOTANIC GARDEN

The Dublin Society was not the only body interested in the foundation of a botanic garden near Dublin towards the end of the eighteenth century. The College of Physicians in Ireland and Trinity College, Dublin, had been involved in the discussions, and a garden for the common use of all three institutions might have resulted had the negotiations not fallen through.[15]

On the failure of agreement with the other bodies, the Board of Trinity College took about three acres of ground at Ballsbridge in the July 1806. The site

15: James Townsend Mackay.

was enclosed with a ten foot high wall, 800 feet of the south-east of which was lined with brick to make it more favourable to the growth of plants.[16]

The Board of the College appointed James Townsend Mackay (Fig. 15) to have the care and management of the new garden. Mackay, born at Kircaldy, Fifeshire, had come to Dublin in 1804 as Assistant Botanist in Trinity College. In his new appointment he was answerable to the Provost and Senior Fellows, and not to Dr Allman, Professor of Botany, who was not associated with the running of the garden, though a collection of medicinal plants was laid out from a list drawn up by him, and he was supplied with specimens and given facilities for lecturing in the garden as required.

Mackay's duties included lecturing and demonstrating to medical and other students in the Botanic Garden. He had a great interest in field botany and took his pupils out to the country to study the native flora. During his time as Assistant Botanist the Board had encouraged his studies by financing trips to the south, west and other parts of Ireland in 1804 and 1805. He was the first to find, in this country, the little Cornish moneywort (*Sibthorpia europaea*) of damp places on the Dingle peninsula and the endemic Irish cress (*Arabis brownii*) of western sandhills, as well as other plants. These studies culminated in his *Flora Hibernica*, published in 1836 with the assistance of the College authorities.

Mackay's familiarity with the remoter parts of Ireland enabled him to refute the statement of the continental botanist, Schultes, who said he had been told by very many Englishmen that 'it is safer to travel among savages than in the west coast of Ireland, which is the reason why the botany of that country is as little known as that of Sardinia'.[17] Mackay named the many interesting plants to be found in the west, including the maidenhair fern, 18 inches or two feet high on Aran, where 'should they find Mr O Maly, the principal resident gentleman, at home, they may perhaps, as I did twenty-five years ago, after spending a pleasant long day exploring the island, sit down with him in the evening to a good dinner, consisting of roast beef, turbot, and other accompaniments, and a glass of excellent claret; and might then return home with somewhat different ideas of the west of Ireland than they had formerly entertained.'[18]

The planting of the garden at Ballsbridge started in the spring of 1808, with trees, shrubs and herbaceous plants. In 1832 two extra acres were added, enclosed with an iron railing and planted with small trees and shrubs as well as a collection of conifers. The final extension of one and a half acres was made in 1848.

The garden attained a high standard in the cultivation of the fashionable plants of the day. Mackay was allowed £20 to £30 a year to visit the principal botanic and other gardens in England and Scotland, where he arranged the exchange of plants. Twice he visited continental gardens and was in correspondence with American botanists, who sent him seeds and plants. In 1822 Loudon in his *An encyclopaedia of gardening* described the garden at Ballsbridge as 'rapidly increasing in riches under the excellent management of its present curator', though only one wing of the intended range of glass had as yet been built, comprising a stove house, 35 feet by 16 feet, and a greenhouse 40 feet by 16 feet. He noted that Mackay had a reputation for the excellent laying out of grounds.

Mackay supported the shows of the Horticultural Society of Ireland with exhibits of rare plants, especially orchid and stove house species. This was much appreciated and at their June exhibition in 1834

> the committee availed themselves of the occasion to present Mr Mackay with a piece of plate, as a mark of the Society's sense of his disinterestedness in declining to be a competitor for prizes, while he continued to contribute the choicest horticultural specimens to their periodical exhibitions.[19]

He could draw on extensive collections in the College Gardens, for by 1852 he could write

> the Trees and Shrubs may be mentioned as very complete, and the Herbaceous and Medicinal arrangements are as extensive as climate and soil admit. In the house collections the Orders or Classes of Cactae, Orchidaceae, Ericaceae, Proteaceae, Palmae, Filices etc, are all extensive, and fully meet the requirements of Medical and other Students.

Mackay's long tenure of office lasted until his death in 1862 and in successive editions of his *Encyclopaedia* (1834, 1850) Loudon noted the high level of maintenance of the Trinity College Botanic Garden under him though he did not hesitate to refer to the then poor state of the garden at Glasnevin. Mackay's successor was John Bain (p. 122).

The College Botanic Garden has benefited through the years from collectors who sent plants from overseas, though on a smaller scale than did the larger Glasnevin Gardens. J. T. Mackay has recorded how former students of the College donated valuable collections of plants. One was Dr Thomas Coulter, who was born near Dundalk in 1793.[20] He went to America early in the nineteenth century, living an adventurous life in the wilds, sometimes surviving only because of his powerful physique and his skill with his rifle when short of food. He explored the flora of California and Mexico, sending to Trinity College Botanic Garden a valuable collection of cacti, described by David Moore[21] as causing a great sensation and stimulating their culture in Ireland and Britain. He returned to Europe about 1834, was appointed Keeper of the College herbarium in 1840, and died in 1843. The big cone pine (*Pinus coulteri*) was called after him, a species which he discovered in California in 1832. This, and Sabine's pine, an allied species, also Californian, have the largest and heaviest cones of all pines; spiny and with edible seeds. Coulter is also commemorated in the Californian tree poppy (*Romneya coulteri*), a plant thrice linked with Irishmen. The genus was named by William Harvey in honour of Thomas Romney Robinson (1792–1882), the infant prodigy who became a famous astronomer at Armagh Observatory, and was the inventor of the cup anemometer.

Thomas Oldham (1816-1878), one-time Director of the Geological Survey of Ireland, sent home four boxes of rare orchids from India, where he had joined the Indian Geological Survey. Another traveller who made a valuable collection of plants and seeds for the College garden, this time form North America, was William Henry Harvey (1811–1866), who, as a schoolboy enthusiast for natural history, was determined to become a scientist. His father was a leading Quaker merchant in Limerick, who took his family on seaside holidays to Miltown Malbay, County Clare. Here the young William developed his interest in seaweeds and shells, subjects on which he was to become a leading authority. His tastes were encouraged at the famous Quaker school at Ballitore, County Kildare. Later his interest in mosses brought him into touch with Sir William Hooker at Kew, who became a life-long friend. At first William Harvey was obliged to go into business, but eventually, after several years of frustration, he got an appointment which enabled him to continue his botanical studies. This was the post of Colonial Treasurer at the Cape of Good Hope, a job which first went to his elder brother. His brother died, however, and William was appointed, only to have two breakdowns in health. Before ill-health forced him to give up the post, by combining his official duties with his enthusiasm for botany, he completed his first important work on African plants, *Genera of South African plants*.[22]

Harvey succeeded Coulter as Curator of the herbarium in Trinity College, though he just failed to get the professorship of botany vacant at the same time, despite the bestowal of an honorary M.D. to increase his chances, a medical qualification being considered a necessity for a professor of botany in those days. In 1848, Harvey was elected Professor of Botany to the Royal Dublin Society, and thus effectively became director of the Society's Botanic Gardens at Glasnevin.[23] During 1849 and 1850 he toured the United States at the joint invitation of the Smithsonian Institute and Harvard University, and it was during this visit that he collected seeds and plants for the Trinity College Botanic Garden. In 1853 he received permission to sail round the world to study natural history and to collect specimens. On his return the Chair of Botany was vacant, and this time he was appointed Professor.

In 1860 Harvey read a paper before the Dublin University Zoological and Botanical Association, gently deriding Darwin's ideas on evolution. He did not mean this to be taken too seriously, for a copy of the paper was found years later, on which he had written, 'This is rubbish – merely got up to amuse an evening meeting of a Private society. W.H.H.'. Nevertheless Darwin had felt ill-used, for he wrote to Joseph Hooker, William's son,

> I was not sorry for a natural opportunity of writing to Harvey, just to show I was not piqued at this turning me and my book into ridicule, not that I think it was a proceeding which I deserved, or worthy of him.

Harvey made amends by sending Darwin a copy of his pamphlet inscribed 'with the writer's repentance, Oct. 1860'.[24]

William Harvey attained great distinction in the world of botany before he died at the age of 55, at the home in Torquay of Lady Hooker, widow of Sir William, his life-long friend, where he had gone in the hope that the mild climate of Devon would cure his consumption.[25]

Another botanist who contributed to the Trinity College Botanic Garden was Arthur F. G. Kerr, of whom his Dutch biographer wrote: 'To most botanists the name Kerr recalls little more than a man who made large botanical collections in Siam and who annotated them in awful handwriting.'[26] Kerr was born in 1877 in the little village of Kinlough, County Leitrim, where his father was a doctor. Arthur was to become botanist to the government of Siam, but first he practised medicine for almost 20 years. He took a degree in botany at Trinity College, Dublin, and then qualified there in medicine. After a voyage to Australia as ship's doctor he arrived in Siam, where he was appointed medical officer of health in the Government service. He became interested in the orchids growing in the hills of north Siam, cultivated them in his garden and made sketches of them. He took the sketches to Kew when home on leave, and was encouraged to collect herbarium specimens of the Siamese flora, then almost unknown. Though he is generally remembered as a botanist with over 21,000 specimens to his credit, in Trinity College he is recalled as the donor of a notable collection of living orchids to the College Garden. Two plant genera and more than 30 species, including a tropical relative of lords-and-ladies, *Amorphophallus*

.3118.

W.J.H.del.

Pub. by S. Curtis Glazenwood Essex Dec.r 1.1831.

Swan sc

4 *Cephalotus follicularis*, the Western Australian pitcher-plant, grown so successfully by John Bain in Trinity College Botanic Garden, Ballsbridge, Dublin; from *Curtis's botanical magazine* (1831), plate 3118

3971.

W Fitch delt.   Pub by S.Curtis Glazenwood Essex Oct 1 1842.   Swan Sc.

5   *Gloxinia tubiflora*, introduced from South America by John Tweedie through Glasnevin; from
Curtis's botanical magazine (1842), plate 3971.

W.Fitch del.ᵗ   Pub. by S. Curtis Glazenwood Essex March.1.1843.   Swan Sc

6   *Androsace lanuginosa,* a rock-garden plant from the Himalaya, flowered during August 1842 in
     Trinity College Botanic Garden, Ballsbridge, Dublin; from *Curtis's botanical magazine* (1843),
     plate 4005.

W. Fitch del.   Pub. by S. Curtis, Glazenwood, Essex June 1 1844.   Swan Sc.

7   *Morina longifolia*, a perennial herb from Asia, flowered in Belfast Botanic Garden during
    August 1843; from *Curtis's botanical magazine* (1844), plate 4092.

J.N.Fitch Lith.

Vincent Brooks Day & Son Imp

L. Reeve & Co London.

8 *Calceolaria deflexa*, a South American slipperwort introduced into cultivation by Messrs Rodger, McCleland & Co., Newry; from *Curtis's botanical magazine* (1879), plate 6431.

8173

M.S.del. J.N Fitch lith.

Vincent Brooks Day & Son Ld imp

L. Reeve & Co London.

9 *Paeonia mlokosewitschii*, an herbaceous peony from the Caucasus, flowered by William Gumbleton, at Belgrove, Cobh; from *Curtis's botanical magazine* (1908), plate 8173.

10   *Buddleja colvilei*, a butterfly bush from the Himalaya, grown at Belgrove, Cobh, by William Gumbleton; from *Curtis's botanical magazine* (1895), plate 7449.

M.S. del. J.N. Fitch lith.

Vincent Brooks, Day & Son Ltd imp

11 *Lomatia ferruginea*, from temperate parts of Chile, flowered at Castlewellan, County Down in July 1906; from *Curtis's botanical magazine* (1907), plate 8112.

kerrii (Plate 14), were called after him, as well as a parasite of fish, for he was also interested in zoology. From 1920, the year of his appointment as Government Botanist, he carried out annual tours in his task of surveying the flora of Siam, travelling by train, car, bullock court, or even by elephant, and then covering great distances on foot. He retired in 1931, and died at Hayes, Kent, in 1942, aged 64.

CORK BOTANIC GARDEN

The Cork Botanic Garden, like that at Glasnevin, owed its foundation to a cultural body. In this case it was the Royal Cork Institution, founded in 1803. This society conducted coursed in chemistry, botany, agriculture, natural history and geology.[27] In 1807 the Governors decided that Cork ought to have a botanic garden, so they leased a five and a half acre site, located at a place called Lilliput, from the Reverend Richard Croly, and in June 1808 appointed a Scotsman, James Drummond (c. 1787–1863), as curator.[28] This appointment was to end 20 years later in near disaster for Drummond, though he went on to re-establish himself in Western Australia, where he became Government Botanist.

During his time in Cork Drummond enjoyed exploring the flora of the county,and soon established himself as a notable field botanist. In 1809 he discovered the splendid large-flowered butterwort (*Pinguicula grandiflora*), and the next year he found, near Castletown Berehaven, the Irish lady's tresses orchid (*Spiranthes romanzoffiana*), two of the most interesting of our native plants. His country rambles were the basis of a series of articles on the plants of County Cork in the *Munster farmer's magazine*.[29]

At home in Cork the Botanic Garden developed under his care and in 1822 was described as containing six acres surrounded by a hedge, with glasshouses in a walled enclosure of one acre near the centre.[30] Security seems to have been impossible, for in May 1826 began a series of robberies of plants. These pilferings were particularly exasperating to Drummond, since he was entitled to augment his salary of £180 a year by the sale of duplicate plants. For six weeks he had employed a watchman but could no longer stand the expense, and started to patrol the garden himself. Then one November night no less than 40 young apple trees were stolen, including some valuable new kinds raised from scions presented to the Royal Cork Institution by the Horticultural Society of London for distribution through the country. The next night Drummond went out carrying a gun to frighten off marauders. He discovered an intruder and charged through a hedge in pursuit. The gun went off accidentally and the robber was shot dead.[31]

This accident and the inquest that followed it must have caused Drummond acute distress. As if this was not enough, the Governors of the Institution found the Botanic Garden a heavy expense despite government support, and the final blow came in 1828 when the Chief Secretary wrote that no grant could be given for the Garden. Drummond wrote an anxious letter to the Governors, anticipating the loss of his job after serving the Society for the best years of his life. He stated that all the property he possessed in the world were his plants in the Garden, and asked that the lease be assigned to him so that he would not have to sell off his plants in a hurry at poor prices. He undertook to continue the supply of specimens for botany lectures as long as he could continue in the gardens without charge. The special committee appointed by the Institution could not see their way to grant Drummond's request; nor did they accept an offer from a local nurseryman, Richard Hartland, to take over the garden provided he was paid £10 a year for supplying specimens for the botanical course at the Institution. Instead they surrendered the lease to Mr Croly, who paid them £20 for removable articles such as tools and re-let the grounds to the celebrated Father Mathew for use as a cemetery[32] and so it remains to this day, with only a cedar tree as a sign of its former use.

Drummond sold his plants from the Botanic Garden by auction, and informed the Governors that he had 'obtained the permission of His Majesty's Government to proceed as a settler to the colony about to be formed at Swan River on the west coast of New Holland'. The committee commended Drummond for his scrupulous attention in leaving the property of the Institution in good order, noting that he had left not only single specimens of all the plants cultivated, but also invaluable beech hedges and large plants which were his own property, and recommended that he should receive six month's salary. Thus ended, through no fault of his own, Drummond's tenure as curator of an Irish botanic garden.

Belfast Botanic Garden

At the other end of the country, too, there was a desire for a botanic garden. In 1828 a notice was circulated in Belfast:

> The people of Belfast have been the first to step forward and form a garden for themselves, a garden the sole property of the inhabitants of the country, supported by the inhabitants and not dependent on any other establishment, not calling in the aid of government, but maintained by the free, independent, voluntary support of a people, the first in the commerce, and certainly not the last in upholding the honour of their country.[33]

This was printed over the name of James Lawson Drummond, Professor of Anatomy at the Academical Institution, and first President of the Belfast Natural History Society. He issued this as Correspondence Secretary of the newly formed Belfast Botanic and Horticultural Society, who were very conscious of the handicap of lacking government support for their projected botanic garden, such as was available to Glasnevin.

Lack of money was to be a perennial source of worry to the Society, and was the main cause of the use of their garden for functions far removed from botany or horticulture.

16: Palm House, Belfast Botanic Gardens, designed by Charles Lanyon; dome executed by Young of Edinburgh; wings executed by Turner of Dublin. (W. Lawrence, reproduced by permission of the National Library of Ireland).

Glasnevin is not crippled, as so many provincial so-called Botanic Gardens are, by dependence on voluntary support, but has an assured income derived from Parliamentary grants. It is not necessary, as in Belfast, to compete with the Circus in tight-rope performances, or to have the grounds injured by the crowds brought together to witness balloon ascents or displays of fireworks.[34]

These words illustrate the difficulties suffered by the Belfast Botanic Garden from its foundation. The Belfast Botanic and Horticultural Society raised £3000 by the issue of shares and managed to keep the garden going for 65 years, but many stratagems were needed to bring in extra money. The terms of admission were changed from time to time; holders of less than four shares in the Company had to pay for entry, and a family ticket was introduced which also admitted the children's nurse. Special terms were offered to those coming from more than six miles away, and to such bodies as the Young Men's Christian Association and the Working Men's Association, provided that at least ten members joined the group. In 1865 a Free Admission Fund was raised by public subscription to encourage the working population to come on Saturday afternoons, when a band was hired. This fund proved too troublesome to administer and instead employers could buy books of tickets for their employees and their families. The opening of public parks put an end to this scheme.

Charges for admission had to be supplemented by other sources of income. Of these, fêtes were more successful financially than the usual kind of flower show. In 1838, for instance, the attractions included, in addition to the ever-popular spectacle of a balloon ascent, archery, boating on the Lagan, dancing, a flower exhibition and a bar. The fêtes became annual events, but their very success led the Society into the situation previously described. Outside bodies were allowed to hire the grounds for a variety of purposes – military tournaments and archery, dog shows and firework displays, Punch and Judy shows and even a display of Zulu dancing.[35]

With the Garden put to such uses it is understandable that a visitor should write

> There is a good deal interesting to be seen in this garden, and a good deal uninteresting. there is a baldness throughout in all we expect to see in visiting a Botanic garden, which the present curator, Mr Johnston, is endeavouring, to the utmost of his power, and within the limit of his means, to correct.[36]

Nevertheless the Society had some major achievement to its credit. In 1839 the foundation stone of the Palm House (Fig. 16) was laid; this is a remarkable building older than the houses at Glasnevin and Kew.[37] The design was by Charles Lanyon who later became a director of the Company, the central dome being executed by Young of Edinburgh, and the wings by Richard Turner of Dublin, celebrated for the palm houses he designed and built subsequently at Glasnevin and Kew.

The other great feature of the Belfast garden, the Tropical Ravine House, was built by Charles M'Kimm, Curator, and his garden staff. They completed the work, done with their own hands, in 1889 and the house attracted many distinguished visitors.[38] In 1897 Burbidge (p. 123) was greatly impressed, stating that it was

> one of the finest and most artistically arranged Fern houses in Europe or in the world. I have certainly never seen so fine and satisfying a collection of Ferns, Bamboos, mosses and climbing or trailing plants under a glass roof before and I have seen a good many glass-roofed gardens and conservatories and ferneries and winter gardens in my time.[39]

Like Bewley's fernery near Dublin (p. 135), the Tropical Ravine House had profited from the pillaging of the Killarney Fern in Victorian times: 'I suspect Mr McKimm has more [Killarney fern] now growing in the Belfast Garden than could now be found in Killarney'.

Charles Druery, the celebrated authority on ferns, described the house more fully in 1903:

I found myself ... on a gallery surrounding a deep ravine, with high sloping sides, and the bottom composed of mounds and rockwork, permeated by winding, roughly concreted paths. This gallery is open to the general public, while the lower portion, which is reached by a series of rough rocky steps like mountain paths, is reserved for specially conducted visitors ... it gives a splendid idea of a tropical or subtropical glen ... Tearing myself reluctantly away from these glimpses of the tropics ... I next went to the conservatories, a fine range consisting of a central circular house, surmounted by a dome of peculiarly graceful outline, whence on each side stretches a wing, the one devoted to plants requiring cool culture, the other to stove plants.[40]

The Society, which from 1840 had enjoyed the title 'Royal' kept the Botanic Garden going until 1894, when it was brought out by Belfast City Corporation. The garden ceased to be the Royal Belfast Botanic Garden, and was opened to the public the following year as the Belfast Botanic Garden Park.

THE HANGING GARDEN OF LIMERICK

An interesting proposal which came to nothing was the offer of a piece of land to the Limerick Horticultural Society for establishing a botanical and experimental garden.[41] Limerick, however, had one extraordinary garden – the Hanging Garden started in 1808 by William Roche, a wealthy banker who 'being much occupied by the care of an extensive banking concern, devised a plan for his personal recreation, to obviate the necessity of occasional absence from his residence.' At the back of his house in George's Street he built lines of arches arising in terraces above one another, the lowest terrace 25 feet high and the highest 40 feet. The side terraces were 150 feet long by 30 feet wide, the central one 180 feet by 40 feet. On top of the arches was a bed of earth five feet thick. A drainage system of lead channels and downpipes was converted in summer for irrigation by closing the downpipes. Flights of steps led from one terrace to another, and from the top there was a fine view of the city and of the winding River Shannon. The highest terraces carried heated glasshouses, some for the production of grapes, pineapples and peaches; others were orangeries and conservatories. These houses were 'united in the angles by globular greenhouses'. The middle arches were lower, 25 feet above the street, and on them vegetables and fruit trees were cultivated, as well as 'flowers of every form, scent and hue'.

Mr Roche's gardens were one of the sights of Limerick. 'Several of our Irish Viceroys and other illustrious strangers have visited this singularly interesting curiosity existing in the centre of a large commercial city and all have departed impressed with admiration of the taste and ingenuity of the worthy and intelligent contriver'. The whole cost him £15,000 but was a shrewd investment, for the cellars under the arches were well adapted to the storage of 2,000 hogsheads of wine, safe from fire or robbery, and at an even temperature from the insulating effect of the mass of soil overhead. The Government took them over at a fine of £10,000 and a yearly rent of £300.[42]

By 1866 the Hanging Gardens were in a ruinous state, and the cellars had been used as a bonding warehouse for many years by the Customs and Excise. Mr Roche's house had been occupied since 1858 by the Limerick Institution, a body founded in 1809, with reading rooms, news rooms and a library.[43] Today the remains of the terraces can be seen, consisting of two arches in Henry Street, now used as a post office store.

HORTICULTURAL SOCIETIES IN IRELAND

The varied plant collections in the botanic gardens stimulated the interest of amateur gardeners everywhere and this increased appreciation of plants encouraged in turn the development of these public collections. As we have seen (p. 26), there were florists' clubs, whose members were devoted hobbyists, cultivating and dressing their flowers for show, concentrating on the perfection of the individual blooms. Nevertheless Loudon complained in 1824, in the second edition of his *Encyclopaedia*, of the lack of flower gardening in Ireland, as distinct from landscaping. He wrote that there were few private collections of plants, though he acknowledged that one of the best flower gardens was Lord Downes' at Merville, near Dublin, 'but in general it may be stated that ornamental culture of every kind is in its infancy in that country'. He hoped that the founding of the Horticultural Society of Ireland in 1816 would lead to an improvement in this aspect of Irish horticulture.

This criticism must refer to the time of his visit to Ireland in 1811, for by 1834 Edmund Murphy, one of the editors of the *Irish farmer's and gardener's magazine*, was able to reply:

> In glancing over the new edition of the *Encyclopaedia of Gardening* ... we were surprised to observe that for want of correct and recent information, the editor was obliged to republish, verbatim, the observations which he made many years ago, and which, although correct then, are by no means so now. [1]

In the same magazine Vindex stated that

since the establishment of the Horticultural Society on its present footing, the cultivation of florists' flowers has become so extended and so much improved, that I prophesy the time is not so far distant when we shall rival, if not beat, our English neighbours in the excellence of those delightful ornaments of our gardens. In some species, such as carnations, pinks, auriculas etc. we have already reached, I may say without much boasting, perfection.

The Horticultural Society was founded by a number of gardeners in the Dublin area, who met at the Rose Tavern, Donnybrook, on 30 September 1816,[2] under the chairmanship of Francis Hetherington, gardener to the Earl of Charlemont. They were conscious that gardening in Ireland had gone into a decline, which they attributed to the departure of so many of the nobility from the country following the Act of Union in 1800. At first the Society was successful; about 200,000 people attended the first show, at which the judges included the Duchess of Dorset, wife of the Lord Lieutenant. By 1830, however, it was found necessary to revise the constitution of the Society. According to Thomas Bridgeford, a prominent nurseryman of Spa Field Nursery, Ballsbridge, who presided at a meeting of the honorary members in the Spadaccini Hotel, Sackville Street, on 9 July 1840, the changes were due to difficulties of management.

> The praiseworthy exertions of its founders were paralysed for want of a more active cooperation upon the part of the nobility and gentry, and from their own inability to devote that time and attention to its affairs which its proper management imperatively demanded. The Society consequently retrograded rapidly, and the late Mr Simpson ... with some other influential members of the Society, waited on some of the gentlemen who now form the Council of the Society, and pressed upon them to take up the management.[3]

The shows of the Society were fashionable occasions, especially the main exhibitions held in the Rotunda Gardens, with bands supplying music, and the attendance of the Lord Lieutenant and his suite. These shows were on a considerable scale and attracted large crowds. At the Spring Show held on 24 April 1835 not less than 2,500 people were estimated to be present. Even at the private shows there were plenty of entries; there were more than 100 dishes of peaches alone at the private exhibition of fruit and dahlias held on 10 September of the same year.

In Ireland, as in Britain, it was the age of stove plants and florists' flowers. The show schedules of the Society for 1840 list the popular flowers of the day. Ornamental plants grown under glass included *Pelargonium*, South African heaths, *Citrus*, *Fuchsia* and *Camellia*. The different types of auriculas were shown separately – green-edged, white-edged and self-coloured. There were classes for *Dahlia*, polyanthus, hyacinths and *Ranunculus*. Tulips and carnations were so highly developed as florists' flowers that there were many classes for them, but roses had not yet reached prominence, there being but two general classes –

'Garden varieties' and 'Chinese and other Hybrids'.The great days of the rose had yet to come.

The lists of fruits and vegetables show how well stocked were the gardens of at least the well-to-do. Pineapples were exhibited regularly, as were grapes, peaches, nectarines and melons. Outdoor fruits comprised apples, pears, plums, apricots, figs, cherries, red and white currants and strawberries. Vegetables appearing in the schedules were cucumbers, asparagus, potatoes, French beans, mushrooms, rhubarb, sea-kale, broccoli (purple and white), lettuce, celery (red and white), carrots and cauliflowers. There were generally five shows open to the public each year, in April, May, June, August and September, with a private exhibition in January for grapes, apples, pears and sometimes cucumbers.

In the year 1839 the Council reported that the Round Room of The Rotunda had become uncomfortably overcrowded at the shows and 'the serious inconvenience thereby inflicted on the female portion of your visitors, imperatively called for increased accommodation.' The experiment was made of hiring marquees for the June exhibition, when 'A long line of marquees, crowded with the most brilliant specimens, extended nearly from the eastern to the western piazza of the Rotunda – forming a delightful promenade, and enlivened by the cheering harmony of a military band.' These arrangements were so successful that the Society bought two marquees in time for the Spring exhibition of 1840, at which the attendance was so great that £250 was taken at the door instead of the more usual sum of about £70.

Some members, however, were disgruntled by the reorganisation of the Society in 1830, claiming that it was the work of a number of amateurs who had a packed meeting for the purpose. John Humphreys, Corke Abbey, Bray, was the leader of the dissidents, and feelings ran high enough to result in the founding, in 1835, of a rival society, the Practical Floral and Horticultural Society of Ireland, which held its first show at Morrison's Hotel on 14 April 1836.[4] Humphreys claimed that this group, soon calling itself the Royal Horticultural Improvement Society, was in reality the original society and the one that first instituted flower shows in this country.[5] There were calls for union of the two societies. Ninian Niven (Fig. 28), lately of the Royal Dublin Society's Botanic Gardens at Glasnevin, respected by all, considered the Council of the Royal Horticultural Society of Ireland to have been very grossly misrepresented.[6] He welcomed the call for union, but this was rejected by Humphreys, who repeated the charges of exclusiveness.[7]

In 1848, *The gardener's chronicle* of London opened a virulent attack on the Royal Horticultural Society of Ireland, accusing it of elitism, of neglecting the interests of working members and of awarding prizes to the nobility and not to their gardeners.[8] These charges were sustained and expanded by a pseudonymous correspondent Hortulanus Hibernicus. He complained that the rules of the Society were not kept, leading to suspicions of the impartiality of judging and even to unsatisfactory payments of prize money.[9] This added to the ire of *The gardener's chronicle*, which wondered 'not that the Irish Horticultural Society is unpopular and therefore ruined, but that it should continue to exit',[10] though acknowledging that some highly honourable men on the Council 'must look upon the proceedings in question with as much disgust as ourselves'. The Duke of Leinster, Lord Charlemont, Tighe Hamilton and J. C. Lyons of orchid fame (p. 96) were among those absolved from the scandals.

The Council replied (but not quickly enough for *The gardener's chronicle*) refuting each accusation. This brought out a rather grudging acknowledgement that the charges in connection with the prizes, at any rate, were unfounded, there having been a temporary difficulty due to the fact 'that somebody ran away with the prize money'.[11]

However, the remaining criticisms were maintained largely on the basis of anonymous letters, *The chronicle* refusing to give the names of the writers, some of whom were stated to be members, or former members, of the Council of the Society. It is evident from this correspondence that difference of opinion existed among Council members regarding the justice of these criticisms.

An attempt was made to heal these divisions by the formation of yet another society, the Dublin Horticultural Association.[12] By now *The gardeners' chronicle* was critical of the Horticultural Improvement Society, and called on it to join the new association[13] but Humphreys remained obdurate.[14] *The gardener's chronicle* repeated many of its charges against the Royal Horticultural Society, being neither appeased by the Council's earlier refutation nor deflected by their public advertisement rejecting the charges. *The gardener's chronicle* called for the dissolution of the Society.[15] This continued campaign was supported by quoting the observations of English visitors to the shows. In particular they were critical of the free-for-alls that took place in the fruit classes at the end. An anonymous visitor from Sussex was 'astonished at the behaviour we witnessed, which could not be compared to anything except a parcel of schoolboys let into an orchard. Some of the ladies close to us were asking each other how much fruit they had got.'[16] That such scenes took place was confirmed in quotation from *The Irish farmers' gazette* describing how at closing time

> a rush was made; the police made no resistance, but rather enjoyed the scene, and the whole of this fine collection of fruit went to destruction in a few minutes, along with a quantity of the plates upon which they were laid, which were trampled underfoot. The attack was instantaneous, and we have not heard that any particular individual has been recognised as leading it on, but we observed some clerks from public offices, and other places very busy in the scrimmage ... and a noted character, who should have set a better example, wearing a white hat, cramming a very large melon into it, and wedged it round with small fruit. This individual was not satisfied with all he could purloin in the fruit way, but filled his pockets, some say unmentionables, with Parsnips, Carrots, Beet, etc. On the whole the scheme was of the most disgraceful character.[17]

The Society complained to the authorities about the lack of police protection, following which a constable was threatened with dismissal, but was fined instead, following representations from the Society.

The campaign against the council had effect. J. C. Lyons and Tighe Hamilton resigned[18] but *The gardeners' chronicle* had not yet finished. It gave a scathing account of the Spring Show, April 1849. Although the Lord Lieutenant, the Duke of Leinster, and Lord Charlemont, as well as more than 1500 visitors attended:

> the gardening public of Ireland had totally deserted it ... as far as good cultivation was concerned we should be glad to enumerate a single plant having the least pretentions to it. ... of course we except some fine old botanical specimens from the Glasnevin Gardens ... there were a few good Auriculas; Hyacinths also were creditable ... vegetables were fine, particularly Broccoli and Potatoes, of which were there was a good supply.[19]

This was contrasted with the Improvement Society's effort two days previously 'which unquestionably was both respectable and meritorious to all concerned'. The *Chronicle* considered that its campaign had won reforms in the Royal Horticultural Society of Ireland.

> We look with satisfaction at this fall of the mighty and rise of the lowly, we would not encourage for a moment the system of rivalry which has sprung up in Dublin ... we have objected to the Royal Society in language sufficiently explicit, for reasons sufficiently plain; but it was to its intolerable management that the criticism was applied, not to the body as a body. That we were right in our objections is abundantly evident from the changes to which the framers of its laws have at last been driven ... For ourselves, we see plainly enough that the exposure, of which we have the honour to be the public instrument, has done its work effectually.[20]

This was too much for *The Irish farmer's gazette*.

> As we are not much in the confidence of either of the Royal Horticultural Societies of Ireland, for reasons best known to themselves, we cannot be accused of being either the partisans or condemners of one or the other; but we really cannot understand why the *Gardeners' Chronicle* should lend itself to such a misstatement of facts ... if it really wishes to give fair play in the contest now going on between the once Practical, now Royal Horticultural Improvement Society of Ireland, and the Royal Horticultural Society of Ireland. ...
>
> We regret to see a bickering, persecuting spirit still kept up by the *Gardeners' Chronicle*, and still more, that it has permitted that which is false to appear in its columns. The statement put forth in the two reports – the first on the Royal Horticultural Improvement Society, and that on the Royal Horticultural Society of Ireland – may pass current with persons in London or elsewhere, but here, or to any impartial eye witness, they only create contempt. We have borne testimony to the excellence of the first exhibition, which, in the plant department, was of first-rate character; but when we see it stated that the vegetables were abundant, and the potatoes fine, we observe too much of the partisan who has scarified truth; for the most miserable trash were exhibited that we have ever seen – they were

actually abortions. Again, in the report of the second show, it is stated that the fruit was generally indifferent: the fact was otherwise; the fruit was excellent ... and the vegetables not only fine, but far surpassed anything of the kind ever exhibited in Dublin at that period of the year ... we would strongly recommend the *Chronicle*, the next time they send a person for the purpose, to impress upon him the necessity of adhering strictly to the truth, and avoid partisanship.[21]

At the same time *The Irish farmer's gazette* criticised J. C. Lyons for supporting the Horticultural Improvement Society's shows with his celebrated exhibits of orchids because of (it argued) a reduction in the value of the prizes offered by the Royal Horticultural Society and then stating that the shows had declined; for keeping the prize money himself instead of letting his gardener have it, and alleged that he was not a disinterested judge. The Improvement Society was also criticised for, it was claimed, trying to draw away support from the rival society's shows by the timing of its own exhibitions.[22]

The *Gazette* now found itself involved in acrimony with both Lyons and Humphreys. Lyons pointed out that the prize money had not been reduced, that he had not had a gardener for 13 years and that though he took the value of the prizes in plate, as was his option, his workmen received their value in money.

Though the dispute with Lyons fizzled out gradually in the correspondence columns, the controversy over the Improvement Society went on vigorously, with anonymous letter-writers weighing in under the names 'Milk of Roses' and 'Hibernicus'. The *Gazette* maintained that its accounts of the respective merits of the shows were correct, and alleged that the Improvement Society had too many 'fillers' in the way of non-competitive exhibits, saying that 'the real merits of an exhibition depend on the number of exhibitors in competition, and not in the almost entire clearance of gardens not for competition ... this does not afford the necessary emulation or stimulus to improved horticulture'.

After some weeks of this correspondence a letter appeared from 'Hortus' which was damaging to Humphreys:

> The discussion which has lately taken place between Mr Humphreys, the sole representative of the Royal Horticultural Improvement Society, and your self has caused much interest amongst its members; it has opened some of our eyes not a little, has made us talk together and compare notes, which in many things, lead to a suspicion that we have been not infrequently duped, by whom time only will tell. None of us can get the least satisfactory clue to the state of the accounts, nor has there been as yet a satisfactory reason given as to why the prizes are not paid.

The letter pointed out some discrepancies in statements from Humphreys relative to finance and it was understood that Mr Tighe Hamilton had offered to pay the outstanding prize monies on condition that Humphreys gave up the books and withdrew his name as honorary secretary, which he refused to do. A demand was made that the Society's accounts be published.[23] This concluded the correspondence.

There is no further mention of the Royal Horticultural Improvement Society in *The gardeners' chronicle*. Though this society lasted at least until 1849,[24] it may have been a casualty of the famine years (1846–1848). The effect of the famine on some estate gardens was calamitous. 'As we now see in many places, the once fine gardens and parterres converted into calf paddocks and sheep pastures, the conservatories into poultry houses, the Pine stoves into piggeries and the mansion houses into pauper bastiles [*sic*]'. Nevertheless, in 1854 *The gardener's chronicle* could report that

> despite the ravages of the famine, the evils of emigration, or the preponderant influence of the Encumbered Estates Court, horticulture not only holds its place, but to a certain extent improves to a high degree in Ireland, as evinced by the productions and attendance at the Royal Horticultural Society's spring exhibition in the Rotunda, Dublin.[25]

It was the custom for prominent members to dine together at a hotel in the evening after the Spring Show, an occasion for many toasts and after –dinner speeches. On 9 July 1840 the Assistant Secretary, Robert Pooler, was entertained at a special dinner in the Spadaccini Hotel, Sackville Street. This was to mark the members' appreciation of his seven years service to the Society, and to present him with 'a very handsome silver cup, value fifteen guineas'. It was at this dinner that Mr Bridgeford made his speech dating the foundation to the year 1817 (the year of the first formal meeting).[26] In subsequent years there seems to have been a misunderstanding, as for a considerable period the Society's writing paper was headed 1830. This, however, must have been the year the Society was reorganised through the efforts of Mr Simpson. Ninian Niven of Glasnevin, at the annual dinner in 1837, referred to his part in this reorganisation,[27] and Robert Pooler himself referred to 1840 as being the tenth anniversary of the new constitution.[28]

The upsurge in horticultural activity in Ireland since Loudon's criticisms is further shown by the founding of horticultural societies through the country. At the annual dinner of the Royal Horticultural Society of Ireland in 1839 a toast was drunk to the local horticultural societies of Ireland. Francis Whitla returned thanks as a member of the Belfast Botanical Horticultural Society, and Robert Pooler observed that there were 17 horticultural societies in Ireland.[29] Those of Waterford, Meath and Belfast were already in existence in 1833, the year in which further societies were founded in Connacht (Ballinasloe), Limerick, Wexford and Kilkenny;[30] Cork followed in 1834.[31] A show held by this society in 1836 included some unusual classes such as those for the best score of almonds, the best lemon and the best orange 'cut with leaves'. There were twelve classes for 'Gorginas or Dahlias', including one for the best new seedling. Present-day lovers of old fashioned flowers will feel nostalgia for the seven kinds of double primroses exhibited, and the 'violets, best four kinds, double, in pots'. The Duchess of Kent was patron of the society, and donated five pounds each year. The second annual report (1836) stated that 'the liberal Annual Donation of Her Royal Highness the Duchess of Kent, for the encouragement of Cottage Gardening and Cleanliness, has been as effective as your Committee could, under the circumstances, have had reason to expect.'

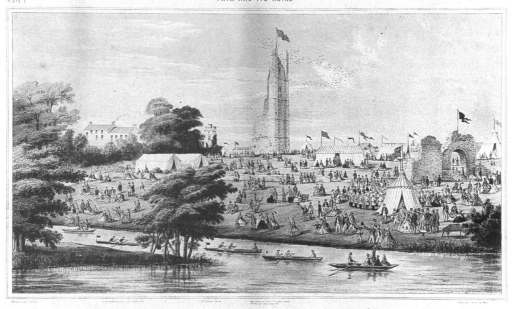

17: Special rail excursions were run to the annual flower show at Trim in the nineteenth century. (Reproduced by courtesy of J. Reynolds)

The shows of these provincial societies were social occasions (Fig. 17) comparable to those in Dublin. For example, the description of the second Spring Show of the Kilkenny Horticultural Society held in The Tholsel on 11 April 1835, written in the fulsome manner of the day in *The Kilkenny moderator*, gives a vivid picture of the scene.

The prizes were awarded and distributed by the hands of that justly esteemed patroness of taste, Mrs Power of Kilfane, prefaced by an appropriate address from William F. Tighe, of Woodstock, Esq. The assemblage on this interesting occasion was brilliant and numerous, and such as might be expected from a neighbourhood which stands distinguished for its taste and beauty.

As might naturally be expected from the progressive skill and spirit of our Horticultural professionals and amateurs, the specimens exhibited were much superior, both in variety and perfection, to those of the corresponding season last year. Hyacinths in all their charming tints crowded the tables in profusion, and perfumed the air with their fragrance, while the Auriculas and Polyanthus exhibited their more perfect forms on every side. A parterre of roses displayed their blooms in every grade of perfection from the gardens of the Marchioness of Ormonde, which likewise contributed a variety of beautiful exotics in flower – Amaryllidae, Cacti etc. etc. Mr Robertson supplied a number of others – such as Australian Acacias, the Berberis fascicularis, Euphorbia splendens and Primula caucasica with Camellias and Heaths in full bloom, which, with a member of beautiful plants from Mr McCraith's nurseries, together with those furnished from the gardens, formed a rich coup d'oeil, at once striking and harmonious to the eye of taste.

Vegetables were piled on the tables in profusion and great excellence; amongst the rest enormous broccoli. It is really astonishing to what a perfection on the culture of that article, so luxuriant at this season, has been brought within the few years past. Endive, lettuce, potatoes, cucumbers, asparagus, rhubarb etc. etc. were to be seen all in a state anticipating the riches of summer.

After criticising the showing of out-of-season fruits, the writer described the floral decorations, which must indeed have added to the 'rich coup d'oeil':

The room and pavilion were tastefully decorated with a Flora crowned with roses, and Medallions set in flowers and inscribed with the names of those distinguished promoters of Horticulture – Knight, Sabine, Lindley and Loudon; and one wreathed with Cypress to the memory of the unfortunate and lamented Douglas, particularly attracted notice.

This latter is a reference to the tragic end of David Douglas, the plant collector who fell into a pit dug by natives in the Sandwich Islands (Hawai'i) for catching wild cattle and was killed by one of the trapped animals.

The Mr Robertson who supplied the acacias, heaths, *Camellia* and other plants to this show was John Robertson, who had a nursery in the area. He was a man of wide interests. He wrote to Loudon's *Gardener's magazine* on disease of fruit trees, the virtues of liquid manure and soot, the identity of grape cultivars, and a mysterious black Irish elm. He was a corresponding member of the London Horticultural Society and contributed to their *Transactions* on the subjects of peach culture, mildew, blight and gum on fruit trees, and the culture of vines and apples. His scientific attitude of mind is illustrated by his articles on the classification of plums, peaches and nectarines, based on their vegetative and fruiting characteristics.

John Robertson could well be called Ireland's most notable pomologist, for he brought to the notice of the outside world many of the apples of Irish origin, some of which became well known in Britain. His letter to the Secretary of the Horticultural Society of London, dated 4 November 1819, contains the first known descriptions of 'Irish Peach' (Plate 18), 'Scarlet Crofton', 'Kerry Pippin', 'White Russet' and 'Ross Nonpareil'. Of these 'Irish Peach', 'Kerry Pippin' and 'Ross Nonpareil' were illustrated in the well-known pomologies published in England by Lindley, Ronalds and Hogg. From Tighe's *Survey of County Kilkenny* we learn that Robertson's nursery covered about 14 acres. He had a fine collection of shrubs, stove and greenhouse plants, raised some 100,000 seedling forest trees annually, and imported clover seed.

Like the founders of the Horticultural Society in Dublin, Robertson was concerned at the decline in gardening that had followed the Act of Union. In November 1829 he wrote to *The gardener's magazine*[32] on the state of horticulture in Ireland, contrasting the low ebb to which it had fallen with the flourishing

18: John Charles Lyons (Reproduced by permission of
Westmeath County Library).

condition of the gardens he knew round Kilkenny at the end of the eighteenth century. At that period there were a dozen gardens or more within a radius of ten or twelve miles of the city, each of which contained pine stoves from 50 to 100 feet in length, 'well stocked and managed by able gardeners from Kew, Hampton Court and other places of note round London. Now we cannot count half the number.' This decline he attributed to the Union having rendered some proprietors absentees, and to the fall in farm prices which 'swept off' others. He recounts how the Dowager Countess of Ormonde had a regular supply of cucumbers through the winter, raised in pine stoves on 'treillages' against the back wall 'though only the other day Mr Aiton, the king's gardener at Kew, had a medal presented to him by the Horticultural Society for the introduction of the practice about London'. Robertson also claimed an early date for the culture of sea-kale in Ireland,[33] quoting a contemporary newspaper article which stated that this vegetable was supposed to be of recent date, the introduction of the then Bishop of Carlisle. However, as far back as 1764 sea-kale was commonly grown in the gardens of Dublin and seed was available in the shops. This plant, now so rare in the wild, was stated to grow then in great abundance on sandy shores around Dublin Bay.

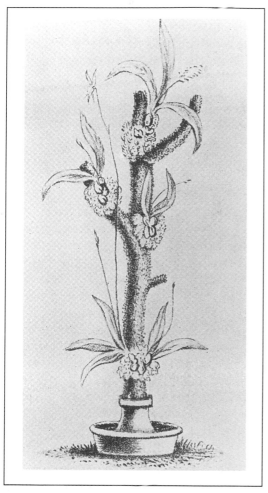

19: Lyons' oniscamyntic stand, to protect plants from pests.

The Westmeath Society was fortunate in having as secretary John Charles Lyons of Ledeston, near Mullingar, one of the most remarkable gardeners of his time (Fig. 18). He was a landowner who might have been expected to interest himself in local antiquities and in such duties as Sheriff for the county. Lyons did these and much else besides, for he loved orchids, was familiar with the great collections at Chatsworth and elsewhere in England, and cultivated them at Ledeston to such effect that he wrote the first book ever published on their culture. Not only did he write it, but he prepared the woodcuts and printed and bound the book himself.

This little volume, *Remarks on the management of orchidaceous plants, with a catalogue of those in the collection of J. C. Lyons, Ledeston. Alphabetically arranged, with their native counties and a short account of the mode of cultivation adopted*, is now extremely rare.[34] It was printed for private circulation only, and was an instant success. When the second edition appeared Lyons was able to say in his preface that it had the approval of such authorities as Paxton, gardener at Chatsworth, Professor John Lindley of London and the directors of the botanic gardens in Belfast, Liverpool, Birmingham, as well as James Mackay of Trinity College Botanic Gardens and David Moore of Glasnevin. The Council of the Royal Horticultural Society of Ireland, to whom the book was dedicated, awarded Lyons a gold medal.

Lyons relates how he received a small collection of orchids from Mexico, which he treated as was usual for other stove plants. Though they grew, and a few flowered, he was disappointed with the results and realised that neither he nor his gardener knew much about them, even to the extent that some were epiphytes and others terrestrial. He soon discovered that 'There has not yet been any work published solely on the culture of Tropical Orchidaceae'. Therefore he studied books describing the environment in countries from which orchids come. On this basis he was able to classify the plants according to whether they grew in dense shady woods, on trees in woodland glades with little sun but plenty of light, or with less exposure to the sun. Very practical directions on the management of orchids follow, with emphasis on careful syringing 'in imitation of a plentiful, gentle shower of rain, let fall on the plants, not driven against them with an upsetting force'. Proper ventilation and resting periods for the plants are also stressed.

He enquired, too, from friends who travelled abroad. On hearing of the extremely heavy night dews that fall in Trinidad he experimented in an 'endeavour to emulate the climate', admitting steam every night for some hours into his orchid house 'the atmosphere of the house resembled a fog ... I could not see a yard before me, yet the plants throve wonderfully. I have found the great moisture injurious to the flowers of some species, others appear to enjoy it much, and to flower freely notwithstanding the great wet'.

This system was contrary to the practice of some of Lyons' contemporaries, who kept a dry atmosphere at night, damping down the glasshouse freely in the morning. In 1838 he invented a steam boiler to facilitate steaming the houses, and while courteously acknowledging the support of 'Mr Appleby, gardener to T. Brocklehurst, Esq, of the Fence, which has been famed for the manner in which these plants have been grown', Lyons claimed a two year priority for his invention when Mr Appleby published a similar system in 1840.

Lyons' steam generator was quite small, two and a half feet long and two feet wide. The lid was fitted with a safety valve, gauges, supply pipe and steam pipe, the joinings 'made good with iron cement, composed of borings of metal, sulphur and saltpetre...the steam is admitted into the house by means of a stop cock at pleasure'. Under the shelving of the house 'runs the steam pipe, perforated at every foot with small holes ... first used a lead pipe but soon found the expansion so great that it got out of shape ... I then substituted the gun barrel gas pipes and they answer admirably'.

Perhaps this generator had evolved from Lyons' experiments in the farmyard, for in 1835 he had published *Remarks on steam for preparing food for cattle.*

Lyons was never satisfied with the growth of orchids in pots or on lumps of turf. He therefore invented his oniscamyntic epiphyte stand.

> The name tho' a difficult one appears to me not to be ill chosen, it is compounded of two Greek words, Oniscus, a woodlouse, and Amynticus, defensive or used in defence against.

The stand considered of an earthenware pan with a raised centre and a hole in it, into which the forked branch of a tree was inserted. The orchid plants were to be attached to the branches with copper wire and their roots covered lightly with moss (Fig. 19). In this way the natural habitat of orchids growing on trees was imitated. The pan was filled with water, thus forming 'a sort of foss, impassable to vermin', hence the name Lyons coined for his plant stand.

So many people applied to Lyons for copies of his book that he was induced to publish an enlarged, second edition in 1845, this time professionally printed. Though enlarged, this edition omitted some of the strong remarks made by Lyons about so-called gardeners:

> There exists amongst the profession unfortunately a set of low fellows, who spend their evenings in pot houses, and their days in cheating their employers. These persons, the dregs of the craft, may be known by a swaggering demeanour, which the simple mistake for knowledge. They are men of assertions, talking down the really well-informed gardener with loud words, slang and braggadocio. At Horticultural Meetings you may see them, dirty and unshaven, in greasy clothes, foul linen, hats and shoes, like their hair, unacquainted with the luxury of a brush; towards noon they liberally perfume the room with porter, peppermint, whiskey and onions, and thus they strut about, the very Parias of Horticulture. On such occasions you may observe them in clusters, perplexing their scanty brains by foolish arguments about nothing. By way of showing their importance, they jostle the ladies who may have the misfortune to be near them, and eventually are consigned to the police, or threatened with it, when their insolence is quieted, and they sneak away. Such persons I do not honour with the name of Gardener.

He had differences of opinion with his own gardener, as when he asked him to stop the vine shoots beyond the bunches of fruit

> but this practice he wholly disapproved of, and the only reason I could ever obtain from him was that the practice was condemned by the *best authors*, but who they were I could never find out from him, his constant reply was, the *best authors*. I shortly after determined on being for the future my own gardener.

He conceded, however, that while laying

> a stress on the necessity of exalting the character of the rising generation of gardeners, it may be imagined that I attribute the want of improvement solely to the Operative, such is not the case; it is but fair to say, that the class do not, nor have not received the encouragement which they have a right to expect.

Lyons was recognised internationally as an authority on orchid culture. His book was translated into German, and he contributed the cultural directions to Sir William J. Hooker's *A century of orchidaceous plants*, published in 1851. In 1853 Professor Lindley described the orchids at Ledeston as by far the richest in Ireland, and named an orchid *Schomburgkia lyonsii* (Plate 12).

Lyons was interested in many other garden plants besides orchids. In 1839 and again in 1841 he printed a *Catalogue of the flowers, bulbs, plants, Orchidaceae etc. at Ledeston*. In this he named large numbers of florists' flowers, such as anemones, of which he had 81 cultivars, as well as 59 auriculas in the self-

WEST MEATH HORTICULTURAL SOCIETY.

EIGHTH EXHIBITION.

JUNE 29, 1836.

P. First prize.
C. Second prize.
D. Disqualified.
O. No claimant.

ORNAMENTAL.

COMPETITORS.	1. Pines, 2lb.	2. G. Flesh Melon 2lb.	3. Melons 3lb.	4. Bl. or R. Grapes.	5. White Grapes.	6. R. Strawberries 24.	7. W. Strawberries 24.	8. Cherries 24.	9. Pinks 12.	10. Seedling Pinks 3.	11. P. Ranunculus 12.	12. Double Stocks 6.	13. Roses 12.	14. Hot house Fruits 6.	15. Green house plants 6.	16. Herbaceous plants 6.	17. Calceolarias 6.	18. H.P. Herb plants 6.	19. Cauliflowers 2.	20. Carrots 24.	21. Parsnips 24.	22. Celery 12.	23. Artichokes 12.	24. Peas.	25. EXTRA Fruit.	26. EXTRA Flowers.	27. EXTRA Vegetables.
1. M. Derum, Gard. to Earl Charleville		P			P	C	P				P								C	C					C	C	C
2. J. Gibbons, Esq				C			P									C	C		P	P	P	P			C	P	P
3. John C. Lyons, Esq		C	C	C	C	C	P									P	P			P	P	C			C	P	P
4. J. Baine, Gard. to Mrs. O'C. Malone																											
5. E. Wade, Gard. to H. M. Tuite, Esq																											
6. Pat. Dronan, gard. to R. Bourn, Esq																											
7. Robert Barlow, Esq																											
8. Mrs Smyth, Larkfield																											
9. John Geraghty, gard. to Lord Kilnain																											
10. Wm Cox, gard. to Mrs. Smyth, Gayb.						P		C				C	P	P													
11. P. Molloy, g. to Mrs. Fetherston, Rocky.								C					P	P									P				
12. Mr. Eaton, gard. to Lady Belvidere																											
13. R. Swift, Esq																											
14. J. Molloy, g. to W. Fetherstonh, Esq																											
15. R. W. Cooper, Esq																											
16. Wm. Reilly, Esq																											
17. Sir Percy Nugent, Bart																											
18. R. H. Levinge, Esq																											

JUDGES. Sir R. Levinge, R. Swift, Esq., Mr George, D. Pollard, Esq. Mr. George, D. Pollard, Esq. Mr. Bridgefort, S. Auchmuty, Sir P. Nugent, Mr. Behan,

20: Show schedule, Westmeath Horticultural Society, 1836, by John Charles Lyons

21: 'Coat-of-arms' by John Charles Lyons for Westmeath Horticultural Society
(Reproduced by courtesy of the National Library of Ireland)

22: Design for Westmeath Horticultural Society by John Charles Lyons.

coloured, green-, grey-, and white-edged classes, together with the names of their raisers. Other plants he grew were polyanthus, pinks, tulips, *Dahlia, Erica,* Cape bulbs and many others. He had a small collection of alpines, including *Ajuga pyramidalis* 'Alba', which is a rare plant today, if indeed it is still in cultivation.

Another book by Lyons, also a rare volume, is his *Grand juries of Westmeath,* printed at Ledeston in 1853. It is sought after not so much for the main body of the work as for the footnotes where amusing and near-scandalous stories are told of families prominent in the county. One odd character, Sir Richard Levinge, 4th baronet, of Levington Park, had some curious architectural and horticultural ideas.

> The south return of the dwelling house was the situation selected for a long grapery, from which he intended to introduce the vines and to train them to the ceiling joists of his own bedroom, which was on the ground floor next to the grapery, for which purpose the room was not ceiled, but the joists were handsomely moulded. He intended to enjoy the fruit when ripe as he lay in his bed, with as little exertion or trouble as possible. The holes through which the vines were brought remain to this day. The vines were introduced, and it is needless to say they neither flourished nor bore fruit, and my respected grandfather was sadly disappointed.

Lyons was active in encouraging horticulture in his home county. He was secretary to the Westmeath Horticultural Society, of which the records have survived of prizes awarded during the years 1834 to 1848.[35] The volume starts with a delightful drawing in pen and ink by Lyons himself of a fanciful coat-of-arms for the Society (Fig. 21). On the shield are shown a pink, an auricula, a rose and an anemone, the whole surmounted by a pineapple as a crest. The supporters are gardeners, one carrying a rake, the other a spade. A scroll underneath reads 'Established in the Year 1834'.

Three shows were held each year, in April, June and August. Hyacinths were popular, as, for example, in the Spring Show of 1835, with classes for blue, for red and for white or yellow varieties. These classes attracted eleven entries, as also did auriculas, which were shown as green-edged, grey- or white-edged and as self-coloured. The classes for polyanthus (six entries) and double primroses (five entries) were better supported than those for double stocks, double anemones, greenhouse plants, exotics and herbaceous plants, where only one or two entries are recorded. Even as early in the year as 5 April a wide range of vegetables was exhibited – asparagus, cucumbers, white and purple broccoli, turnips, potatoes, French beans, cabbage and mushrooms. Seven entries of apples and one of pears indicate skill in the storage of fruit. The summer show was held in Murray's Hotel, Mullingar, on 27 June.

> The arrangements were perhaps the very best that could be devised and the ingenuity and judgement of Mr Lyons, with whom they originated, were conspicuous in the simplicity and accuracy of detail which they presented.

Immediately after the adjudication and previous to the admission of the public, printed reports of the Show were struck off by means of a small Ruthven press, and in readiness for distribution. A seedling mimulus raised in the Secretary's (Mr Lyons) garden was particularly admired, being considered by the professionals the finest variety hitherto raised, far surpassing the *Mimulus smithii*. The ground colour of the flower is a delicate lemon colour, and the spots, five in number, of a rich clear crimson, a blood colour. It has been named the *Mimulus Westmeathiensis*, in compliment to the Marquis of Westmeath, patron of the Society.

At these summer shows grapes, strawberries and cherries were popular classes, but fruit came into its own in the August shows, as in 1834, with classes for peaches, nectarines, apricots, greengages, gooseberries, white currants and grapes. There were competitions for the largest and heaviest melon as well as for the best flavoured specimen. Extra prizes had to be provided for cherries, figs and oranges. The flower classes included carnations (bizarres, flakes, selfs and picotees), double stocks, *Dahlia*, herbaceous and greenhouse plants. Vegetables on show were carrots, parsnips, onions, celery and broccoli. The judges included David Moore of Glasnevin and Thomas Bridgeford, the Dublin nurseryman. The prizes awarded by the Society at their shows included silver tablespoons, teaspoons, sugar tongs and medals. No other proceedings of the Society have come to light, but occasional comments in the margins of those surviving give us glimpses of incidents, as in June 1839 when Lyons 'cut for medal with Derum and lost'. At that show one exhibit of strawberries was disqualified as being wild fruits. At the summer show of 1840 a note was made of the 'collection £2–19–0. Deduct lost by waiter 1 [shilling].'

J. C. Lyons died at Ledeston in 1874, aged 82. His widow placed a mural tablet to his memory in Mullingar church on which she could truly record that 'His highly cultivated tastes and varied talents were successfully directed to more than one branch of science and art'.

Today Ledeston is fast falling into a melancholy ruin, standing near the shores of Lough Ennell. Nothing remains to indicate all the horticultural activities once carried on there save the remains of a walled-in garden with faintly seen foundations of the greenhouses in which orchids once flourished safely on their oniscamyntic stands. The press on which Lyons printed his books is preserved in the County Library, Mullingar.

The fate of Ledeston is an appropriate note on which to close this account of early nineteenth century gardening in Ireland. Though Ninian Niven, like John Claudius Loudon, was to foster the development of the new, middle class owner gardener, the famine years, so tragic for the peasant population, were the ruin of many landed proprietors.

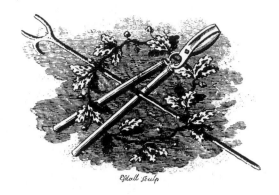

Esdall sculp

GARDENING IN IRELAND IN VICTORIAN TIMES

The evolution of the Victorian garden took place in an attempt to organise into a system of design the floral wealth which resulted from the botanical and horticultural advances of the early years of the century. When this plethora of plants was combined with the variety of architectural styles for which the landscape gardener was required to provide a setting, the outcome was not a single style of gardening but a wide variety of styles, each often used in tandem with another, to give a cosmopolitan aura. The full range of historical European styles was disinterred and amplified by an array of plants derived from almost every corner of the globe into which the European empires had reached. Even those from climates very different from that of Europe could now flourish in the artificial atmosphere of the Victorian hothouse.

The triumvirate of architectural styles which reigned in the early decades of the century consisted of the Neo-classical, the Italianate and the Early English. For each there was an appropriate garden setting, the creation of which became part of the task of the architect who often chose to ignore, or subordinate to his design, the recent horticultural advances. In Ireland, the most influential garden in the first of these styles was that laid out about 1825 by the architect C. R. Cockerall around the Neo-classical house which he had designed for James Lennox Naper at Lough Crew, County Meath.[1] It focused on a fountain in the form of a stone basin raised on a pedestal in the antique mode. On either side was a sunken panel delicately decorated with jewel-like beds of flowers, and gravel walks led to an apse-like orangery the wings of which enclosed a sunken nymphaeum of classical statuary and rockwork after the manner of the Ancients.

The second of the styles was the Italianate which was based on the design of the Italian villa of the Renaissance. For climatic reasons these villas had been

23: Lakeside walk, Johnstown Castle, Co. Wexford, by Daniel Robertson c. 1840.

built in airy hillside locations so that their gardens descended from the house in terraces, retained by decorative stone walls and joined by flights of often magnificent stone steps. This style was first introduced to Ireland by an architect, Daniel Robertson. His first tentative essay took the form of a terrace wall, upon which a line of classical statuary balanced (Fig. 23), at a discreet distance from the main garden of Johnstown Castle, County Wexford.[2] A later more confident expression of this approach was his essay in seven descending terraces in front of Castleboro, another house in the same county.[3] They led from the house to a stone water-gate on the river, a feature derived from those terraces which act as landing stages from the lakes to the gardens of the villas around lakes Como and Maggiore. Though this work was followed by a commission to design stone balustrading for a terrace at Kilruddery, County Wicklow,[4] his best remembered achievement is his design for the garden at Powerscourt (Fig. 24) nearby.[5] Of this only the first terrace, with its steps modelled on those in the garden of the Villa Butera near Palermo, and a lakeside grotto guarded by reclining figures in stone, were ever completed; for his patron, the sixth Viscount Powerscourt, died on a journey back from Italy where he had gone to buy statuary for his projected garden. When his son undertook the completion of the garden 25 years later, he did not avail himself of Robertson's plans but instead commissioned a group of contemporary landscape gardeners to provide him with ideas. It was from an amalgam of

24: Powerscourt, County Wicklow. A layout in the Italianate style. (Photograph by W. Lawrence, reproduced by permission of the National library of Ireland).

25: Leinster Lawn and Merrion Square, Dublin. Public gardening in Victorian times. (Photography by W. Lawrence, reproduced by permission of the National Library of Ireland).

26: Terenure House, County Dublin, residence of Frederick Bourne, a pioneer of the natural style
of gardening, who opened his garden to the public.

these with those of Robertson that the garden was completed under the
direction of the seventh viscount.

The last of the triumvirate of architectural styles was the Early English. It
was used by the versatile Robertson at Wells, County Wexford,[6] which James
Fraser noted in the *Travellers' guide* of 1843, had been 'recently altered to the
early Tudor style of architecture and the grounds around the mansion, and the
approaches to it, are in the process of formation in a style conformable thereto'.
The conforming approach was a straight avenue, a fashion which had been out
of popular use for half a century. Other examples of straight approaches to such
houses during this period survive at Morristown Lattin, County Kildare,[7] and
Dunleckney Manor, County Carlow, the latter another Robertson design.[8] Here
also survived until recently a formal garden of sundials and topiary work which
was appropriate to the Early English style of the house.

The architectural influence was soon tempered by the rising popularity of
two landscape gardeners, James Fraser (1793–1863) and Ninian Niven
(1799–1879), both of whom, although born in Scotland, spent some time in one
or another of the Dublin botanic gardens before establishing their respective
practices. They both combined a thorough knowledge of practical horticulture
with a sensitivity to the advantages of a formal garden layout. Born in
Edinburgh, Fraser worked in the Trinity College Botanic Garden during
Mackay's time.[9] He then became a gardener at Dartfield, the house of Henry
Blake in County Galway, where he met M'Leish when the latter was asked to
make suggestions for the planting.[10] His reputation began to flourish after he

had come to Dublin to be head-gardener at Terenure House, which, according to Loudon's *Encyclopaedia*, had the most complete arboretum in the country (Fig. 26). The writer of the encyclopaedia went on to say of Fraser as a person that he was 'an excellent botanist and gardener as well as a man of general information'. In 1825 he contributed an invaluable essay 'on the present state of gardening in Ireland' to *The gardener's magazine*, a periodical conducted by Loudon.[11] After M'Leish's death in 1829 Fraser decided upon assuming in public the profession of landscape gardening[12] which for the remainder of his years he combined with the writing of a series of popular guide books for travellers in the country. *The handbook for travellers in Ireland*, *The handbook for the lakes of Killarney*, *The handbook for Dublin* and *The guide to the county of Wicklow* all ran to many editions over the succeeding years. Although it is for these that he is now known, Fraser himself appears to have judged his landscape gardening as the more important of his two pursuits.

His approach to landscaping was conservative. His patrons were drawn, at a time of increasing social change, from the old landed gentry, and his work was concerned with the making of ornamental demesnes in the manner of the preceding century. His accounts in 1834 of the demesnes he improved at Saunders Court, County Wexford, and Gowran Park, County Kilkenny, indicate this approach. Of the first he wrote:

> Thirty years ago, the demesne was abandoned and the trees prostrated ... it is now in an advanced state of renovation ... already the young plantations mark out the long and flowing boundary lines ... the beautiful and highly varied surfaces broken by several narrow glens and ravines, adorned already with the growth of natural copsewood.[13]

And of the second:

> The demesne is in a transitional state. Even now in the incipient state of the improvements the outlines of the young plantations, enclosing a large tract of the beautiful grounds to the south of the house, can be traced.[14]

The care he takes to explain the flowing outlines of his new plantations and the variety of undulating surface produced by earthmoving and modelling in the interior of the demesne put us in mind of the eighteenth century designs of 'Capability' Brown. His delight in the growth of the natural copsewood at Saunders Court, however, would have earned the approval of the later school of Picturesque landscapers. Any doubt as to whether his approach and style was primarily subject to their influence may be cast aside on reading the reports he prepared for alterations to be made in the demesnes of Castle Coole, County Fermanagh,[15] and Castlemorres, County Kilkenny.[16] In each he criticised the existing plantations as being too thin, and the practice of allowing them, as in the Brownian tradition, to be grazed by cattle by omitting any protective fencing. He also commented that the variety of trees which had been chosen theretofore, had been too limited. In proposing to remedy what he saw as defects, he recommended the thickening of the existing belts of trees, in one case by as much as tenfold, fencing them against the depredations of the grazing herd, so encouraging the growth of a picturesque and luxuriant underwood of shrubs and young trees, and the planting through the woods of a wider array of tree species which would include many conifers. His talents in the creation of the old-fashioned landscape park were employed as late as 1855 when the intrepid Misses Gascoigne raised for themselves a large Gothic mansion at Castle Oliver, County Limerick, and required Fraser to make a suitable setting for it.[17]

Like Humphrey Repton and other gardeners from the Picturesque period, Fraser was not averse on occasion to introducing novel elements – formal flower gardens and specialist plant collections – into his designs. In his influential plan for the garden at Ashridge Park, Hertfordshire, Repton included such features as an American garden, a rosarium and a parterre with a fountain.[18] He, however, felt obliged to excuse himself for so doing on the grounds that the lie of the land was so flat no amount of artificial earthmoving would make of it a piece of picturesque parkland, were it not to be enlivened by such attractions. The eighteenth century prejudice against flowers near the house was still so strong that he did not position these novelties in full view of the windows but distributed them at random and discreetly throughout the neighbouring shrubberies. Fraser, when he was faced with similarly unpromising sites at Adare Manor, County Limerick,[19] and Castlemartyr, County Cork,[20] proceeded in an almost identical way. Of the first he recounted in 1843 that its surface was flat but that the grounds contained a great variety of shrubs, majestic trees and shaded walks. Of his arrangement of the second he is more explicit:

> Though the surface of this demesne is flat ... the grounds are adorned by rich shrubberies, extensive plantations and venerable trees and ornamental gardens of different characters connected by beautiful pleasure grounds.[21]

This might almost be a description of Ashridge. One of these 'gardens of different character' was the *Camellia* garden, designed to show the various beauties of that plant and another a flower garden encircling the ruins of an old Norman keep.

The garden Fraser designed for Curraghmore, County Waterford, was the most advanced of his productions for it included not only an oval flower garden around the eighteenth century Shell House in the grounds but also a set of three formal parterre gardens around the house.[22] It was perhaps due to his inexperience in this novel mode that the principal parterre went dramatically wrong during the course of its construction. His scheme of four sunken panels was to stretch from the house to the side of the lake but when they began to dig them it was found that they gradually began to fill with water due to the fact that their new reduced level was lower than the water-level of the lake. This must have caused him some embarrassment as the panels were hurriedly filled

27: Ninian Niven.

in and left flat as they are to-day. On another side of the house he designed a formal American garden, the beds of which were filled with the spring-flowering *Magnolia* and *Rhododendron* then being imported. Their formal arrangement may be contrasted with the more natural woodland settings in which the Himalayan *Rhododendron* were planted when they were introduced later in the century. Fraser died in 1863 at the age of 70 as a result of complications arising from a chest cold, in his house at Westland Row, Dublin.[23] His obituary states that his fame had spread so far in latter years that his talents had been frequently employed in England and in Scotland, and lauds his good-humoured urbanity and hospitality.

His chief rival, Ninian Niven, was by contrast a Victorian *par excellence*. Unlike Fraser, he did not spend time in the layout of landscape parks, by then an outmoded medium of landscape gardening, but rather devoted himself to the creation of large formal gardens for a wide variety of patrons, drawn not only from the old landed gentry but also from the new industrial and entrepreneurial classes. The Gardenesque style, with its small-scale shrubberies and winding paths, was unsuitable for the large gardens and public parks which were often required to accommodate crowded garden parties and fêtes which were a feature in the social life of the Victorian age. Niven, therefore, turned to the classical French garden for inspiration. Its wide paths and alleys had been evolved to contain the similarly large crowds of courtiers at Versailles and other grand palaces. He nonetheless considered that it could not be transferred to the Irish context without alteration, for he professed the superiority of the natural approach even though 'as regards the modern style of it an extreme of curves and windings have [sic], in many cases, been entered into'.[24] The solution, which he was to use for the remainder of his life, was what he called his 'intermediate' style in which the wide spaces and paths of the French manner would be bent into the winding curves of the natural style.

Niven (Fig. 27) was born at Kelvin Grove, near Glasgow, of a gardening family.[25] When Ninian was 14 years old he decided to follow the family tradition, and was apprenticed in the gardens of Bothwell Castle, notable for their collections of rare plants. He intended to become a plant collector, and on completion of his apprenticeship, he returned to Glasgow to study drawing and painting, as a means of illustrating his finds, but was recalled to Bothwell to take charge of the flower garden there.

A short period as gardener at Belladrum House, Inverness, followed. While there he was offered the post of gardener at the official residence of the Chief Secretary for Ireland, Lord Glenelg, in The Phoenix Park, Dublin.[26] He remained there for eight or nine years, showing his talent for landscape gardening by remodelling its garden, earning thereby the praise of Loudon for 'the best-managed garden in Ireland'.

Niven's taste for landscaping made him critical of the villa gardens he saw in the neighbourhood of Dublin, complaining that they were 'as regularly belted and clumped as ever a fortification or prison was surrounded with a wall', shutting out the view of 'the splendid and glowing scenery, which almost on every side surrounds them – unless perhaps some of the more elevated outlines of the Wicklow or Dublin mountains are to be seen overtopping this tantalising screen'. He pointed out that the view from the house should be considered and advised that vistas should be opened up by careful cutting out of the trees in the surrounding belt.[27]

Perhaps it was a dweller in one of these villas that came forward to defend them against Niven's description. Vindex wrote in the *Irish farmers' and gardeners' magazine*

> I happen to be tolerably well acquainted with the environs of Dublin, and I do unhesitatingly assert that there is as much, if not more diversity in the appearance as well as in the localities of its villa residences than can be met with in any other part of the kingdom of the same extent.[28]

This pseudonymous correspondent complained that to follow Niven's suggestions would open up nearer views of the neighbour's stable or gable end. Thus Niven found himself in controversy, as he was to find himself later over his plans for Glasnevin, this time with one 'J.C.'.

Niven succeeded John Underwood in 1834 at Glasnevin having been selected in preference to David Moore, then at Trinity College Botanic Garden. He found the Botanic Gardens at Glasnevin in such a state that drastic measures were needed which immediately involved him with 'J.C.'. He seems to have been a devoted utilitarian and like Loudon would 'throw down Westminster Abbey if it stood in the way of his wheelbarrow'.[29] The proposals that aroused such ire were the abolition of the Irish garden (Hortus Hibernicus) on the grounds of there being so few plants peculiar to Ireland and also the removal of the Pecudarium or Cattle Garden. The area thus made available was to be an experimental garden for potatoes, turnips, peas and farm grass mixtures. Niven wished to build one or two model cottages near the river to demonstrate the value of allotment gardens, these to be worked by the tenants of the cottages. 'J.C.' accused the Royal Dublin Society of planning to convert the Botanic Garden into a kitchen garden, with 'turnips thrust among the tube-roses [sic]'.[30] He objected to spoiling the sylvan beauty of the river with cottages surrounded by leeks and cabbages; but it was the proposed destruction of the Hortus Hibernicus that made him particularly angry. His letter was published with a footnote by the editor, Edmund Murphy, pointing out that 'J.C.' had confused the term 'peculiar to Ireland' with 'indigenous to Ireland' and that the Irish garden contained no rare plant.[31] This left Niven with little to reply to, especially as other correspondents came to his defence. Joseph Hamilton of Annadale Cottages, Dublin, in particular approved of Ninian's taste in landscaping, praising his ideas on opening up views:

> A few large trees which stood between the garden and some distant objects of peculiar interest have been judiciously cut down. The Sugar Loaf Hill, near Bray, St. George's splendid spire and steeple and the bishop's handsome mansion house, may now be seen to very great advantage through the newly-created vistas, while more than a sufficiency of well-grown trees remain on every side for ornament and shelter.[32]

Niven found the collection of plants very run down. He went over to England on the invitation of Lord Mountnorris, who gave him 600 species of plants. Other gardens that helped were Wentworth, Fitzwilliam, Chatsworth and Sheffield Botanic Gardens.[33] With all these additions to the collections and with improvements in layout, Niven was able in 1838 to publish his *Visitor's companion to the Botanic Gardens* for the benefit of the increasing numbers being attracted to the Gardens. 'Such a work will appear the more desirable when it is recollected to what extent the visitors to this delightful resort are annually increasing: having, during the course of the last four years advanced from seven to upwards of twenty thousand.'[34]

Wade and Underwood had given personal tuition to apprentices. Niven continued to train apprentices, and a training course for gardeners has continued at Glasnevin ever since.

To gentleman pupils, facilities are presented, of an inviting description, towards the attainment of useful and practical information, connected with botanical science or rural affairs, a species of knowledge of the utmost importance to gentlemen in general, but to country gentlemen in particular.[35]

Niven had his problems with vandalism.

Several depredations having been committed ... any person or persons so detected will run the risk of being made public examples. It is pleasing, however, to think that such acts of wantonness and bad taste have been comparatively few ... However trifling it may appear for one person to take a small portion of even the most common plant, it is not so when the many would thus help themselves ... and this would leave us so completely at the mercy of such persons as, eventually, to produce the most distressing dilapidation.

It was necessary to warn against bribing the young men in the garden, though he believed their integrity had withstood the temptation.

In his short stay of five years at Glasnevin Niven accomplished much. In addition to all he did to restore the Gardens he found time to contribute to the periodicals of the day, including Loudon's *Gardener's magazine* and won a gold medal from the Royal Dublin Society for an essay on the cultivation of the potato. His name was included in the list of contributors announced in the prospectus of *The gardeners' chronicle*, showing that he was considered to be among the most notable horticulturists of the day even after he had resigned from Glasnevin.

In 1838 he resigned to set up on his own as a landscape gardener and nurseryman at the Garden Farm, Drumcondra, Dublin. He styled himself 'Professor of Landscape Gardening' and advertised a course of lectures

both Theoretical and Practical, on Agricultural and Horticultural Science ... to be delivered by him on the Tuesday and Friday of each week throughout the Season Terms Eight Guineas (including all charges) for the course – payable in advance... N.B. – Early notice of intention will oblige, addressed by letter, Garden Farm, Drumcondra.[36]

The Drumcondra nursery developed into a considerable undertaking. In 1864 there were acres of strawberries and other soft fruits. Peaches, grapes, apples, pears and plums were grown for the Dublin market, as well as vegetables. 'The peculiarities of vegetable culture at Drumcondra would be well worth recounting for the benefit of gardeners, young and old; but I had not time to get accurate particulars. It may, however, be noted that the suds from a great washing establishment adjacent is a very active agent which Mr Niven carefully conducts to many of his crops'. There were ornamental plants too, including conifers, some in pots for sale, *Sedum*, *Sempervivum* and so on, the whole 'compounded of a very small infusion of farm, a good half of market garden, a fourth of nursery garden, a slice of alpine ground and two or three of experimental horticultural buildings, with a slight dash of the botanic garden'.[37]

28: Killakee House, County Dublin, where the landscaping by Ninian Niven was admired by William Robinson. Photograph by W. Lawrence, reproduced by permission of the National Library of Ireland).

His long and influential career as a landscape gardener began auspiciously as he had just laid out a parterre below the windows of the Vice-regal Lodge in The Phoenix Park.[38] It was encircled by an enfilade of Irish yews (*Taxus baccata* 'Fastigiata') and a raised walk with a stone balustrade on which stood rows of flower-filled vases. This formal arrangement was counterbalanced by a series of meandering walks which led through trees into a surrounding wilderness. When Niven's next project, the establishment in The Phoenix Park of a national arboretum, was abandoned[39] he betook himself to France to examine at first hand the gardens designed by Le Nôtre at Versailles and other similar places.[40] On his return he had the opportunity of applying his study, for he was asked by James Pim, a Dublin businessman, to design for him a place of public entertainment and instruction for Dubliners of all classes, who would, nevertheless pay to enter.[41] Their instruction was to be catered for by the erection of an observatory for gazing at the stars, and also geological and botanical displays, their entertainment by the organisation of fêtes, band concerts and theatrical events. For these gardens Niven first put into practice his 'intermediate' style dividing them by axial paths, the first of which wound down from the old castle which was by the entrance gates into a valley flooded by a lake and then, crossing by a bridge, ascended a hill upon the top of which the observatory was placed and the second, crossing it at a point where the great palm house stood, wrapped itself around the perimeter of the eminence. Neither the gardens nor the designs for it survive, only a lengthy description by Niven.

After this he was to contrive a series of grand designs for the gardens of the leading country houses of the time – Nutley Park, County Dublin, Kilkenny Castle, County Kilkenny,[42] Killakee, County Dublin (Fig. 28),[43] Baronscourt, County Tyrone,[44] Santry Court[45] and Templogue House,[46] County Dublin – all characterised by a similar approach: straight gravel walks with solemn rows of Irish yews in each, defined sunken lawns, sometimes enlivened with statuary, a flower-filled vase or a bed of annuals. This arrangement would end, in the Italian rather than the French manner, with a stone balustrade, leaning over which one might survey the extent of an eighteenth century landscaped demesne rather than gaze, as one might in a formal French garden, into a formal vista. In every case, its strict formality was contrasted with the natural lines of the paths which curved away from it into plantations of specimen trees, usually conifers – redwoods (*Sequoia sempervirens*), deodar (*Cedrus deodar*) and cedars of Lebanon (*Cedrus libani*) – a sombre diet which was leavened with hollies, junipers and laurels, which, though many were variegated, nevertheless contrived to maintain the dignified solemnity treasured by Victorian taste. However often the circumstances of a particular site required adaptations of the basic formula he never succumbed to the extravagant artificiality which, with its thousands of bedding plants, coloured gravels and intricate patterns of clipped hedging, was typical of the Victorian garden in England. In the gardens at Killakee and in those which he designed for the Great Dublin Exhibition[47] of 1863, Niven laid out formal beds of evergreen azaleas rather than the more usual annual plants. At Killakee, also, and at Woodtown Park[48] nearby, his descending terraces were teased into arcs decorated, unusually for him, with rings of clipped box. In the gardens at Templeogue House and Santry Court, such decorative planting becomes almost vestigial, its restrained effect relying only on the counterpoint between the long horizontal lines of the successive levels of lawn and the vertical forms of rows of Irish yew, a tree that became as important in Irish and English gardens as the cypress in Italy. This tree was found by George Willis between 1740 and 1760 when hunting hares on the hills above Florence Court, County Fermanagh. He came to a limestone rock called Carraignamadagh (Rock of the dog) and he noticed something strange in the appearance of two small plants of yew – sufficiently strange for him to dig them up. One he planted in his own garden, and the other he gave to his landlord, Lord Mount Florence (later the first Earl of Enniskillen). It was fortunate that Willis shared his find, for the plant in his own garden died in 1865, but the other still survives at Florence Court. It was from this tree that the first cuttings were given to the nurserymen, so it is the ultimate parent of all the Irish yews in cultivation.[49]

It is remarkable that George Willis should find two plants of this fastigiate sport, assuming that they were indeed distinct seedlings and not a double-stemmed plant that he was able to split into two rooted pieces. The Irish yew is considered to be a juvenile form in which the upright form and radial arrangement of the leaves associated with the seedling stage have persisted indefinitely, although this does not prevent the trees from flowering or fruiting freely. The seeds, however, do not give true Irish yews since the original tree was female, as are all those propagated vegetatively from it and the berries result from pollination by males of the ordinary form. It was surprising, therefore, when male Irish yews began to turn up in England. These were traced to Barnham Nurseries, Bognor, and it is surmised that for once a seedling of Irish yew bred true for the fastigiate habit of growth, or that it could have been a case of sex reversal, a phenomenon not unknown in other plants.[50] Whatever its provenance, the Irish yew became a *sine qua non* of the Victorian garden.

Niven's horticultural background, his intense interest in plants for their own sake rather than the mere colour they might contribute to a design and the restraint shown in his plans for formal gardens all combined to make his work attractive to the coming generation of gardeners, among whom William Robinson was the most prominent. When the latter wrote accounts of seven Irish gardens for *The gardeners' chronicle* between 1863 and 1865 no fewer than five of the seven he chose were either wholly or partly laid out by Niven.[51]

Many of the lesser features in Niven's garden anticipated those which were later promoted by Robinson in his book *The wild garden* (1870) and by others of his generation. As early as 1837 when Niven put forward his ideas for the public gardens at Monkstown, he broached the notion of a flower border in which the seeds of the annuals might be sown 'broadcast',that is, at random, rather than in the strict lines of the more normal sowings of the period. In the same plan, he proposed in a similar anticipation of the wilder approach of the Robinsonian garden, that some of the trees and shrubs should be planted in 'promiscuous' groups. The informality of his scheme for the American Garden at the Great Exhibition, also a foretaste of the rhododendron gardens of later years, was in sharp contrast to the regularity of earlier designs, such as those of Daniel Robertson, for the same kind of garden.

Niven's commissions for official gardens, in addition to those at the Vice-regal Lodge included those for the lodges of the First Secretary[52] and the Under-Secretary,[53] both also in The Phoenix Park.[54] Among the parks which he laid out for the public's pleasure were the People's Gardens in The Phoenix Park,[55] the Public Gardens and those of the Royal Marine Hotel, Dun Laoghaire and the Public Park at Blackrock,[56] another of Dublin's seaside suburbs. Unfortunately, the design for the last for which he was paid £20, had not been executed by the time of his death. His public spirit manifested itself when he replanted at his own expense an avenue of London planes down the centre of Dublin's principal thoroughfare, Sackville Street (now O'Connell Street). Unfortunately it was not to prove a fitting memorial to him as the trees died not long afterwards, the roots being poisoned by the gases escaping from the leaky sewers under the street.

Throughout his life he had written occasional verse, some of which was collected into a book and published under the title *Redemption thoughts* in 1869.[57] The following extract written on a hill overlooking Killiney Bay near Dublin is an example of its modest flavour:

> When I am dead and gone, that lovely bay
> That spacious sea, will still its curving waves
> Roll in; so tranquil now, so smooth, so bright
> And gently murmuring; and yon blue sky
> Will still reflect its beauteous tints, so rich
> On thy calm bosom.

He had enjoyed remarkable health throughout his life and worked in his garden up to the day he died, aged 80, in 1879. He was regarded as a cheerful and warmhearted personality, so that his funeral, though held at an early hour for privacy, was attended by many friends. His son, James, in continuation of the family tradition, was curator of Hull Botanic Garden.

Such was Ninian Niven's genius that in 1993 two gardens designed by him were chosen as worthy of restoration by the European Union under the 'Gardens of historic interest' scheme. These were the Iveagh Gardens, Dublin, laid out for the Great Exhibition of 1865, and that at Hilton Park, County Monaghan.

Born in Dundee in 1808, Niven's successor as curator of the Botanic Gardens at Glasnevin, David Moore (1808-1879) (Fig. 29) bestrode the horticultural world of Ireland, as Niven had done the world of garden design. We know of Moore's early career through information provided at the request of *The gardeners' chronicle* in 1871.[58] He was apprenticed to Mr Howe, gardener to the Earl of Camperdown at Camperdown, near Dundee. There he laid the foundation of his great knowledge of plants, for the collection was regarded as one of the most complete of that time. He became foreman there, but then moved to the nurseries of James Cunningham of Comely Bank, Edinburgh, where there was another notable collection of plants. In 1829 he moved to Ireland to take up the position of assistant to J. T. Mackay, Director of the Trinity College Botanic Gardens.

Under Mackay he developed a great interest in the Irish flora, which led to his appointment to the post of botanist to the Ordnance Survey of Ireland. During the course of this work he prepared a manuscript catalogue of plants observed in the county of Londonderry in 1834 and 1835.[59] In 1837 appeared his account of the botany of the parish of Templemore, in the first volume of the *Memoirs of the Ordnance Survey of Londonderry*.[60] However, the Survey did not publish further volumes on the same scale, despite the compilation of much material.

Moore was to retain his interest in field botany all his life. In 1838 he became Curator of the Royal Dublin Society's Botanic Gardens at Glasnevin. In the 1860s he collaborated with A. G. More of the Dublin Museum to publish, in 1866, *Cybele Hibernica*, long the standard work on the distribution of the plants native to Ireland.[61]

29: David Moore.

The Society's Botanic Gardens contained a 'Natural arrangement of British plants', which Moore described as one of the most interesting and useful in the garden, and one much used by visitors.[62] The maintenance of this was the occasion of several field trips to collect plants. On account of his familiarity with the flora of Antrim and Derry he was allowed to make a visit there during the first year of his appointment to Glasnevin. The plants he brought back included two that he discovered while worked for the Ordnance Survey. One was a grass *Calamagrostis stricta*, now known to be a rare native of Britain also. The other was a sedge *Carex buxbaumii* which he had found on an island in Lough Neagh.[63] It was subsequently exterminated by grazing. In Britain this sedge grows only in a bog in Inverness.

The following year (1840) he spent a month in Clare, Cork and Kerry collecting plants.[64] In 1841 and 1842 he was in Westmeath, where he found a rare stonewort (*Chara tomentosa*) in Lough Ennel and another rare sedge (*Carex appropinquata*), and also obtained exotic plants for Glasnevin from J. C. Lyons of orchid fame (see p. 96) and from James Naper of Lough Crew. In 1854 he found the pyramidal bugle (*Ajuga pyramidalis*) on the Aran Islands. In all he added seventeen or more 'firsts' to the Irish flora.[65] The scale of his efforts can be measured by his comment that 'I have collected with my own hands, having for this purpose travelled over a large portion of Ireland, from east to west and from north to south, and from sea level to the tops of the highest mountains.'[66]

David Moore was indeed a great traveller. Apart from these botanical excursions he made many visits to botanic gardens and nurseries at Kew, Liverpool, Hull, York, Manchester, Edinburgh and Glasgow. During a tour through Scandinavia, Germany and Belgium in 1863[67] his interest in field botany was again useful, this time in prompting him to collect rare alpine and herbaceous plants from their natural habitats in Norway. In Germany and Belgium he obtained scarce and valuable palms for the new glasshouse at Glasnevin. In his continental travels he covered a vast amount of ground, visiting in addition Holland, Italy, France, Russia, Austria, Spain and Portugal.

Moore's work in enriching the collections at Glasnevin was greatly helped by donations sent from abroad. His brother Charles who was Curator, and later Director, of the Royal Botanic Garden, Sydney, New South Wales, sent many plants in Wardian cases. These were closed glass cases invented by Dr. Nathanial Ward, a London physician, who got the idea when he came upon a fern growing spontaneously in a corked bottle. These consignments included tree ferns four to seven feet high. Plants were sent in return to Sydney, Trinidad and Jamaica.

Another sender of plants was Edward Madden (1805-1856)[68], of whom Moore wrote: 'Large supplies of seeds from the Himalayan Mountains have been sent by Major Madden of the Royal Bengal Artillery, a member of the Royal Dublin Society, whose exertions on behalf of the Botanic Garden could scarcely be overrated'. He had sent seeds of rhododendrons, conifers and other plants, not to Glasnevin alone, but also to Trinity College Gardens, to Belfast and to Kew during the period 1841 to 1850. His name is not widely known among gardeners today, though he is commemorated in the beautiful, scented but tender *Rhododendron maddenii*. He deserves to be remembered for several notable plants which he introduced into cultivation. These include the giant Himalayan lily, *Cardiocrinum giganteum*, of which the stems are used to make musical pipes in their native country, and also *Lilium wallichianum* and *Cassiope fastigiata*, considered by Bean to be the prettiest *Cassiope*. At Glasnevin grows a tree-like specimen of *Abelia triflora* that is a direct link with Madden as it was raised from seed collected by him. Madden's interests were botanical but he had a garden in India from which he sent home living specimens of *Lilium wallichianum* and other plants. He retired from the army in 1849, after staying as long as possible to earn his pension, as he was dogged by ill-health. He collected herbarium specimens at Aden, Suez, Cairo and Malta on his way home to settle in Edinburgh where he worked on his herbarium specimens from the Himalayas.

Seeds were also received at Glasnevin from other collectors in many parts of the world. In this way Moore was instrumental in distributing to gardens such plants as *Cardiocrinum giganteum* and pampas grass (*Cortaderia selloana*). He was the first in Europe to raise the latter, from seeds received from John Tweedie of Buenos Aires in 1841, who sent many species including *Gloxinia tubiflora* (Plate 5).

Moore's years at Glasnevin were marked by the inevitable trials of any person in charge of a major garden. In his very first year he had to contend with the devastation of the 'Great Wind' of the night of 7 and 8 January 1839,[69] a storm that became legendary in Ireland. He had finished cataloguing all the plants in the greenhouses and stove house and was starting on the herbaceous plants when the winds began that were to reach a hurricane force that night. Many large trees in the gardens were blown down, fortunately mostly common species, and their removal improved the appearance of the garden, except where they had screened the view of Glasnevin village. The clearance of the debris took so much time that completion of the re-arrangement of the herbaceous plantings had to be abandoned for that season. In his own words it was a year 'almost unprecedented in this country for the unfavourableness of the weather for gardening and botanical operations'. This was a mild comment on such a tornado, which blew down part of the wall along the road to Glasnevin village, though the Botanic Gardens suffered comparatively little damage to its structures.

In his first report of the general state of the Royal Dublin Society's Botanic Gardens, David Moore was able to say that 'so far as neatness and cleanliness went, I found it in such order as did much credit to my talented predecessor', but he soon had trouble over maintenance of the glasshouses. In 1840 he drew attention to the decayed and tottering state of the lower range of hothouses near the entrance gates, regarded by the architect as being beyond repair.

Just then the Society was going through a difficult period owing to a dispute with the government over its constitution and responsibilities, even involving a threat to the Society's annual grant. All the glasshouses therefore were neglected and leaked. The lower range had to be propped up to prevent the whole front from falling forward *en masse*. However, by 1843 the difficulties with the government had been resolved, and Moore was able to report that the Society had taken up the problem of the glasshouses 'with spirit' and a fine range of wrought iron conservatories were started with the help of private subscriptions from members of the Society. These, with money from reserve funds, supplemented the £4,000 contributed by the government. Though by the end of 1846 the wings of the new range had been finished and filled with plants, the central conservatory continued to be a source of frustration for another four years, being without any means of heating. In his report for 1851 Moore was able to state that the efficiency of the heating apparatus and the general suitability of the house were proven. The plants made rapid growth after their removal to the new conservatory, where bananas and plantains were able to ripen their fruits. The Octagon House was repaired and a young Norfolk Island pine once more was placed in it, recalling the original purpose for which the house had been built.

The great water-lily of the Amazon, *Victoria amazonica* (*V. regia*) first discovered in 1837, was the plant sensation of the 1850s. David Moore was determined that Glasnevin should have it quickly. In 1851 he built a 15 feet square brick and cement tank in one of the houses of the old range to grow it on a small scale while he pressed the Society to provide a special house. This was started in 1853 but it was not ready until the end of May 1854, too late for *Victoria amazonica* to flower that year. In 1855 he was able to report triumphantly that 'the beautiful conservatory which had been built for the purpose of cultivating the *Victoria amazonica* and other tropical aquatic plants had proved suitable.' The first flower opened on 13 August and flowering continued until the middle of September. The leaves were fully five and a half feet in diameter. This magnificent plant continues to be cultivated in the same house to this day.

David Moore lived in an exciting time for the lover of trees. Prior to the nineteenth century the conifers available were European – Scots pine, silver fir, Norway spruce and European larch. Then, from 1827 onwards, came the arrival of the exotics. David Douglas had been sent to North America by the Horticultural Society of London and from there he sent home so many conifers that he wrote: 'you will begin to think that I manufacture pines at my pleasure'.[70] Other introductions came from China, Japan and South America.

Moore was energetic in developing the arboretum at Glasnevin, which he had found in an unsatisfactory state due to overcrowding. Some species had been planted in triplicate, others were minor varieties. He thinned these, and removed the willow collection, since Niven had planted duplicates in a more suitable location near the river. The newly introduced conifers which were planted included Douglas' introductions from north-western America, Mexican species such as the remarkable *Pinus montezumae*, so fine at Glasnevin today, the graceful but tender *Pinus patula* and the Himalayan *Cedrus deodara*, *Pinus excelsa* and *Picea morinda*. The last three were regarded by Moore as of the greatest importance both as ornamental and valuable timber trees. The deodar, so familiar today, was then very new, having been introduced to Europe in 1831.

Other now familiar trees especially mentioned by Moore as novelties included *Pinus insignis*, *Abies nobilis* and even *Cryptomeria japonica*, which he planted out in the open ground to test its suitability for our climate. In 1855, he recorded the acquisition of 'the extraordinary coniferous tree called *Wellingtonia gigantea* [= *Sequoiadendron giganteum*], which was discovered a few years ago in upper California and is found to be sufficiently hardy in Britain'. With such an influx of new species began the fashion for conifers, so Moore could write 'the coniferous or Pine family, which of late years have become so great desiderata among planters'.

David Moore died in the same year, 1879, as Ninian Niven. He was a Scotsman to the end, in speech if not in name. 'After fifty years' familiar discourse there was no imitation of the mellifluous tones of the Dubliner and the straightforward directness of his speech, as well as the accent, betrays the North Briton'. His life was a remarkably full one. He built the Glasnevin Botanic Gardens up to the highest standards in equipment and plant content, travelling widely to obtain interesting plants for the collections. He was the first to hybridise the curious pitcher plants. *Sarracenia* x *moorei* (*S. flava* x *S. drummondii*)

30: Frederick William Burbidge.

(Plate 17) was exhibited by him at the Botanical Congress in Florence in 1874.[71] Many other hybrids were raised and unsuccessful attempts made to cross *Sarracenia* with *Darlingtonia*. He published a *Handbook for the Botanic Garden of the Royal Dublin Society* (1850). His duties did not stop at horticulture for he carried out experiments on farm crops on behalf of the Society. He advocated cutting down the haulms of potatoes before full maturity, a measure against blight still practised to-day. Other crops he studied included clover, rye, barley, kohl rabi, and vetches. He had a special interest in manures for the farm. In spite of all of these activities Moore still found time to become one of the country's leading botanists. He could well lay claim to the full quotation from *The Aeneid* from which the Royal Dublin Society derives its motto: *Quae regio in terris nostri non plena laboris?*

John Bain, Moore's contemporary at the nearby Trinity College Botanic Gardens was of a more retiring nature. Although he was born in Ireland in 1815, his parents were Scottish. He was first Foreman and later Assistant Curator to Mackay, under whose influence he became an expert in the native flora of Ireland. On the death of Mackay in 1862, Bain succeeded him, and under his care the gardens became noted for the cultivation of such insectivorous plants as sundews (*Drosera* spp.), pitcher plants and the strange *Cephalotus follicularis* of Western Australia (Plate 4). This plant is rarely grown well, but Bain's specimens were very robust, a large pot containing so many pitchers that they over-lapped each other, and trailed down the sides of the pot in such profusion that they almost hid it from view.

Though Bain was of a retiring nature his company was sought by many notable contemporaries, not all of them botanists. The Reverend W. Ellis, a well-known plant collector and missionary, who is said to have refused the bishopric of Madagascar, sent him orchids from his important collection in England, including species that Ellis himself had discovered and introduced to cultivation.

John Bain never married, and on his retirement in 1878 went to live with his niece at Holyhead, Wales. He kept up his interest in wild flowers, as related by his successor, F. W. Burbidge. Together they would walk miles to see rare plants, such as the marsh gentian (*Gentiana pneumonanthe*), unknown in Ireland. He died in 1903, and was buried in Mount Jerome Cemetery, Dublin[72].

The next Curator, Frederick William Burbidge (Fig. 30), born at Wynneswold, Leceistershire in 1847[73] received hs earliest education at the local village school.[74] His father was a farmer and fruit grower,[75] but Frederick soon showed his preference for gardening and he was ambitious to improve his education. He entered the Royal Horticultural Society's Garden, then at Chiswick, and was so keen on drawing and painting that he also attended classes in art, winning a first prize of £4, which he spent on a microscope. From 1868 to 1873 he was at Kew, after which he joined William Robinson (p 133) on the staff of *The garden*. He was now a busy journalist, contributing (among other works) to a series in the journal, called 'Garden flora', each of his articles being accompaned by a coloured plate. Here Burbidge's artistic talent found scope in several good pictures. That of daffodils from Barr's nursery (1883) shows a grace and naturalness that is somewhat lacking in the plates of his book *The Narcissus: its history and culture* (1875), which was long a standard work. His paintings for *The garden* included several of orchids, such as a splendid one of the yellow, olive, brown, and purple *Oncidium macranthum*, drawn from a specimen grown at Straffan House, County Kildare. He published a book *The art of botanical drawing* (1873), another *Cool orchids*, and yet another, *Propagation and improvement of cultivated plants* (1877), which was much praised. Burbidge was indeed a prolific writer of books at this period, others being *Domestic floriculture* (1875), followed by *The chrysanthemum* (1884), *Wild flowers in art and nature* with J. G. L. Sparks (1894) and *The book of the scented garden* (1905).

In 1877 and 1878 Burbidge made a break with the life of a journalist, travelling in Borneo for the famous nursery firm of Veitch and Sons accompanied by Peter Veitch. This expedition resulted in the introduction of several striking plants. *Nepenthes rajah* is a remarkable pitcher plant with leaves five or six feet long in the wild, though only half that length in cultivation, ending in great purplish-brown pitchers capable of holding two pints. This species was to be particularly associated with Glasnevin, for Frederick Moore was the only grower who really succeeded with plants from the original introduction, from which he was able to supply specimens for *Curtis's Botanical magazine* in 1905.[76] Among the orchids Burbidge discovered in Borneo was the beautiful *Cypripedium lawrenceanum*, regarded as one of the most attractive species. Sir Joseph Hooker named *Burbidgea* after him, a genus of herbaceous plants of the ginger family (Zingiberaceae), founding it on *B. nitida* (Plate 15), an orange-scarlet flowered species whch Burbidge discovered growing on moist shady rocks in Borneo. Burbidge was doubly commemorated by the citation in *Curtis's botanical magazine* for the plate was from his own drawing and Hooker's words were 'I have named this interesting discovery in recognition of Mr Burbidge's eminent services to horticulture, whether as a collector in Borneo, or as author of *Cultivated plants, their propagation and improvement*, a work which should be in every gardener's library'.

Burbidge was very ill with malaria while in Borneo and returned in a very weak condition. He wrote a book on his experiences called *The gardens of the sun* which won much approval on its literary merits.

When Burbidge went to Trinity College Botanic Gardens as Curator in 1879 he was already well known. He became a member of the Royal Irish Academy, of the Royal Dublin Society and of the Scientific Committee of the Royal Horticultural Society of London. He was an honorary life member of the Scottish Horticultural and Botanical Society, a Veitch Memorial medallist and one of the original recipients of the Victoria Medal of Honour.

While at the College Botanic Gardens Burbidge hybridised, in 1880, *Calceolaria pavoni* with *C. fuchsiaefolia* and raised *C. x burbidgei*, a greenhouse pillar plant which Gumbleton of Belgrove (p. 142) named after the raiser.[77] This hybrid proved to be especially useful as it flowered chiefly during the winter. Burbidge was Curator of the College Botanic Gardens for 26 years, and did much for its reputation. In recognition of these services, and of his literary work, the University of Dublin, in 1889, conferred on him an honorary M.A. degree, the citation including a witty reference to the work of Burbidge on *Narcissus* being such that Narcissus himself, admiring himself in the water, would have been astonished at what had been done for him by the art and skill of Mr Burbidge. A measure of his pride in this occasion is shown by the many reproductions of his portrait as a good-looking young man in cap and gown which appeared in contemporary journals. In 1904 a volume of his old journal *The garden* dedicated to him, shows him as an elderly man in the year before his death. His friend and predecessor as Curator, Frederick Moore, referred to his love and enthusiasm for his work, his minute knowledge of plants, including their structural details, and his loyalty to his friends.[78] An anonymous note in *The garden* (1906) referred to him as a stalwart champion of the rights of gardeners, but having little or no sympathy with the new woman-gardener movement. At first it seems surprising that Burbidge should occasionally have used Veronica as a *nom-de-plume*[79] in *The garden* but he probably thought of it in the botanical rather than in the female sense.

Of the other botanic gardens founded in the flurry of the earlier part of the century, the early demise of the Cork institution has already been noted. That at Belfast continued to have financial and administrative difficulties. The garden finally took shape under Daniel Ferguson who was curator from 1836 until his death in 1864. He wrote *A popular guide to the Royal Botanic Garden of Belfast* (1851). He was succeeded by his son, William Hooker Ferguson, who had trained under Hooker at Kew. After allegations of mishandling of money connected with the sale of plants and members' subscriptions, he resigned in 1868.[80] As a result of an advertisement in *The gardeners' chronicle*, Joseph Forsythe Johnston, a foreman in Manchester Botanic Garden, was appointed head gardener – not curator – out of 80 applicants, with a free house and £80 a year. This was £20 less than Ferguson had received, but two years later his salary was raised to £100 and he was styled Curator. Johnston stayed for nine years and retired in 1877 after a dispute over how much free time he was entitled to, and also over his dismissal of his foreman Charles McKimm. The extra free time which he took appears to have been in the pursuit of a landscape gardening career, for it is as the latter he describes himself in the title page of his book *The natural principles of landscape gardening* (1874). The opening lines indicate the abstract and not a little pompous quality of the work: 'The arrangement of vegetation is a matter of such moment as to require little justification in advocating its needfulness'. It is divided formally into three sections called 'Books'. The first, the most theoretical, is concerned with Beauty, having sub-sections entitled 'The feelings for True Beauty', 'The general principles of Beauty', and 'The detailed observation of Beauty'. The second Book contains a lengthy dissertation on 'The laws of order' and their application to landscape design by attention to lines of sight, lines of distance, places and the site. The last deals with 'The principal effects and styles of scenery' among which he discusses those of woodlands, shrubberies and pineta. The philosophical nature of the book, coming from a man whose career began in practical gardening affords an example of the Victorian capacity for self-education and self-improvement. He was succeeded as curator by the man he had dismissed, Charles McKimm.

A similar capacity marked the career of Joseph Paxton (1801–1865), who rose from his early position as a working gardener to become a colossus not only of Victorian gardening but also, because of his architectural, engineering and entrepreneurial talents, of the Victorian age.[81] He served the sixth Duke of Devonshire, called 'The bachelor duke' and one of the period's foremost patrons of horticulture, first as head gardener, then as steward and finally, as close friend and confidant. He first came to Ireland in 1840 to advise the duke on his Irish seat, Lismore Castle, County Waterford. He stayed only a short time, however, and nothing conclusive seems to have been done. Ten years later, the duke brought him again to Lismore and this time a series of works was inaugurated which was to occupy the next eight years, that is, until the duke's death in 1858. The principal effort was concentrated on converting the castle itself from near ruin into the romantic and picturesque pile overhanging the deep valley of the River Blackwater which we see today. The gardens were also renovated. On his first visit he wrote to his wife that he and the duke had spent some time looking at the plantations and deciding where thinning and

31: Derrycunnihy Cottage, County Kerry. A nineteenth century picturesque cottage set in a typical naturalistic garden of the period. (Photography by W. Lawrence).

replanting were necessary; and he noted the mildness of the climate, remarking particularly on 'the myrtles and hydrangeas and other greenhouse plants' growing without protection.[82] On his visit in 1852 it was the park which again was the centre of his attention, for he worked on laying out new drives and approaches and opening up views and prospects through the woodlands.[83] In 1858 he wrote to his wife of the grapery being constructed in the kitchen garden.[84] It was perhaps also on this occasion that a hothouse was constructed there, an example of one of Paxton's excursions into the world of mass-production, known as 'Paxton's hothouses for the million'.[85]

During his professional visits, he took time off to visit his sister whose husband was employed on the estate of the Viscount de Vesci at Abbeyleix, County Laois, and his daughter who was married to the rector of Mothel, County Waterford, and for whom he designed a rectory and garden.[86] He also visited the sights, both natural and horticultural. On his first visit in 1840 he had been impressed by the size of strawberry trees (*Arbutus unedo*) growing by the lakes of Killarney[87] and had travelled northwards to Mount Shannon, County Clare. Here he saw the conservatory constructed by Lord Clare to plans which he had provided some time before.[88] It is now derelict but was described in the *Irish farmers' and gardeners' magazine* as ' a metallic splendid curvilinear roofed conservatory'.[89] It must have been fascinating as it was designed during the same period as Paxton was erecting one of the wonders of Victorian England, The Great Stove at Chatsworth in Derbyshire. In 1844, he paid a visit to the garden of Lady Tighe at Woodstock, County Kilkenny, and reported again to his wife: 'it is the best-kept place in Ireland, the lady being rich and personally fond of gardening. She has applied our wall at Chatsworth and it answers beautifully. Of course I am a great lion in Ireland'.[90] His reference to the wall appears to be to the Conservative Wall at Chatsworth, which took the form of glass cases erected against a garden wall to protect and conserve tender fruit. On his next visit in 1858, the year of the duke's death, he made an excursion to the gardens at Newtown Anner, County Tipperary, and Curraghmore, County Waterford, where he admired and commented upon the progress of the gardens then being laid out by James Fraser.[91] His last visit was in 1862 when he sailed to Belfast, visiting the Giants' Causeway, the natural rockwork wonder of the north Antrim coast and stayed with Lady Londonderry at Garron Tower 'where she was very pleased to see me and would have kept me a week.'[92] It must have been on this excursion that he, as recounted in an article by F. W. Burbidge, laid out the garden at Narrow Water Castle, County Down. This consisted of a balustraded terrace and parterre around the castle and pleasure grounds leading off to a walled garden in terraces descending from a range of greenhouses at the top.

Two of his assistants and possibly a third, were to give designs for gardens in Ireland. Edward Milner, his chief associate, responsible for the extraordinary gardens around the Crystal Palace when it was removed to Sydenham in London, and who had an international practice covering a number of European countries, gave two.[93] One was for a pair of sunken flower beds which now forms part of the great garden at Powerscourt,[94] and the second at Gibbstown Park, County Meath, for Mr Gerrard, whose wife had been a lady-in-waiting to Queen Victoria and who may have required a garden of a quality which would reflect her former station.[95] The interest of both lay in the fact that the geometrical pattern of their flower-filled beds was delineated not in the usual way of clipped box-hedging but by a cut-stone tracery. He was preceded to Ireland by James Howe who also had worked at Sydenham. Calling himself a landscape engineer, he carried out no less than five commissions here. All of his designs are marked by vigorous scroll-work patterns emphasised by panels of coloured gravels in a manner which was typical of the high Victorian style in England, but the gorgeousness of which was eschewed by Ninian Niven and the Irish designers of the same period. One suspects it was a desire for the more elaborate Victorian style which prompted Howe's patrons in Ireland to employ him. In 1863, *The gardeners' chronicle* described his panelled parterre in front of Straffan House, County Kildare, the seat of the Barton family of Bordeaux wine-merchants.[96] In 1865, he was working at four places in different corners of the country. At Leyrath, County Kilkenny, he supervised the construction of a parterre designed by W. A. Nesfield in a style complementary to the rich Italianate character of the new house.[97] At Temple House, County Sligo, which had been rebuilt in a balustraded classical style in 1860, he enriched the setting with a parterre of unwonted richness for Ireland.[98] At Powerscourt he contributed one of the many schemes considered by Lord Powerscourt for the garden[99] and at Castle Leslie, County Monaghan, he carried out what must have been his last commission, for his consequent demise was described by Lord Powerscourt thus:

> Curiously enough, Mr Howe died shortly after the plan was completed of drink. He had been at Glaslough, County Monaghan, laying out improvements for Col. Charles Leslie and was taken with delirium tremens and left and only got him to Sydenham where he lived, in time to die there.[100]

A more interesting landscape gardener who came to Ireland was William Brodrick Thomas of 52 Wimpole Street, London. One of his grandfathers was Lord Midleton who had a large estate in County Cork. He lived as a bachelor at Wimpole Street with his unmarried sister, Fanny, who was deaf and dumb but perfectly *compos mentis*. According to family legend, he, in his later years, lived on the ground floor, and she above, but they could not be got together, as he was too bulky to get upstairs and she, too infirm to come down. He was a great trencherman, which may account for the fact that he appears to have been unoffended by the differing attitudes of his employers – some asked him to dine, others sent him to the servants' hall, where he used to enjoy himself hugely.[101] He was exceedingly fashionable as a designer, enjoying the patronage of the Prince of Wales and his circle. For the Prince he made two lakes at Sandringham House, Norfolk, decorating one of them with artificial rockwork provided by James Pulham and Sons, of York, one of the specialists in that

Victorian genre. Even the Prince was taken aback by the cost, describing Thomas as 'a gentleman not to be described as inexpensive'. The ubiquitous Lord Powerscourt requested him in 1866 to prepare an alternative plan to that furnished by Howe the year before, for his garden, and subsequently recounted:

> Mr Thomas came to Powerscourt and stood on the upper steps. There was a high hillock between the house and Juggy's Pond. He said: "The first thing to do is to take away 'the stomach'." The 'stomach' hid nearly half the pond from view at the windows of the drawing room. Then he drew the plan. His idea was to formalise the plan and make it more like a fountain basin and the design would have been simple but it was considered better to leave the pond in its natural state.[102]

It is interesting that he should have drawn his plan on site rather than later when he returned to his office.

He then followed Howe to Glaslough, but not with any greater success. Lord Powerscourt wrote:

> Mr Thomas left Powerscourt and went to Col. Leslie at Glaslough to design for him what Mr Howe had been unable to do, and also to mark certain trees which were to be removed to clear a site for a new house and terraces; Col. Leslie employed Mr Broderick Thomas about a week, his fee being five guineas a day and his expenses to mark the trees, which he did by placing visiting cards on the trees which were to be removed.

Colonel Leslie was relating this to Lord Powerscourt who said "What did you do, did you cut the trees?" "No", said Colonel Leslie, "no sooner was Thomas off by the train than I went and took all the visiting cards off again."[103]

Apart from noting the civilised mode by which the trees to be felled were marked, it is also but fair to Thomas to point out that his client at Glaslough appears to have employed a number of architects as well as landscape gardeners before he finally made up his mind as to which scheme for the house and garden he wished to adopt. Another of his designs was carried out at Baronscourt, County Tyrone, the seat of the Duke of Abercorn. This comprised an extensive parterre edged with scrollwork beds and rows of Irish yews.[104] His last work here was his plan for St Stephen's Green, Dublin, in 1879. The Green had been in the ownership of Lord Iveagh, a member of the Guinness family, who determined upon handing it over to the citizens of Dublin for their enjoyment, but only after he had first paid for its transformation into a park of a scale and magnificence befitting the centre of Dublin. He commissioned Thomas to prepare the designs which were centred around a new lake.[105] With its dripping cliff of rockwork erected by James Pulham and Sons at one end it is very similar to the one he had made at Sandringham. Unfortunately, Thomas was too ill to supervise the work and the task fell to William Sheppard, a Dublin landscape gardener who for many years had been assistant to Ninian Niven.

Sheppard had commenced his own practice on Niven's death in 1879 and by 1886 he was able to advertise –

WILLIAM SHEPPARD
LANDSCAPE GARDENER &c
(Successor to Mr N. Niven)
CHARLEVILLE, CHURCHTOWN, DUNDRUM, DUBLIN
Will be happy to wait on the Nobility and Gentry on all matters connected with Parks,
Pleasure Grounds, Gardens and Woods.
Surveys made and Plans prepared for new Gardens, Lakes, Ornamental Ponds,
Waterfalls, Caves, Boat Houses, and all kinds of Rockwork, Ferneries, Horticultural
Buildings, Roads, Drainage &c.
ESTATES VALUED
W. Sheppard has been patronised by the Right Honourable the
EARL of CARYSFORT K.P. to superintend the making of New Gardens &c at
Glenart Castle, Arklow,
Co. Wicklow;
Right Honourable LORD ARDILAUN,
St Anne's, Clontarf, Dublin, to superintend the execution of the works of
improvement in St. Stephen's Green Park and also by other Noblemen and Gentilmen
in different parts of the United Kingdom.

Sheppard's designs for the public parks at Palmerston[106] and Harold's Cross[107] in the south Dublin suburbs continued the Victorian tradition but his two known designs for private gardens at Glencormac[108] and Clonart,[109] both in County Wicklow, looked forward to the wild Robinsonian style. The remains of the dripping pool designed by him still exist at Glencormac.

The fashionable Victorian garden became so complex that it required specialist designers to carry out some of its main features. Apart from Mr Pulham, already mentioned, Mr Bracken of Chester designed rockwork features, the most spectacular of which, in Ireland, was the fernery at Roebuck Castle, County Dublin.[110] Although the great English firms of Ormson,[111] Mackenzie and Moncur,[112] Boulton and Paul,[113] Cranston[114] and Richardson[115] erected conservatories too numerous to mention, those in curvilinear iron work by Richard Turner of the Hammersmith Works, Ballsbridge, Dublin, were the most original and the most elegant of all. Although his designs for the Palm House at the Royal Botanic Gardens, Kew, the National Botanic Gardens, Glasnevin,[116] and the Belfast Botanic Gardens[117] are well-known, some of his unexecuted projects are often forgotten. His commended design for the Crystal Palace of the Great London Exhibition of 1851 was only rejected in favour of that of Paxton on the grounds of cost and speed of erection. At the exhibition he showed a brass model of a Winter Garden for the Wilhelmshoe Palace of the King of Prussia in Berlin.[118]

Many of his smaller glasshouses like those for the Vice-regal Lodge (now Aras an Uachtaráin),[119] Edermine, County Wexford, Rath House, County Laois, and Bellevue, County Fermanagh have only recently become known.[120] They were all characterised by an extreme of lightness which was achieved by his intuitive but daring grasp of engineering design. Like most Victorian ironmasters he also supplied the extensive market for garden sculpture and architectural features in cast iron. The gates, gate-lodge and fencing at the entrance to Mayfield, Portlaw, County Waterford, the seat of the Malcolmson family, provide glimpses of an interesting medley of his designs.

No fewer than four firms seized on the success of the Turner tradition to produce curvilinear conservatories or other ornaments themselves. The Malcolmsons, with interests in cotton milling, ship-building and coal-mining were one of the foremost of Ireland's families of the Industrial Revolution. As an offshoot of their ship-building yards in Waterford, they began the Neptune Ironworks which produced cast-iron furniture characterised by a wealth of naturalistic detail; fern, ivy, and oak leaves being used as the principal decorative motifs.[121] The second such firm was James Pierce and Sons of Wexford, which firm has only recently gone into liquidation. Pierce erected conservatories in collaboration with Richard Turner, as at Edermine, County Wexford[122] as well as on his own. Although the largest of the latter would appear to be the roof over the Gothic Conservatory at Johnstown Castle, County Wexford. the most elegant is surely that still extant at Castlebridge in the same county. The third ironmaster of the Turner school was Robinson of Dublin. The only house known to have been erected by him was that designed by Lanyon and Lynn at Ballywalter, County Down.[123] The last of the group was the firm of Ross and Murray (at one time called Ross and Walpole) who erected the great conservatory at Abbotstown, County Dublin, for Lord Holmpatrick.[124] The other specialisation of this firm was in the design and erection of light iron suspension bridges which are a feature of some Irish gardens. (The earliest of its kind, though its designer is not known, is at Birr Castle, County Offaly.[125]) The best known pair is at Mount Usher, County Wicklow. There is an almost forgotten pair at Straffan, County Kildare. Richard Turner also designed garden bridges but the lightness of his structures was achieved by passing tension cables under rather than over the bridge in the usual way. One example was at Cahir Park, County Tipperary,[126] and another at Lismore Castle, is so close to it in design that it is also attributed to him. An exception to the Irish tradition of curvilinear ironwork was the work of the Dublin firm of Mallet, whose rectilinear designs do, however, follow the native tradition of using abstract or foliate decorative ornament.[127]

The absence of figurative ornament in Irish art goes back to the Celtic period. Those who wished to have statuary or fountains with figurative decoration were obliged to purchase them abroad. William Smith and Company of Glasgow, for example, appears to have made the centrepiece of Ninian Niven's design for the distiller, George Roe at Nutley Park,[128] near Dublin, for its description fits that illustrated by them in *The Irish builder*.[129] Ironmasters from no less than three European countries – Kahl & Co of Potsdam, Geiss of Berne and Bartezat of Seine-et-Oise – fabricated the statuary for the restoration of the seventeenth century garden at Kilruddery.[130] The usual marketplace for these ornaments was one or other of the great industrial exhibitions which were so characteristic of European life at the time. The great cast-iron fountain which stood in the parterre at Curraghmore was bought for £3,000 by Lord Waterford at the Great Paris Exhibition of 1863.[131] At the same exhibition, Lord Powerscourt bought the gates known as The Golden Gates which guard one of the secondary entrances to the demesne.[132]

While these artists were at work it seemed as if the continuing elaboration and increasing complexity of all aspects of Victorian gardening were proceeding to a point of absurdity, and, indeed, many were convinced that it had already reached that point by 1870, for in that year, the wind of change blew its strongest yet in the shape of a book entitled *The wild garden* by William Robinson, whose ideas are still a strong influence in gardening today.

WILLIAM ROBINSON AND HIS IRISH CIRCLE

I saw the flower gardener meanly trying to rival the tile or wall-paper men, and throwing aside with contempt all the lovely things that through their height or form did not conform to this idea ... The choke-muddle shrubbery, in which the shrubs kill each other, shews betimes a few ill-grown plants, and has wide patches of bare earth in summer over which pretty green things might crowd.[1]

Thus William Robinson saw the flower knots and parterres of the Victorian era, and the dull shrubberies of the time, on his return from wanderings in the 'orchid-flecked meadows of [Buckinghamshire] to the tumbled down under cliffs on the Essex coast'. He had been collecting wild flowers as part of his job in Regent's Park, where there was a small garden of British plants which had to be kept up.[2] This was William's first job in England, and from these ideas he was to develop the movement that became a revolution in gardening. This was the revulsion from the geometric designs executed in bedding plants in favour of the natural style of growing plants which is so well suited to Ireland, the country from which he had fled. 'Robinson came of a family of small farmers-countrymen of respectable standing in County Down'[3] though the place of his birth in 1838 remains uncertain.[4] While he was still a boy his father, who was agent to Lord St George in County Mayo, eloped to America with Lady St George, leaving behind a wife and family. Though William went to America with his brother, traced his father and demanded money from him,[5] he started his career in reduced circumstances as gardener's boy at Curraghmore, County Waterford, the estate of the Marquis of Waterford, where his first job was to carry water from the river to the glasshouses. During the last year of his life thoughts turned back to those early days, and he sent a copy of his *The English flower garden* to the head gardener there for the use of the young men in the bothy, stating that he had once lived in that bothy himself.[6]

32: William Robinson, portrait by the French artist Carolus-Duran.

We next hear of him as foreman gardener at Ballykilcavan, County Laois.[7] The garden there was one of those old-fashioned gardens of great charm, as later described by him. There was no parterre, just a pleasant setting of lawns and trees, with an old walled garden in which flowers, fruit and vegetables grew in close but happy proximity. There was a range of hothouses containing tender exotics, and, in 1861, when Robinson quarrelled with his employer, Sir Hunt Johnson-Walsh or with the head gardener, he vented his spleen on these plants. One night he put out the fire in the hothouses, left the ventilators open and fled to Dublin.[8] The reason for this extraordinary action is not known. It may have been a clash of personalities, for Robinson was to have many during a long and pugnacious life, perhaps arising basically from the early trauma he had suffered as a result of his father's elopement.

The manner of his departure must have made it unlikely that he could obtain another position in Ireland, but the young man gained an interview with David Moore, curator of the Botanic Gardens at Glasnevin,[9] and through him secured an introduction to Robert Marnock, curator of the Royal Botanical Society's Garden, Regent's Park, London, where he resumed his horticultural career.[10]

Robinson's ideas on gardening style must have been influenced by the beauties of the 'orchid-flecked meadows' in which he wandered in the course of his job with Regent's Park, leading to the notion that as far as possible one should follow nature in the approach to garden design. In expressing doubts about the design of Victorian gardens he was in accord with William Morris and a generation of poets, writers and architects of the Pre-Raphaelite movement who, for similar reasons, were in revolt against the Establishment in their own fields. Morris had written of the Victorian flower garden 'Another thing ... too commonly seen, is an aberration of the human mind ... it is technically called carpet gardening.'

A further influence was the Irish Victorian garden which, particularly through its chief exponent, Ninian Niven, had avoided the excesses of its English counterpart. Four years after his flight from Ireland he was back there to prepare descriptions of Glasnevin and Trinity College Botanic Gardens, Ninian Niven's nursery, The Phoenix Park and two private gardens for a series of articles in *The gardeners' chronicle*.[11] Four articles were devoted to the garden of T. Bewley at Rockville, near Dublin. This was a garden after his own heart.

> ... perhaps the very sea of floral monotony by which we are surrounded may have a good effect stimulating men of wealth and taste to take an opposite course, and revel in rarity; but, be the cause what it may, places where specialities and novelties are thoroughly well catered for, are fortunately easily to be found in the neighbourhood of London and some other large cities. Thus one displays a mine of orchidaceous wealth, another glows with the most wondrously painted foliage plants and a third is adorned with illimitable diversity. At Rockville all these are done, some of them in an unrivalled manner, and much more besides. The orchids alone are of great value, and sufficient to make the fame of a ducal garden; the plants of remarkable foliage I have never seen surpassed; I believe Rivers himself has no such orchard house, which at Rockville combines the comforts and advantages of a winter garden and Persian fruit grove; while for Ferns and a Fernery you might go to Buenos Ayres, to Borneo, and examine all the glass erections from St. Petersburg to the sunny shores of the Mediterranean Sea, where such things cease to be a luxury without finding a more unique scene, or one in which Ferns – from the largest arborescent species downwards – look or do better, or are more richly displayed than in the great Fernery at Rockville.

Rockville was a garden on a lavish scale. Robinson describes 'a sort of half-grot greenhouse structure', planted with Killarney fern, rockwork planted with alpines, orchid houses with double glazing (the result of Mr Bewley's own experiments), stove houses, another fern collection (with, alas, hundreds of Killarney ferns) and the orchard house containing 1,000 feet of shelving for forcing strawberries, oranges, figs, vines, limes, shaddocks, citrons, lemons, peaches, nectarines, loquat, guava and two myrtles with edible fruits (*Myrtus ugni* and *M. apiculata*). In the garden was a glazed rustic arcade of tufa rock planted with *Camellia*, *Rhododendron* from Sikkim and Bhutan, myrtles, roses and honeysuckles. Rare conifers, hardy ferns, tea and China roses were among other features of the garden.

Among the Ferns was a fine specimen of the singular *Athyrium filix-foemina Frizelliae* which was originally obtained from the Devil's Glen in Wicklow and fell to the lot of Mr J. Bain of the College Botanic Gardens – just the person into whose hands a curiously choice thing ought to fall.

No wonder Robinson was dazed after seeing round this garden.

The condition of an individual who would attempt to digest during a single day the results of the labours of hundreds of men cleverer than himself, as exhibited at an industrial exhibition, would not be by any means an enviable one towards the close of his well-meaning experiment. In some such condition did I emerge from the examination of Mr Bewley's plants; but with the conviction that the time could not have been better spent than in seeing, on the whole, the finest collection of exotics to be found in any private garden of the United Kingdom. So, calling to mind a passage from Loudon written some thirty years ago, in which it is stated that the chief things to be found in the gardens of Irish gentlemen of that time were potatoes, I smiled and bid goodbye to Rockville.

The other private garden was Killakee (Fig. 114), laid out by Niven, the property of Mrs White, widow of the 'late Colonel White who found it a barren waste supporting here and there a few miserable cottiers.' The garden was on the slopes of Montpelier, 700 feet up, on the east side, and with magnificent view over Dublin and the sea. Robinson wrote

I was glad to see but the slightest dash of bedding-out proper in this garden ... I have yet to see the place in which the unities, so to speak, of good taste in laying out and keeping gardens, both geometrical and natural in style, are better preserved than at White's of Killakee.

The geometric features included 'a fine circular fountain, with a bronze Neptune in his car of shells drawn by sea-horses, a pair of very symmetrical specimens of *Araucaria* [*araucana*], about 24 feet high, standing one on each side of the lawn to the right and left of the fountain', balustrades, terraces, massive iron gates, chain tents, a conservatory by Turner and a fernery with gothic arches. The less formal features included 'beds of a permanent and chaste character, containing Kalmias, Vacciniums, Rhododendrons, Heaths, Azaleas and a hundred shrubs, which highly relish the mountain air, and agreeably associate with the statuary placed about.' It was a truly remarkable garden

margined by wildly diversified woods, which, with the bleak hilltops around, looking much as they did when our 'noble savage' ancestors gleaned the Blackberry brakes for food, and ate the pignuts when they could get them; and the lordly progenitors of our nobility dashed after the wild wolf when on the look out for a garment.

William Robinson's developing ideas were further influenced by the public gardens of Paris. He had become horticultural correspondent of *The Times*, a prestigious position for a rebellious 29 year old, and went to Paris in 1867 to report on the Paris Exhibition of that year.[12] He also contributed articles to *The field* and to *The gardeners' chronicle*, and was agent for the nursery firm of Veitch. He admired the way in which the beds in the Paris gardens 'did not depend for their effect on the manner in which our gardeners over the last twenty years have violated nature's laws by the use of crude schemes of rude colour but on the subdued colours and dramatic forms of many hardy and sub-tropical foliage plants'. He did not, however, hesitate to criticise when he saw costly and unnecessary embellishments. When he reported in his book *Gleanings from French gardens* (1868) that the French were thus superior in many aspects of gardening there was a patriotic furore in the correspondence columns of *The Times*. Robinson had from the beginning an eye for the controversial subject and a pen with which to bring if effectively before the public. By this time, however, he was beginning to win the support of a number of influential men, such as the Very Reverend Reynolds Hole, Dean of Rochester, an acknowledged plantsman and writer, to whom Robinson later dedicated an edition of his great book *The English flower garden.*

Robinson's opinions in favour of the garden as a place for the cultivation of plants in a natural manner received further impetus from the developing interest in alpine gardening. Alpine gardeners grew their plants in more or less simulated settings of natural rockwork. 'With this rather than with bedding gardening,' Robinson wrote, 'you have communion with Nature.'[13] He went to Switzerland to study alpine plants in their native environment and there met Henri Correvon, who was to remain a lifelong friend and contributed to many of his publications. The lessons of this visit were given tangible form in the publication of his *Alpine plants for English gardens* in 1870.

Robinson's advocacy of the natural style of gardening was also favoured by the movement to revive the old-fashioned English garden, which had disappeared from the grander country houses, but had survived in the more conservative cottage garden. The revival was begun by the poets, painters and architects of the Pre-Raphaelite movement. William Morris tried to create a medieval garden at his Red House from fragments of medieval illuminations. Topiary, trellised walks and bowers, and high clipped hedges all formed backgrounds for old-fashioned flowers like hollyhocks, sunflowers, lilies, roses and jasmine. The orchards, vegetable and flower gardens were happily intermixed as in the best cottage gardens and wooden gates, stone walls and flights of steps were made in the way of the traditional craftsman rather than in cast iron or stone from the factories of the Industrial Revolution. Both William Morris and another famous adherent of the movement, John Ruskin, contributed articles to the early issues of *The garden*, a periodical founded by Robinson in 1870.[14]

These various and still developing ideas did not receive their first explicit expression until the publication of *The wild garden* in 1870. In this Robinson first set down the new principles of gardening, beginning with a quotation from Bacon: 'I wish it to be framed as much as may be, to a naturall wildnesse'. It was

33: Formal garden at Johnstown Castle, where the grounds were laid out in the Italianate style by Daniel Robertson, c. 1840. (Photograph by W. Lawrence, reproduced by permission of the National Library of Ireland).

Robinson's opinion that gardening had been developing in a perfectly natural way until about 20 years previously, when the arrival of half-hardy bedding plants, and the usurpation by the architect of the gardener's traditional role, had combined to lead the art down a blind alley. The gardener must reclaim his lost domain by reorganising gardens so that they perform again their traditional function as places where plants are grown rather than stages on which merely architectural patterns are traced.

The most comprehensive and important expression of his ideas came with the publication of *The English flower garden* in 1883. This was to become, without doubt, the single most important gardening book of the next century. No fewer than 15 editions appeared during this period, under the auspices of Robinson himself. A further edition, revised by Roy Hay, appeared in 1956. The book takes the form of a miscellany of articles by Robinson himself and by other leading flower gardeners of the day, around a common theme – that of the naturally designed flower garden. He conceived the promotion of this new idea to terms of a battle, writing that it was 'a muster of skirmishing parties'. The language he used was calculated to tease his opponents. He called their parterres 'floral rugs', their fountains 'water squirts' and their grass slopes 'railway embankments'.[15] He insulted Paxton and his assistant Milner by writing of their great gardens of Chatsworth and Sydenham as being 'designed as they might be by a theatrical super who had suddenly inherited a

THE GREAT ARAUCARIA IN THE GARDENS AT WOODSTOCK, KILKENNY—Height 50 Feet.

34: Monkey puzzle, *Araucaria araucana*, at Woodstock, Inistioge, County Kilkenny.

millionaire's fortune'. Robinson asked his readers to turn away from such formal follies and take nature as their model, and in the same way as an earlier movement towards the natural, that of the early eighteenth century, he asked them to take the principles of landscape painting rather than architecture as their guide. In making living pictures in the garden he felt that only natural species of plants should be used. He preferred the 'natural' character of such plants to the 'unnatural' forms and variegations of many hybrids. For the same reason he disliked 'sports' of any kind, though these are often prized by the collector. No false nationalism would allow him to approve, therefore, of the upright Irish yew; he much preferred the common kind. Of large trees he preferred the more natural habit of the evergreen oak or cedar of Lebanon to the more architectural, and therefore to his eye more artificial, shape of those trees much planted by the Victorians, the giant redwood (*Sequoiadendron giganteum*) and the monkey puzzle (*Araucaria araucana*) (Fig. 34).

Robinson's idea was that if one could gather a whole range of exotic plants from all the continents of the world, from Australasia, Asia, Africa and the Americas as well as the best European plants and set them down together in one place in such a way as to make it appear that they had all occurred there naturally, then one might have some idea of a natural paradise, or more fancifully, a garden in Eden. Such an effect might only be achieved with a wide variety of plant types – trees, shrubs, bulbs, herbaceous plants and alpines all interplanted and thriving happily together. No mere collection of trees in an arboretum, or shrubs or alpines on their own, no matter how naturally laid out, could become a Robinsonian garden as they would be limited to one plant type alone. The paradisiacal mixture was to be no jumble, however. Robinson advised his followers as to the best arrangement to achieve the desired effect. First of all the house should be set down on a spreading lawn, which was to be conceived not as a bowling green of perfect grass but as a sort of garden meadow planted with colonies of bulbs and flowers in groups derived from the study of the grouping of wild flowers. The lawn should follow the natural lie of the ground and should not be artificially levelled or terraced. Neither should its shape be cut up with flower beds, as this would detract from its status as a meadow. All planting should be confined to the borders of the lawn, where its edge should be varied with many recesses and projections to form a natural and flowing outline. This type of mixed border was thenceforward to become one of the characteristic elements of the twentieth century garden. It should be planted first with shrubs. 'Give the bushes room to fully attain their natural forms' and 'they should not be planted so much lumped together, but in open groups with beautiful hardy bulbs and flowers in between', wrote Robinson. The bulbs and flowers on the other hand might be lumped together and planted densely: 'Have no patience with bare ground and cover the border with dwarf plants'. Trees and shrubs should be planted not as single specimens but in natural groups. Climbers should be set 'to throw a delicate lacework of flowers over trees and shrubs rather than posts or other artificially made supports'. Plants should be chosen for their form as well as their colour, and the latter should be quiet rather than unnaturally bright. Paths and steps are reduced to a minimum in number and size, as also are other architectural features, as they are merely impediments whose care takes up valuable time which the gardener should spend tending the plants, and in any case such utilitarian features tend to spoil the paradise effect.

Throughout his life Robinson kept in touch with a number of leading Irish gardens. When he visited Trinity College Botanic Garden in 1865 he met the new Curator, John Bain (p. 122). In Ireland Robinson had friends as interested in natural plant species as he was, and there were gardens there from which he could draw examples of natural planting for *The English flower garden*. F. W. Burbidge at Trinity College Botanic Gardens (p. 123) continued to contribute a number of long articles and photographs. W. E. Gumbleton of Belgrove, County Cork, one of the leading plantsmen of his day, wrote the article on *Eremurus*. The illustrations in later editions included the snowdrop planting at Straffan, County Kildare and the planting of daffodils in natural groups at Belmont, County Carlow. The content of the earlier editions was confined to the hardy herbaceous flowers that can be grown in these islands, but the interest of the gardening world in the growing number of hardy trees and shrubs then being imported into Europe was soon reflected in later editions; so much so that the title came to reflect the content of the book inaccurately, there being an increasing number of trees and shrubs and a decreasing number of flowers described as time went on. In the milder Irish climate tree and shrub gardening became more important than flower gardening which, however, retained its popularity in England. The references to Irish gardens become more frequent, therefore, in the later editions. The half-hardy trees and shrubs at Castlewellan, County Down, Fota, County Cork and Kilmacurragh, Mr Acton's garden in County Wicklow, are frequently noted. Fine foliage plants and plants of fine form which Robinson particularly appreciated are illustrated by *Gunnera* at Narrow Water Castle, County Down. He also illustrated the rapid growth of plants in Ireland by those he had seen growing in the garden of Mr Beamish at Ashbourne, County Cork. Although most of these referred to southern hemisphere plants which grow particularly well in Ireland, he also quotes at length Hudson of Glenville Park, County Cork, now the seat of Mark Bence-Jones, on his 25 years experience of cultivating and hybridising *Rhododendron*, especially those of Sikkim and Bhutan. The lists of kinds planted in the garden are interesting as an example of the rhododendron mania of the late nineteenth century.[16]

Robinson's especial praise was reserved for the garden at Mount Usher (Fig. 35), County Wicklow, of which he said it was quite unlike any other garden that he had ever seen,

> a charming example of the gardens that might be made in river valleys, especially those among the mountains and the hills. In such places there is often delightful shelter from violent winds, while the picturesque effect of the mountains and the hills offers charming prospects from the garden.

His appreciation of Mount Usher's setting is elaborated in detail: 'the eye wanders from the Torch Lilies and the Gladioli, to the blue Agapanthus and then to the Pine and Fir clad hills' and 'to see it in time of Lilies, Roses, Peonies, Poppies and Delphiniums is to see much lovely colour amongst the rich greenery of the rising woodlands'.[17] The Robinsonian style was to give Ireland over the next 50 years some of her most splendid gardens. Those at Derreen and Rossdohan, County Kerry, Annes Grove in County Cork and Rowallane in County Down are continued today in this style. The last garden in Ireland to be laid out in the pure Robinsonian manner was Creagh, County Cork; made by Mr and Mrs Peter Harold-Barry, it owes nothing to post-Robinsonian styles, being a wild and natural planting of native and exotic species by an old lakeside and its adjoining woodland on the mild shores of Baltimore Bay.

In the library of the National Botanic Gardens, Glasnevin, are volumes inscribed 'Gumbleton Bequest' and in the National Gallery of Ireland, Dublin, is a picture similarly labelled. These legacies to the nation recall one of Robinson's correspondents, William Edward Gumbleton, who, like him, was an eccentric bachelor, an art collector and music lover as well as a gardener.[18] He was the last of a family long settled in County Cork, and when he died in 1911, aged 71, Sir Frederick Moore of Glasnevin wrote an obituary note describing him as 'a man of strong character, fearless in his criticisms and very tenacious of any opinions he had formed, after due observations, about plants, and it is not to be wondered at that he was not always a favourite.' Nevertheless he was secretary to several charities and left money to many such bodies in his will. Indeed, Moore referred to 'his large circle of intimate friends who thoroughly understood him and appreciated his high qualities'.[19]

After a period at Oxford, William Gumbleton travelled abroad with his mother, studying music and art before settling down at Belgrove in County Cork, where he built up a remarkable garden, from which plants were sent to be illustrated in *The gardeners' chronicle, The garden*, and in *Curtis's botanical magazine*. Among the 13 illustrations of plants from Belgrove in the latter will be found *Arctotis gumbletonii* (Plate 13), a daisy with deep orange red flowers. The editor, Sir Joseph Hooker, wrote that the genus *Arctotis* was in need of revision.

> In the meantime I have the pleasure of naming this beautiful plant after my friend W. Gumbleton, Esq., of Belgrove, Queenstown, Ireland, who raised and flowered it, and to whom horticulture in general and the Botanical Magazine in particular, are indebted for procuring and liberally distributing many new and interesting plants.

Gumbleton had a methodical approach, collecting all the species he could of certain genera, growing them in his garden and comparing one with another. In this way he became known as an authority on *Begonia, Salvia, Dahlia, Arctotis, Gnaphalium, Gynerium* (now called *Cortaderia*, the pampas grasses) *Nerine, Campanula, Kniphofia,* and other plants.

He was interested in many shrubs. Contemporary accounts refer to *Berberidopsis, Ceanothus, Olearia,* 24 species of *Philadelphus,* a variegated form of

35: Mount Usher, County Wicklow; a fine garden in the Robinsonian style.
(Photograph by David Davison).

Chamaecyparis lawsoniana and a 'whole series of ornamental *Pyrus*' (probably *Chaenomeles*) growing at Belgrove. F. W. Burbidge gave an account of Belgrove in *The gardeners' chronicle* in 1896[20] from which we can picture the varied features of the garden. A conservatory at the west end of the house was filled with *Pelargonium* varieties imported from France, a fine seedling *Santpaulia* of Gumbleton's own raising, and various greenhouse shrubs and bulbs. Across a gravelled walk was a lawn in which beds had been cut to present 'a brilliant picture of regulated floriferousness and vigour'. Hardy and half-hardy bulbs, herbaceous plants and shrubs were all packed into what must have been a remarkably well filled garden.

Belgrove was a combination of trial grounds and a botanical garden. Samuel Arnott, of snowdrop fame, visited the garden in August 1908.[21] Although he described the garden proper as not large and principally occupied by small beds and borders, he proceeded to list large numbers of genera of annuals which Mr Gumbleton was testing there as well as shrubs and herbaceous plants. Elsewhere on the property he was impressed by the 'magnificent collection of Cortaderias, one of the most complete in existence in any British [*sic*] garden ... and a splendid collection of upwards of 30 Kniphofias, including the newest hybrid varieties planted in clumps, among these being the really good variety named in honour of W. E. Gumbleton'. Arnott also noted a collection of hybrid *Yucca*.

The botanical aspect of the garden at Belgrove is shown by Arnott's mention of such species as *Abelia triflora* (first introduced from the Himalayas to Glasnevin in 1847), *Cladrastis lutea*, *Daphniphyllum glaucescens* (= *D. macropodum*), *Magnolia campbellii*, *Nuttalia cerasiformis*, the deciduous holly (*Ilex montana*), *Stephanandra tanakae* (introduced to Kew only in 1893), *Olearia virgata*, the golden chestnut of California (*Castanopsis chrysophylla*) and 21 American species of *Crataegus*, to mention a few plants at random from Arnott's list. Gumbleton was prompt in obtaining recently introduced species, as, for example, *Cotoneaster franchettii*, first raised in France about 1895 from Chinese seed, and the choice *Viburnum carlesii*, now well known but then a scarce plant of which a single specimen sent to Kew in 1902 was the first introduction to Europe. Gumbleton grew *Lilium henryi*, first sent to Kew by his compatriot Augustine Henry in 1889, though later sent in quantity by E. H. Wilson. He also had the choice yellow peony *Paeonia mlokosewitschii* (Plate 9) still an uncommon plant, first described in 1897.

Fruit trials were another feature at Belgrove. In the kitchen garden were 100 varieties of gooseberry and an 'extensive number' of strawberries. As well as fruit and vegetables there was a collection of day lilies (*Hemerocallis*), and water-lilies grew in tanks. On the walls there were rare shrubs (*Feijoa*, *Mutisia* and *Fremontodendron*). Belgrove must indeed have been a remarkable garden.

In 1899 William Robinson dedicated a volume of *The garden* to Gumbleton. The citation records a *Begonia* named *B. lemoinei* bloomed for the first time 'in this kingdom' at Belgrove in 1875, 'precursor of such a splendid strain which now adorns our houses and gardens'. In 1892 Belgrove was the scene of the first flowering of *Buddleja colvilei* (Plate 10). *Eremurus himalaicus* had already flowered there in 1881, the first time in Europe. This event caused some heartburnings to John Smyth of Rathcoursey, Ballinacurra, also in the county of Cork. In 1890 he wrote to *The garden*, criticising the plate in *Curtis's botanical magazine* and went on to say 'I am a bit jealous over this plant as I was the first to grow it from seed sent me from India nearly twenty years ago by Major Lloyd ... I gave plants of it to the late Reverend Harpur Crewe and to Mr Gumbleton; both flowered it before I did.'

Copies of some of Gumbleton's letters to Robert Lynch, Curator of the University of Cambridge Botanic Gardens from 1879 to 1919 are preserved. These give an impression of a prolific writer, not afraid to beg for plants, not only for himself but also for his aunt and for such friends as J. Poë of Riverston, County Tipperary (p. 148). He was, however, a willing donor, even to his own detriment. He refers to the loss of a female plant of *Nuttalia cerasiformis* as 'unfortunately given away, I don't know to whom, as any lover of shrubs visiting my garden can take away from thence anything they may fancy that I have duplicates of, so I now have only two males and am most anxious to get a female or berries to sow from which one may come'. His reputation as a peppery character is borne out by repeated strong complaints that Lynch's paper on *Arctotis* had not appeared. 'I really think you might get it done now after more than a year's incubation and send it to the Chronicle'. Then follows '

More than three weeks ago, before leaving home on the 11th ult. I wrote to you asking you several questions about the long-delayed Arctotis article, whether you wanted any spare bulbs of Jersey Ixia I might have this year over and above my own wants etc, and I certainly think you might have answered my letter before now. I was very near stopping on my way back to town from the Norwich Musical Festival and paying you and your garden a flying visit, but on enquiring at the station was informed that the narrow-minded and illiberal company did not permit the breaking of a journey on a return ticket, so I had to come on to town and postpone my visit to next spring or summer.

Gumbleton contributed to William Robinson's journal, *The garden*, but took issue over the praise given there to *Physianthus albens*, a climber, half-hardy, and which, in his opinion, was a dull dingy and utterly worthless plant, quite unworthy of being figured in the coloured plate in *The garden*. 'I have been instrumental in having it turned out of more than one friend's greenhouse.' He was taken aback when this letter appeared in print, and he complained to Lynch that his criticisms were meant for the editor's eyes only.

From Belgrove Gumbleton wrote about plants to people all over the world. The day before he died he wrote to William Watson, Curator of the Royal Botanic Gardens, Kew, about such rarities as *Mentzelia conazaltii*, *Eupatorium pazcuarense* and *Encelia adenopoda*.[22] How many gardeners of today have heard of these plants? Gumbleton was one of a band that included such authorities as Harpur Crewe and F. A. Bowles. Such friends came to stay at Belgrove, to spend the day going systematically through the collections and in the evening looking up references in their host's comprehensive library of botanical and horticultural books. Though not sharing Bowles' gentleness of manner Gumbleton had many characteristics in common with him. Both men were bachelors; both were authorities on *Crocus, Colchicum, Narcissus* and *Galanthus*. No doubt they stimulated each other in these interests and Bowles refers to plants he had seen growing at Belgrove in his books *My garden in Summer* and *My garden in Autumn and Winter*. In these we get a glimpse of Mr Gumbleton 'waving his umbrella, which in all weathers accompanied his garden rambles' and perhaps Gumbleton shared his friend's impatience with herbarium specimens (Mummies, Bowles called them) for Sir Frederick Moore deplored that he 'could not be induced to make botanical studies or keep dried materials, hence much of his work is lost'.

Sir Frederick also recalled how Gumbleton's umbrella could on occasion be used as a weapon of offence.[23] On one occasion, just after Sir Frederick had been appointed to Glasnevin, Mr Gumbleton was announced accompanied by John Bennet-Poë of Riverston, Nenagh and Edward Woodall from England. Gumbleton's umbrella was used freely that day, to bang on the flags of the Aquatic House when correcting Frederick's pronunciation of a plant name, and even to slash down a plant to which he objected. Plants were attacked in other gardens as well as his own, to cries of 'Tush, tush' – a term he applied to plants which displeased him.[24] A form of *Olearia virgata* which he 'got from the ignorant, most presumptuous Gauntlett bloomed with me this year and is utter Tush'.

Little remains today at Belgrove to mark all William Gumbleton's efforts. His house has gone, but the wandering visitor can trace the walled garden, now partly grazed, with the remains of glasshouses and brick-built water tanks and can follow the stream, marking how it was once dammed to form ponds. Bamboos and double marsh marigold still linger there. There are the remains of a twenty foot *Feijoa sellowiana* and a few *Cordyline*, but perhaps the greatest relic is a magnificent tree of the pink magnolia (*Magnolia campbellii*) about 75 feet high, considered to be perhaps the largest specimen in Ireland or Britain.[25] Next to it is a fine *Davidia involucrata* (dove or handkerchief tree).

Gumbleton is still remembered in the district as an oddity, small in stature, balding and very pompous. In his garden and out of it his actions were such as to be remembered long afterwards. He took a delight in pointing out that some of his plants were the only specimens in Ireland, even if they were not doing very well. This exasperated some of his friends like the Beamishes of nearby Ashbourne House, who prided themselves on growing only plants which flourished in the locality. Visitors sometimes teased him; one, told that there were no weeds at Belgrove, found a dandelion and said, with a sweeping gesture of the arm, "What rare exotic have we here, Mr Gumbleton?"[26] His visit to the garden at Merville, Cobh, is remembered for the way in which he corrected his host for using the old generic name (*Vitis*) for the Virginia creeper; "*Ampelopsis veitchii*. Not a vine, but like a vine. You will remember that, won't you?"[27] With his musical friends, too, he had differences of opinion. Legend still recounts a scene in the Bank of Ireland, Cobh, where Gumbleton and the bank manager, disagreeing on the tune of the aria 'Il Balen' in 'Il Travotore', each sang his version in the public office. To the end Gumbleton maintained his eccentricity, being buried, not in a graveyard, although he was the son of a clergyman, but in the grounds of Belgrove, where his grave near the walled garden is marked by a plain limestone slab inscribed with his name and dates.

Sir Frederick Moore had described Gumbleton's library as the richest botanical library in Ireland, so it can be imagined that it was with some excitement that he learned that it had been bequeathed to Glasnevin, he to decide what books to keep, the rest to go to the Royal Horticultural Society's Lindley Library in London. In a letter T. P. Gill, Secretary of the Department of Agriculture and Technical Instruction for Ireland, authorised Sir Frederick to travel by rail to Cork to inspect the books. From this we get an example of the customs of the time. Sir Frederick and William McArdle could go second class, with 7s 6d per night subsistence. An office assistant could go too, but third class, and with 5s 0d per night.

Sir Frederick felt his responsibilities in deciding which volumes to retain. He wrote to Bowles, who was an executor of Gumbleton's will. Bowles replied, regretting the passing of 'our kind old friend' and reassuring Sir Frederick that he would be justified in keeping all the books for Glasnevin and recommending that any inferior sets should be sold to help towards a better housing of the rest.

36: Augustine Henry, plant collector and forester.

On Bowles' advice William Wesley, booksellers of London, were appointed valuers. They put an estimate of £500 on the collection. In the upshot the Lindley Library got bound runs of *The garden*, *The gardeners' chronicle*, and a small number of cases of books. So today the National Botanic Gardens, Glasnevin, possesses such treasures as works by Redouté on Liliaceae, Andrews on geraniums, Sibthorp's *Flora Graeca* and a long run of *Curtis's botanical magazine*. Gumbleton is remembered in Ireland for these, for his picture and perhaps in Oxford, for he left his books in foreign languages to the Taylorian Institute of Foreign Languages, but these cannot now be traced.

On the other side of Cork harbour, some miles from Belgrove, lived Gumbleton's friend, William H. Crawford[28] of Lakelands (1812–1888) (p. 168), creator of another garden favoured by the mild climate of the south coast of Ireland. A notable event which occurred here in 1844 was the first flowering in the British Isles of *Magnolia campbellii*, a native of the Himalaya, described by Bean as 'perhaps the most magnificent of the magnolias'.[29]

Lakelands was described as a fine old house, full of rare books, pictures and engravings. At the door stood two large tubs with large specimens of *Philesia magellanica*, four to five feet in diameter. This dwarf evergreen shrub with carmine red tubular flowers two inches long, is still regarded as a special plant where it grows well, as at Rowallane, County Down.

Lakelands was a remarkable garden,[30] the grounds planted with trees and shrubs from the Himalayas and the southern hemisphere. These included a rare and tender *Araucaria angustifolia*, a Brazilian monkey-puzzle, more than twelve feet high and well shaped, the pendulous-branched Huon pine (*Lagarostrobus franklinii*) from Tasmania and the plum-fruited yew of Chile (*Prumnopitys andinus*), the latter about 50 feet high. Firs and spruces included *Abies venusta*, *A. grandis* and the tiger-tailed spruce (*Picea polita*) of Japan. On the house itself grew vigorous plants of *Berberidopsis corallina*, which must have been a splendid sight in autumn, as they were unusually high – up to 20 feet – and carried the long red flowers abundantly. The outdoor rhododendrons included *Rhododendron thomsonii*, *R. falconeri* and the delicate *R. dalhousiae*, the latter flowering freely. Glasshouses contained a rich collection of orchids and rare Himalayan *Rhododendron*.[31] One genus in particular is associated with Crawford; that is *Brownea*, called after that Irish friend of the great Linnaeus, Patrick Browne of Jamaica and Mayo (p. 36). This genus of tropical trees and shrubs flowers mainly in winter, with heads of orange or red blossoms, and was a great speciality at Lakelands. Crawford grew them in his greenhouses, in tubs or in a sunken border. They grew so tall that the branches had to be tied down to prevent them pushing through the roof. Rather than prune them back he later added a roof several feet above the old one. When Gumbleton saw the *Brownea* he was much impressed by *B. macrophylla* with its gorgeous *Rhododendron*-like orange-scarlet blossoms scattered over the tree from top to bottom. *Brownea* x *crawfordii* is a hybrid (*B. grandiceps* x *macrophylla*) raised by Crawford and named after him by William Watson of Kew.[32] Gumbleton wrote an account of these plants for Robinson's periodical *The garden*.[33]

It was on a cold and wintry day that Gumbleton brought Burbidge of the Trinity College Botanic Garden to see Lakelands. They received a warm welcome and were shown over the whole garden by the owner 'whose face shone with delight as one after another of his floral treasures drew forth some exclamation of surprise'.[34] Yet Crawford was generally regarded as an ascetic, though unsparing of expense when it was in a good cause.[35] His good works are commemorated in the Crawford Municipal College of Art and the Crawford Municipal Technical Institute. The former Botanic Garden of University College, Cork, benefited by the erection of a range of glasshouses.[36]

Crawford's death on the night of 18 October 1888, was in keeping with his quiet and retiring life. He had been to his club that day, and feeling unwell, asked his doctor, whom he met there, to prescribe for him. He dined at home as usual, and settled down to read afterwards in his fireside chair. The next morning he was found there by his servants, having suffered a heart attack after they had left him for the night.[37]

John Bennet-Poë, friend of Gumbleton and of Robinson, and a contributor to *The English flower garden*, lived as a boy at Riverston, County Tipperary, where he raised good varieties of plants with such success that 'Riverston Variety' was regarded as a hall mark of distinction. In particular his form of the Christmas rose (*Helleborus niger*) was described as a particularly free flowering, robust plant with white, rose tinged flowers four inches in diameter on red spotted stalks.[38] He put up the first exhibit in Ireland of daffodils at a flower show, that of the Royal Horticultural Society of Ireland in 1885.[39] Four years later he moved to London, where he became interested in the commercial possibilities of daffodils, joining a syndicate formed to distribute the new kinds being raised by Engleheart. He attained distinction in the councils of the Royal Horticultural Society of London, was a trustee of the Society's Garden at Wisley and was a noted exhibitor of daffodils, tulips, auriculas and orchids.[40]

A strange and little known extension of the Robinsonian ideas was its application to cemeteries, for William had strong ideas on the subject of cremation. In 1880 he published his *God's acre beautiful*, re-issued in 1889 as *Cremation and urn burial, or the cemeteries of the future*. This small book has a frontispiece showing such a cemetery of the future, with trees, lilies, *Yucca*, *Hosta*, lawns and Grecian temples. Despite this there is little in the rest of the book for those who would wish for such a landscape instead of tombstones. There are descriptions of what he regarded as the horrors of ordinary burial, and illustrations of the cinerary urns of the ancients. The book was dedicated to Sir Henry Thompson, President of the Cremation Society of England, and to Sir T. Spenser Wells, 'in acknowledgement of their public services in advocating a mode of sepulture harmless to the living, and which admits of beautiful and enduring memorials to the dead'.

From 1885 William Robinson lived at Gravetye Manor, Sussex, a house with an estate of over 1000 acres, which he developed from a neglected state according to his own ideas, and lived a bachelor's life, no woman being allowed into the house. Even though Gertrude Jekyll was a great friend, she was entertained to tea only in the summer house. He did, however, love children, in spite of his many eccentricities.[41] None but wood fires were allowed in the manor house, and he was particular about the quality of the fruit and vegetables he ate.[42] For the last 26 years of his life he was confined to a bath chair, or travelled round his estate in a caterpillar-wheeled motor car. His disabilities did not prevent him from keeping up his interest in artistic matters, for until near the end of his days he would motor up to London to visit picture galleries and art exhibitions. He died in 1935, aged 96, 17 years after his death was mistakenly reported, an obituary having appeared in *The Daily Telegraph* in January 1928, only to be retracted with apologies two days later.[43] To this day the great gardens of Ireland reflect his taste and style.

At the time that Robinson's literary efforts were encouraging the cultivation of species from overseas the numbers of such plants being added to following the explorations of Augustine Henry (1857–1930) (Fig. 36), greatest of Irish plant collectors, who spent 19 years in the Far East.[44] He was the son of a flax merchant in County Londonderry, and after taking his B.A. at Queen's College, Galway, he went to Queen's College, Belfast, where he took his M.A. degree and then entered for medicine. Sir Robert Hart, on a visit to Queen's

College, encouraged Henry to enter the Chinese Customs Service, a chance meeting which directed Henry to the scene of his botanical labours. First, however, he had to finish his medical studies, and he discovered he could do this more quickly by going over to Edinburgh.

His first lengthy stay in China was at Yichang, a few miles downstream from the Yangtze Gorges. Here the flora was varied and beautiful. Initially his interest in botany was stimulated by his being asked to investigate plants used by the Chinese as sources of drugs. Though he continued to be primarily a botanist, sending thousands of important herbarium specimens to Kew, he also sent seeds and living plants. Very many of these became well-known garden plants. To mention but a few, he discovered *Actinidia deliciosa* (as *A. chinensis*), the familiar kiwi-fruit of commerce. A small leaved holly – *Ilex pernyi* – and the catkin-flowered *Itea illicifolia* are quite widely cultivated. The popular *Lilium henryi* is one of Henry's Chinese lilies. *Rhododendron augustinii* and *R. auriculatum*, *Sarcococca humilis* and *Syringa reflexa* are among the garden-worthy shrubs discovered by him or by Chinese assistants under his direction.[45] As well as botanic gardens, private patrons have been important channels for the introduction of exotic plants to our gardens. Henry sent plants and seeds to A. K. Bulley, founder of the well known nursery, Bees Ltd., whence was to come a curator for Glasnevin (p. 165).

On his return to Europe Henry spent a period at the Royal Botanic Gardens, Kew, working largely on plants of his own collecting, and while he was in London there occurred one of these chance meetings which lead to great things. Henry had been invited to speak to the Royal Horticultural Society on his Chinese lilies. H. J. Elwes was in the chair, and the two men struck up a friendship which resulted in their collaboration on the famous *Trees of Great Britain and Ireland* in seven volumes, always a rare work as only 500 copies were printed. Henry made a particular contribution to the naming and botanical description of the trees, and devised ingenious keys for identification based on leaves, twigs and on the position of buds, so that the species could be identified even in the absence of flowers and fruit.

In 1913 he accepted the newly created Chair of Forestry at the Royal College of Science, Dublin, where he lectured to forestry students and also to students of agriculture and horticulture whose courses included forestry.

By the time he died in 1930 he had achieved an international position with membership or honorary membership of societies in France, Belgium, Finland, Czechoslovakia and Poland. He was on the council of the Royal Arboricultural Society of England, on the Scientific Committee of the Royal Horticultural Society of London and on the councils of the Royal Dublin Society and of the Royal Irish Academy. The silver medal of the Societé Nationale d'acclimatation de France was awarded to him in 1923, and in 1929 the Botanical Institute of Peking dedicated to him the second volume of *Icones et plantarum Sinicarum*, a collection of drawings of plants. At the National Botanic Gardens, Glasnevin, the Augustine Henry Forestry Herbarium stands to his memory, with a plaque

37: Sir Frederick Moore.

recording the labours of his widow, Alice, in sorting, arranging and labelling his tree specimens, about 10,000 in number.

Henry's friend, Frederick Moore (Fig. 37), also became one of the closest friends of William Robinson. Although William had been helped by Frederick's father at a critical point in his life, neither of the Moores contributed to *The English flower garden*, perhaps on account of the demise of one and the youth of the other at the time of its publication.

Frederick was born in the Botanic Gardens at Glasnevin, where he had his first encounter with plants at an early age. He and his brother were playing soldiers with wooden swords made from plant stakes when they met a group of tall plants, bigger than themselves and therefore foes worthy to be slashed to the ground. Alas for the boys, these were plants of *Cardiocrinum*, flowering for the first time, and objects of great interest and admiration to the staff and to the public. Retribution soon followed in a painful fashion.[46] Nevertheless Frederick's love of plants soon developed and as a schoolboy in Hanover in 1870 he was allowed to grow plants of his own. He went along to the Herrenhausen Gardens to beg the director for a little prepared soil and came away with a present of bulbs in addition.[47]

Sir Frederick reminiscences of those early days indicate a rather stern Victorian father deciding what should be done with his son. On the advice of a friend, head of the Indian Woods and Forests Department, David Moore did not put his son into the forestry service, but started him on a horticultural career. He was set to learning the names of plants in Glasnevin, and attended the Royal College of Science, Dublin. Soon, however, he was informed that arrangements had been made for him to work at Van Houtte's nurseries in Ghent. There Frederick worked long hours without payment, as a voluntaire, living in humble lodgings and working in the nursery from 6 a.m. to 8 p.m., sometimes with Sunday morning duty from 5 a.m. to 1 p.m. Three mornings a week he went to lectures in the Botanic Garden School of Horticulture. These were mostly given by nurserymen and he found them of great value, but even more so the practical demonstrations of budding, grafting and the pruning and training of fruit trees. Even on free Sundays Frederick and his fellow students would explore other nurseries in and around Ghent. From Ghent he moved to the Univerity of Leiden Botanic Garden; here, too, he took a course or lectures and practical classes, this time at the university. The fluency he acquired in French, German and Flemish was to be an asset in his later continental travels as Keeper of the Royal Botanic Gardens, Glasnevin.

Frederick returned to Ireland in 1876 on his appointment as Curator of Trinity College Botanic Garden, where his father had been Foreman from 1829 to 1834. He remained there for three years, succeeding on the death of his father in 1879 to the post of Curator at Glasnevin Botanic Gardens.[48]

The Palm House, so severely criticised by William Robinson, had been badly damaged by storms, and had to be replaced urgently. The new house, the Great Palm House, was completed in about six months early in 1884, to the great satisfaction of the Board of Visitors and their president, the Duke of Leinster, who congratulated Moore on his 'great care and attention during the alterations whereby all the valuable plants of the Palm House had been preserved without any loss or damage', a more happy outcome than John Underwood's unfortunate experience at the building of the Octagon House 65 years previously (p. 67). Indeed Moore earned the confidence of his superiors during his first seven years at Glasnevin; Professor Valentine Ball, Director of the Science and Arts Museum, in his annual report referred to 'Mr Moore's excellent administration of the very responsible duties of his post, and the excellent temper and judgement shown by him in connection with the relations between him and his staff. I am, I feel sure, only stating what is already well known and fully realised by the Department'. Moore's ability to win the devotion of his staff was outstanding, and it was referred to again on his retirement by William Watson of The Royal Botanic Gardens, Kew.[49]

Frederick, like his father, travelled much abroad, keeping in touch with private and botanic gardens in Britain and on the Continent. His definition of the duties of the curator of a botanic garden included that of collecting good plants and distributing them. In 1893, for example, on his way to the Botanical Congress at Genoa, he visited 13 gardens in the south of France and in Italy. He

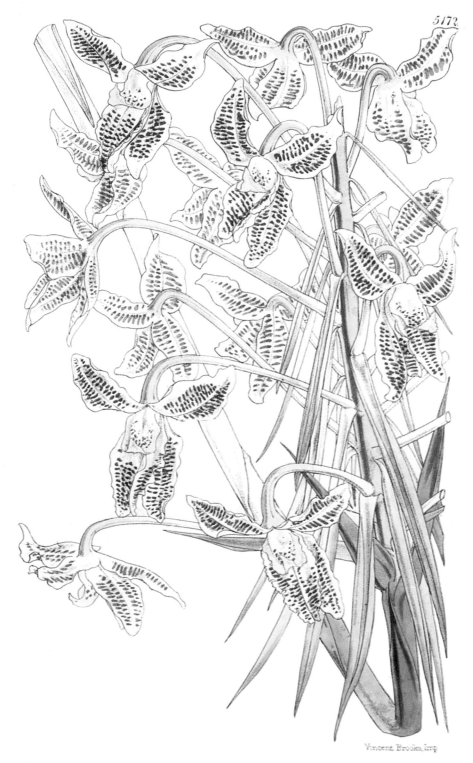

Vincent Brooks, Imp

12 *Schomburgkia lyonsii*, a Jamaican orchid, named after John Charles Lyons of Ledeston, Mullingar; from *Curtis's botanical magazine* (1860), plate 5172.

13 *Arctotis gumbletonii*, a perennial from Namaqualand, South Africa, named after William Gumbleton of Cobh; from *Curtis's botanical magazine* (1901), plate 7796.

14   *Amorphophallus kerrii*, a tropical lords-and-ladies from Siam (Thailand), named after Dr. A. F.
G. Kerr, and grown in Trinity College Botanic Garden, Ballsbridge, Dublin; from *Curtis's botanical magazine* (1917), plate 8692.

15 *Burbidgea nitida*, a ginger from Borneo, discovered by and named after F. W. Burbidge; from *Curtis's botanical magazine* (1879), plate 6403.

M S del J N Fitch lith.   Vincent Brooks Day & Son Ltd Imp.

L. Reeve & Co London

16 *Deutzia purpurascens*, a shrub from China, supplied to the Royal Botanic Gardens, Kew, by Daisy Hill Nursery, Newry, County Down; from *Curtis's botanical magazine* (1900), plate 7708. (x 0.9).

17 *Sarracenia* x *moorei* and *S.* x *popei*, two of the earliest hybrid pitcher-plants raised at the Royal Dublin Society's Botanic Gardens, Glasnevin, in the 1870s, by David More and William Pope; from *The garden* (1886), plate 566. (x 0.7).

18 Apple 'Irish Peach', introduced by John Robertstown of Kilkenny; from *The Herefordshire pomona* (1879-1885), vol. 1, plate 19 (detail).

19 Rose 'Irish Brightness', 'Irish Star' and 'Irish Pride', new Irish-raised roses from *Rose Catalogue for 1903 & 1904* issued by Alex. Dickson and Sons, Royal Irish Nurseries, Newtownards, County Down.

38: Charles Frederick Ball.

was especially impressed by the Parc Tete d'Or at Lyons, the Jardin d'Acclimatation at Hyères, by the good cultivation practised at the Florence Botanic Garden, and by Thomas Hanbury's garden at La Mortola, on the borders of France and Italy. He concluded: 'the various botanic gardens were remarkable rather for the strength of certain groups of plants than for the excellence of the collections in general, and in none of them are the collections as good as at Glasnevin'.

Frederick Moore was one of the original recipients of the Victoria Medal of Honour, instituted in 1897 by the Royal Horticultural Society of London to celebrate the sixtieth year of the reign of their patron, Queen Victoria. Moore was among those present on 26 October 1897, when the medallists were entertained to luncheon at the Hotel Windsor, Westminster, by the President and Council. 'The company then adjourned to the Drill Hall, where a large number of persons had assembled to witness the interesting ceremony of presenting the medals'. The other recipient from Ireland was F. W. Burbidge. Moore was to be the last survivor of the company gathered to receive their medals on that October day.

39: John W. Besant.

Moore's great success as curator of Glasnevin has overshadowed his other services to horticulture. In 1909 the Royal University of Ireland conferred on him the degree of M.A. *honoris causa* 'in consideration of his high scientific position and of the valuable assistance he has given the university in connection with the practical examinations of the university'. He played a large part in the early efforts of the Department of Agriculture and Technical Instruction to encourage fruit growing, in cooperation with his brother-in-law, Professor Campbell, then Secretary to the Department.

The range of Frederick Moore's activities was impressive, for in addition to all these undertakings he found time to serve as honorary secretary to the Royal Horticultural Society of Ireland and to the Royal Zoological Sociey of Ireland. He was a member of the Council of the Royal Irish Academy, and Consulting Botanist to the Royal Dublin Society. He was a plant breeder too, receiving the Veitch Memorial Medal from the Royal Horticultural Society of London for seedling *Lachenalia*. These included some called after his friends, such as W. E. Gumbleton, or after his pupils, for example May Crosbie.[50] His knighthood was conferred on him in July 1911 during the visit of King George V to Ireland.

In Sir Frederick's reviews of the position of Irish horticulture written in 1906, 1910 and 1915,[51] we get an account of the changes in Irish gardens as seen by him.

> There appears to [have been] a steady decline in the popularity of indoor gardening, and I regret to say in the class of plants grown indoors. Collections of stove plants, of hard wooded plants, of ferns, of orchids, and of many old and popular occupants of our conservatories have become less numerous, and but few specimens are to be found. These have been replaced with plants of rapid growth, plants which can easily be discarded when shabby, and quickly replaced with a fresh batch, and with annuals. Show Pelargoniums, Ericas, Epacris, Eriostemon, Acacias, Diosmas, Genetyllis, Azalea, Camellias, Crotons, Dracænas, Anthuriums, Orchids, have made space for Cyclamen, Primulas, Cinerarias of various sections, Schizanthus, Campanulas, fibrous and tuberous rooted Begonias, Mignonette, Zonals, Deutzias, deciduous Azaleas, and similar plants ... One difficult subject may not only be said to have held its own, but to have made rapid and remarkable progress, that is the carnation. ... Formal bedding out continues to disappear ... Of old favourites the rose still reigns supreme, and continues to advance all along the line. ... Herbaceous plants, alpine plants, and rock-gardens, aquatics and bog gardens, and flowering shrubs are the specialities one finds receiving most attention in present-day gardening. . ... Take such popular *genera* as Delphinium, Trollius, Spiræa, Phlox, Penstemon, Iris, Pæonia, Anemone, Papaver, Campanula, Helianthus, Aster, Kniphofia, Eremurus, Lobelia, and will anyone contend that there has not been progress in this department. Amongst the alpines the advance is even more marked. ... in Aquatics the same story may be told. ... A pond, not taken up with spouting dolphins and mis-shapen fairies, or nymphs in impossible and contorted positions, but ... framed with edgings of Primulas, Calthas, Iris, Lysimachia, Orchid, and other plants which delight in the swamp. Is not this progress?

He goes on to refer to Lemoine's new hybrid *Deutzia* and *Philadelphus*, then appearing from France, and to the new species and hybrids available in other genera. Cacti had fallen from fashion:

> an enthusiast who still gives up valuable indoor space to a collection of Cactaceae is regarded with grave suspicion as to his or her sanity. True, occasionally here and there a specimen of some of these may survive and be pointed out as a curiosity, the name of which is probably unknown ... although at one time many houses were filled with them, and the splendid specimens which were exhibited at the principal shows were marvels of skilful cultivation.

Frederick Moore knew the gardens of Ireland particularly well, and was associated with the development of many of them, such as Mount Usher, Kilmacurragh and Headfort. He realised that the Botanic Gardens at Glasnevin was not a suitable locality for the cultivation of the many new *Rhododendron* species and many of the other plants coming in from the expeditions of Farrer,

Forrest, Kingdon Ward and their contemporaries. He enriched Irish gardening greatly by distributing these plants throughout the country, to gardens where he knew they would be appreciated and cared for.

Armytage Moore of Rowallane described the enjoyment of those who accompanied him on tours of these gardens:

> To find Fred Moore in his true element, to enjoy him at his best, one needed to accompany him, as the writer has often done, through many of the best gardens of the British Isles. His versatility was as characteristic as his natural modesty and his absence of dogmatism. In another's garden he appeared to forget his own, and abstaining from comparisons, shared the enthusiasm of his host, thereby paying a thoughtful and touching compliment.

Sir Frederick's assistant at Glasnevin was Charles Frederick Ball (Fig. 38). He was an Englishman, born in Loughborough, Leicestershire, and he received his early training in the nurseries of Barr and Sons before entering the Royal Botanic Gardens, Kew, in 1900. Two years later he was appointed sub-foreman in the herbaceous and alpine department. He then tried market gardening in cooperation with his brother, but this form of gardening did not appeal, and after a year he returned to Kew, whence he moved to the Royal Botanic Gardens, Glasnevin, in 1906.[52]

Ball was a keen plantsman and enjoyed plant-hunting on the Continent. In 1911 he went to Bulgaria to visit the famous rose-growing area of Kazanlik, where attar of roses was prepared. He was received by the King of Bulgaria, who complained that English nurserymen were doing their best to exterminate some rare Balkan plants such as *Lilium jankae*, the yellow turk's cap lily of Bulgaria and Serbia, by excessive collecting. This complaint did not prevent them from becoming friends, and they found a common interest in their love of alpines, of which there was a fine collection in the palace garden, besides rare ferns and hardy orchids. One hazard of gardening in Bulgaria was very heavy hail, which could tear to ribbons the broad leaves of such plants as *Veratrum*. Ball described how 'bombs' were kept in readiness in the garden, to be fired at the approach of a storm, causing the hail to fall in another place.[53]

He travelled to the Rila Mountains to botanise there in company with Herr Kellerer, who was in charge of the King's alpine garden, and who is commemorated by *Saxifraga* x *kellereri*. On the way they admired corn fields blue with annual larkspur, which there takes the place of corn poppies at home. To Ball the three most wonderful sights were *Primula deorum* (a primrose of the section Frondosa), bordering the streams in countless thousands, *Rhus cotinus* (= *Cotinus coggyria*) covering acres, and *Haberlea rhodopensis* on shady perpendicular crags near the Shipka Pass, sometimes in tufts two to three feet across, in full flower. It was here that Herr Kelleher ran back, calling excitedly, "Weiss, weiss". He had found a lovely white flowered plant of the *Haberlea*.[54]

At home, Ball was editor for a time of *Irish gardening* and contributed several articles to that monthly journal on plants and plant-hunting trips in the Alps. He was keen on hybridising, and at Glasnevin crossed barberries,

Mahonia, *Calceolaria*, flowering currants, *Campanula* and *Escallonia*; he is commemorated by the well-known *Escallonia 'C. F. Ball'*.[55]

A life so full of promise for horticulture was to be cut short tragically. After war broke out he joined up and was sent to the Dardanelles. There amongst the hardships of trench life he still found pleasure in plants. He sent seeds to Glasnevin and wrote 'a knowledge of plants and botany always makes a walk interesting and conveys much useful information'. Olives, brooms, sea-lavender, sea-holly and other plants helped to take his mind off the trials of war, as did the receipt of at least one copy of *Irish gardening*. He had a narrow escape when landing, being knocked over by a piece of shrapnel, but was saved as he happened to be carrying a sandbag, which took the force of the impact. It was when he had been sent to a rest camp, after being in the thick of the fighting, that he was hit again, and this time wounded mortally.

The next Assistant Keeper at Glasnevin was John William Besant (1878–1944) (Fig. 39). Like so many good gardeners he was a Scotsman, coming of a family of gardeners. He was born at Castle Huntley, Perthsire, the eldest of three brothers, all of whom attained notable positions in horticulture. One brother, W. D. Besant, became Director of Parks, Glasgow; another J. G. Besant was Superintendent of Parks, Harrogate, and both served terms as President of the Institute of Parks Administration.

John Besant came to Glasnevin with much experience behind him. In his early years he worked in several well-known Scottish gardens – Rossie Priory, Alloa Park and Callendar. He was at the Glasgow Botanic Gardens from 1899 to 1901, then going to the Royal Botanic Gardens, Kew, where he was sub-foreman in the flower garden department. He was remembered there for his part in the social life of the students, especially as a good cricketer.

It was during a visit to Bees Nurseries, Cheshire, in 1905 that Sir Frederick Moore met Besant, then assistant manager. He was impressed by his keenness and the enthusiasm that made him so willing to stay on that Saturday afternoon to show his visitor round. Sir Frederick urged him to apply for a vacancy that came up at Glasnevin in 1907. He was appointed, and in 1920 became Assistant Keeper. On the retirement of Sir Frederick in 1922 Besant succeeded him. For 22 years he was Keeper, and was widely known as a keen plantsman and knowledgeable grower. He contributed many articles to the gardening journals, including *The gardeners' chronicle*, *Journal of the Royal Horticultural Society* and to *Irish gardening*, which he edited for some years. He was awarded one of the first five gold medals of the Royal Horticultural Society of Ireland, was an Associate of Honour of the Royal Horticultural Society of London, President of the Dublin Naturalists Field Club and of the Kew Guild. He died in September 1944, aged 66 years.[56]

When Sir Frederick retired in 1922 the Moores had to find a place to live. In Lady Moore's own words the search was long and difficult. They wanted a walled garden, a lime-free soil and soft water. These they found at Willbrook, an attractive Georgian house of medium size, to the south of the city, towards the Dublin Mountains, though the soil was not ideal, being a heavy clay.

40: Lady Moore, photographed in 1964 with a group of *Cardiocrinum giganteum* var. *yunnanense* in her garden at Rathfarnham, Dublin.

Lady Moore (Fig. 40), herself a keen plantswoman, took a leading part in creating the garden. There does not seem to have been much there in the beginning, for all she mentioned were three fine old purple beech trees, a big sycamore, and a good *Wisteria* on the house. The approach was through a field; here the railings were moved back and the trees and shrubs planted which were to be the first impressions of gardening visitors, such as *Nothofagus dombeyi* which quickly grew to a tall specimen with a clear trunk, *Picea breweriana* with its weeping branches, the spire-like *Picea omorika* and the dangling fruits of that ornamental spindle, *Euonymus planipes*.

The walled garden had probably been a vegetable garden, as it continued to be, but with the replacement of the old fruit trees and the creation of herbaceous borders. Here memory recalls a few of the many plants for which

Willbrook was noted, including the dove-blue flowers of *Helleborus torquatus*, though Lady Moore considered the name to be doubtful. Very lovely too, was *Paeonia* 'Emodoff', said to be a hybrid between *P. emodi* and *P. officinalis*, raised by Sir Frederick in his early days. By the ironwork garden gate *Tropaeolum polyphyllum* spread widely in a gravelly bed, and on the nearby wall a 14 ft specimen of *Itea ilicifolia* was prominent. This species was discovered and introduced by Augustine Henry.

Lady Moore's surviving notebook shows how friends far and near contributed to the making of the new garden at Willbrook, and is an indication of how many had benefited from the encouragement and generosity of the Moores while they were at the Botanic Gardens at Glasnevin. Frederick Moore's wide knowledge of nurseries at home and and abroad enabled him to obtain many good plants. Many bulbs were planted, particularly snowdrops of many kinds from E. A. Bowles and H. J. Elwes. The Straffan snowdrop came direct from Straffan House, where Fred Streeter was head gardener, later to become a personality in the gardening circles of England. *Crocus* species, forms of *Iris unguicularis*, *Erythronium*, *Dodecatheon*, *Narcissus* and tulip species must have formed a notable collection of spring flowering plants. Numerous unnamed *Rhododendron* species still under collector's numbers came from Headfort, though Lady Moore records that large leaved kinds were not a success, even in specially prepared beds. Species of the Triflorum series did well. Other great gardens and gardeners of the day that donated plants included Kilmacurragh, Sir John Ross-of-Bladensburg, The O'Mahony, Shaw-Smith of Ballawley Park, Howth Castle, Rowallane, Mount Usher, Murray Hornibrook, Lionel Richardson, as well as many people with smaller gardens.

Phylis Moore became well known abroad for her knowledge of plants. She contributed to the garden journals of the day, with articles keeping such Irish gardens as Rowallane,[57] Mount Usher, Kilmacurragh and Fota[58] before the public eye, as well as writing on particular plants. In 1934 she and Sir Frederick were invited by the Royal Horticultural Society of London to be their representatives and judges at the spring flower shows in the United States of America. She has left us her impressions of that visit. During her time there she encouraged the founding of the American Rock Garden Society, so much so that at the fiftieth anniversary celebrations she was recalled as the 'true godmother of the American Rock Garden Society'.[59] She was President of the Royal Horticultural Society of Ireland for the years 1950–1952, and conveyed the greetings of the Society to the Royal Horticultural Society of London on the occasion of the sesquicentenary of the latter.

At Willbrook the Moores entertained gardening friends from near and far and encouraged many young people to become keen gardeners, one such being E. B. Anderson, who went on to become one of the leading plantsmen in Britain. Visits to Willbrook are recalled vividly by R. D. Trotter, one time Secretary to the Royal Horticultural Society of London, who wrote of the generous hospitality, the comfortable armchairs each side of a warm fire in the study, the apples ripening on the mantelpiece, the stories of famous Irish gardens and their creators, and the journeys round the garden from which the visitor never came back empty handed. Graham Stuart Thomas has also written appreciatively of his visits to the Moores, of the good plants in the garden, including his special interest, old garden roses, and of how his visits to Irish gardens with Lady Moore prompted him to collect the more unusual herbaceous plants. Phylis Moore's friends remember her kindly way of hinting that she would like a plant she admired: "Do you think that plant might have a little brother?" They would agree with Graham Thomas' summing up of her character as 'keen, kindly, and with a good sense of humour'.[60]

THE YEARS OF THE GREAT PLANT BREEDERS

The late nineteenth century and the early part of the twentieth century was not only a time of botanical exploration overseas, but at home new plants were entering gardens from a different source. This was through the efforts of plant breeders, amateur and professional. The eighteenth and early nineteenth century florists had been concerned with the improvement of such plants as the auricula, the carnation, the dahlia, the hyacinth and even the gooseberry. We have seen how important were such florists' flowers in the early Dublin and provincial horticultural shows. Now the rose, the daffodil and flowering shrubs were to be the fashionable plants and Irish growers were to take a leading part in developing new kinds.

DICKSON'S AND McGREDY'S ROSES.

Two names in particular, Dickson and McGredy, are inseparable from the story of the modern rose. The first Dickson to come to Ireland, Alexander, was born in 1802 at Whitebog Farm, Hawthornden, near Edinburgh. He was no more than 15 years old when his parents sent him as an apprentice to the gardens of Dalhousie Castle, thus starting him on the career that was to lead to the founding of the famous firm of Dicksons of Newtownards, County Down. At Dalhousie Alexander attracted attention through his skilful cultivation of rare plants sent home from Canada by Lord Dalhousie. This led to his first employment in commercial horticulture at Cunningham's Comely Bank Nurseries, Edinburgh. Here he continued to develop his talent for the cultivation of uncommon plants, becoming especially interested in *Camellia*, *Epacris* and heaths, which were among the fashionable stove and greenhouse plants of the day. He hybridised South African heaths and raised many good seedlings, thus foreshadowing the great interest in plant breeding that was to bring fame to the Dickson family.

After several years at Comely Bank, Alexander Dickson returned to private service, this time in Ireland. He took charge of the gardens of William Montgomery of Greyabbey, County Down. While there he made friends with John Harvey, a local nurseryman, who was so impressed with Dickson's character and ability that when Montgomery died Dickson was offered the position of manager of Harvey's nursery – an offer that was accepted.

Once again Alexander found himself in commercial horticulture, this time for good, for in 1836 he decided to set up on his own. Commercialism did not narrow his pleasure in gardening, for he continued to hybridise plants, working in such diverse subjects as sweet peas and tomatoes, as well as indulging in rose breeding in a very amateurish way.[1]

Alexander Dickson died in 1880. His sons, George (1830–1914) and Hugh (1834–1904), had taken up rose breeding in a more specialised manner, Hugh later branching out on his own at Belmont, Belfast. It was under George that Dicksons of Hawlmark (a name adopted to identify the Newtownards firm) first became famous for new roses. During his lifetime the firm won 446 gold medals for new seedlings (Plate 19). He was himself awarded the Victoria Medal of Honour in 1907, the first of three generations of the family to receive this high award. By now he was an old man, but still maintained a keen interest in the seedling roses, even though he had to be wheeled out in a bath chair to see them.

George's son, Alexander (1857–1949), inherited his father's enthusiasm, and started hybridising roses in 1879. It was in 1887 that the first Dickson roses to be awarded gold medals were shown at the National Rose Society's show. These were hybrid perpetuals – 'Earl Dufferin', 'Ethel Brownlow' and 'Lady Stewart' – now no longer grown. By 1908 the *Journal of horticulture* noted that out of 66 prize-winning cultivars no less than 25 had been raised by Dicksons. Then, just before George's death, the firm introduced 'George Dickson' one of the most celebrated roses ever raised. 'Etoile d'Hollande', 'Christopher Stone', 'Shot Silk' and 'Betty Uprichard' are Dickson productions known to all interested in the culture of the rose. By 1963 the firm aimed at introducing at least three new cultivars each year, and so eagerly were these anticipated that it was necessary to produce 10,000 bushes of a new kind before it was released to the public.

Alexander II died in 1949, aged 92. He had taken a prominent part in local affairs, serving on the Down County Council for many years, for some of them as chairman. He presented a mayoral chair made of gold medals won by his firm to the borough of Newtownards. Dicksons held royal warrants from Queen Victoria, Kings Edward VII, George V and George VI. Alexander himself had been made a Chevalier of the Order of Merit by the French government.[2] His son Alexander, third of that name, was the third successive member of his family to be awarded the Victoria Medal of Honour, and the first to be conferred with an honorary degree, Bachelor of Agriculture, by The Queen's University,

Belfast, in recognition of his own and his family's contribution to horticulture. In 1968 the Royal National Rose Society presented him with the Dean Hole medal for outstanding service to the rose. He died in 1975, leaving his son, Patrick, to continue the award-winning progress of the firm.

McGredys, that other great Irish firm, was founded by Sam McGredy (1828–1903), a head gardener who went on to set up his own nursery, leasing ten acres of land close to Portadown, on which he put up a small greenhouse. From this nursery, which he started in 1880, Sam sold general nursery stock, including apple trees for the orchards of County Armagh. His hobby was the raising of show pansies and it was his son, Sam McGredy II (1861–1926), who started the breeding of roses, first exhibiting his new seedlings in 1905. It was his success in winning a gold medal with 'Countess of Gosford' that encouraged him to expand his hobby into a more serious undertaking. These were the years when it was the fashion to name flowers after relatives of the raiser, or after notable people. Sam's introductions included such once-famous roses as 'Mrs Herbert Stevens', 'Lady Alice Stanley, 'Mrs Charles E. Pearson' and 'The Queen Alexandra Rose'. Seventeen years after winning the first medal he had won 51 more, as well as 29 certificates, and had been awarded the Dean Hole medal of the Royal National Rose Society.

Sam McGredy III was 29 years old when his father died and he became head of the firm. The success of the breeding programme continued unabated on an even larger and more scientific scale. The famous rose 'Mrs Sam McGredy' was called after his wife Ruth. Then disaster struck, for Sam III died suddenly in 1934, when the next Sam was only two years old. Then came the war, and the necessity to produce food instead of roses. The survival of the firm was due mainly to the efforts of Walter Johnston, brother-in-law of the late Sam McGredy. At the age of 20 the fourth Sam McGredy took over and initiated a new and still successful era in the family firm – an era that saw the arrival of such winners as 'Daily Sketch', 'Elizabeth of Glamis' and 'Mischief'. The book, A family of roses (1971), by Sam McGredy and Sean Jennett, well describes the atmosphere of a big nursery growing and breeding roses. Not only are triumphs recorded, but also accidents such as the unintentional burning of tens of thousands of seedlings during fumigation, and the destruction of £20,000 worth of stock through the use of the wrong spray mixture.

SLIEVE DONARD AND ITS SHRUBS

It was in 1905 that William Slinger, working in a small nursery in the north of England, felt that the time had come to look for wider scope and better pay, for he had earned a reputation as a skilled grower of roses. He answered two advertisements in trade journals and received favourable replies from Ireland and from Cheshire. Since Dicksons, the famous rose firm at Newtownards, offered one shilling more per week than did the other firm, Slinger took the job. In this way arrived the family that was to make Slieve Donard nursery one of the best known in Ireland, Britain, and beyond.

Dickson's twelve coppers were a better investment than they knew, for in William Slinger they found an enthusiast who flung himself into his new opportunities. Those were the days of eager interest in the showing of roses, more particularly dressed blooms displayed as florists' flowers in boxes and baskets. So numerous were these shows that Slinger could find himself crossing the Irish Sea every night of the week, arranging flowers on the show bench, going back for more and travelling from one show to another to receive flowers brought over by a colleague in the firm. With such intense activity it can be imagined that arrangements did not always go smoothly. One unfortunate messenger arrived at the docks only to find he could not remember where he was going with the roses. All he could recall was that the name of the place began with M. *Bradshaw's guide* was consulted and Milford, South Wales, was chosen as the place, with disastrous consequences through the non-arrival of the roses at Millom, Cumberland.

The custom of dressing roses on the exhibition bench also led to tense situations. William's son, Leslie, remembered that as a boy he used to see his father watch for the approach of the judges, and at the last moment remove the woollen ties holding together individual blooms that threatened to be overblown.[3]

Willie, as he was known to his friends, soon had another opportunity for advancement, an opportunity greater than he realised at the time. He joined James Coey, a wealthy amateur plantsman, of Larne, County Antrim, who had taken over the Donard Nursery in Newcastle, County Down. The nursery had been founded in 1904 by Thomas James Ryan, son of the head gardener at Castlewellan, seat of the Annesley family.[4] A catalogue, undated but probably for 1921, shows that Coey specialised in daffodils, offering expensive hybrids raised by Engleheart and others, as well as a general collection of over 100 kinds. He was a successful exhibitor, winning medals for dry bulbs as well as cut flowers at the London and Birmingham shows.

On the death of James Coey, Slinger took over the nursery as a going concern. As Leslie, his elder son, shared his father's interest in plants, it was decided that he should have wider training before entering the business. He worked at Aldenham House and at the Royal Botanic Gardens, Kew, before returning to Newcastle. Meanwhile William had started the plant hybridising for which the firm was famous, by crossing forms of the wand-flower (*Dierama pulcherrimum*). Some 40 seedlings were raised and named, mostly after birds. Since these were tall plants, up to four feet in height, the breeding of a dwarf race for the smaller garden was the next step. This followed from two chance gifts, the first being seed of a dwarf species, now known to be *Dierama dracomontanum*[5] from South Africa in 1938. These dwarf hybrids were given appropriate names like 'Ariel', 'Puck' 'Titania' and 'Oberon'.[6] Leslie was encouraged to take up plant breeding, and it was characteristic of the keen eyes and imagination of the Slingers that he worked on *Escallonia*. Already they had 'Donard Seedling'. Leslie crossed 'Slieve Donard' (a seedling from 'Donard Seedling') with *Escallonia organensis* 'Pennickii' to obtain a new type having a more compact habit and brilliant flowers. These new hybrids included 'Apple Blossom' (from which sported 'Peach Blossom'), 'Pride of Donard', 'Donard Radiance' and 'Donard Star'.[7] These fine shrubs are still with us, but it is harder now to come by the lovely wandflowers raised at Slieve Donard.

Though the *Escallonia* varieties are perhaps the most widely celebrated productions of the firm, Leslie worked also on *Viburnum carlesii* for several years, producing 'Donard Pink' (also named 'Aurora') with deep rose coloured flower buds, and the vigorous 'Diana'. *Potentilla fruticosa* 'Tangerine', a very distinct colour break, was obtained by breeding, but P. 'Longacre Variety', with its spreading habit and large yellow flowers, was a chance seedling in a Newcastle garden. Careful selection, as distinct from deliberate crossing, gave such good plants as *Cupressus macrocarpa* 'Donard Gold'. In addition to their own productions the Slingers had an eye for good plants occurring in other gardens such as *Meconopsis x sheldonii* 'Slieve Donard' and cooperated in their propagation and distribution; in this way also were established in cultivation the *Chaenomeles*, *Hypericum* and *Primula* from Rowallane, all bearing the name of that famous garden. In 1935 the Slieve Donard nursery introduced *Forsythia* 'Lynwood Variety' from Miss Nora Adair's garden in Cookstown, County Tyrone. As well as these successful efforts at plant improvement there was time for prize winning exhibits at Chelsea and Southport, and the building up of the nursery as a well-known centre for good plants. No less than 28 different forms of *Iris ensata* (= *I. kaemferi*) and 36 different montbretias (*Crocosmia*) were listed, a contrast to the present-day tendency to cut down and standardise. Though not daffodil breeders, the Slingers were very successful exhibitors of this flower at the great shows of the inter-war period at Chelsea and Birmingham. Such a high pitch of horticultural enthusiasm and endeavour could be sustained only by dedicated plantsmen, so perhaps it was inevitable that the nursery should have come to an end in 1976 following the death of Leslie Slinger in November 1974.[8]

WATSONS OF KILLINEY

It could be said that the nursery firm known later as Watsons of Killiney was founded by chance. If old William Watson of Douglas, Lanarkshire, had not married again, or if his son William had got on well with his stepmother, there would have been no nursery in Ireland. As it was, William junior packed up, went down to the boat and sailed to Dublin in 1856.[9] He started gardening in a small way on the north side of the city, his particular enthusiasm being the cross-breeding of *Pelargonium*, then a very fashionable flower. Ferns and carnations were other interests. In 1881 he moved to bigger premises at Clontarf.[10]

With age and increasing deafness William had to give up his social activities, such as his honorary secretaryship of the Dublin Horticultural Club, in 1877, and later had to hand over his business to his sons James and John.[11] He had five sons, all of whom were connected in one way or another with agriculture or horticulture. One of them, David, was a pharmaceutical chemist, but preserved a link through his interest in agricultural chemicals. His exhibit of spraying appliances earned commendation at the Spring Show of the Royal Dublin Society in 1910. William, the eldest, became managing director of Paul and Vincent, fertiliser and animal foodstuff manufacturers, but continued to take a keen interest in the family firm. It was on his advice that his brothers bought Kilbogget Farm, Killiney, "even" he said, "if you have to beg, borrow or steal".[12] This was a splendid move for the firm, to a site with a mild climate and a favourable soil. John specialised in shrubs, James in roses and fruit[13] and in all these the firm gained a reputation for the high quality of their plants, and were known for the wide range of species and cultivars they offered.

Watsons of Killiney were noted for the series of coloured brooms (*Cytisus scoparius*) which originated at Kilbogget. 'Lord Lambourne' with scarlet-crimson wing petals and cream coloured standards, attracted attention at the 1927 Chelsea Show on account of the vivid colouring of the flowers and was given an Award of Merit. 'Dorothy Walpole' was another strongly coloured seedling, with crimson and rose petals, which won a similar award, as well as a First Class Silver Medal when shown at Ghent, Belgium. Other brooms from Killiney were 'C. E. Pearson', 'Killiney Red'[14] and 'Killiney Salmon'. Other cultivars, such as 'Elizabeth J. Watson' are less well known as they were introduced late in the life of the nursery.

Seedlings of Lawson cypress (*Chamaecyparis lawsoniana*) were also selected at Watson's nurseries, but not in time to become widely distributed. One, named 'Kilbogget' has a compact habit and comparatively light green foliage. Its chief attribute is its shape, which makes it a useful screen in smaller gardens. Other seedlings were 'Moonlight', with silvery foliage, and 'Killiney Gold' which looks its best as a young tree in summer time, since it is the young shoots that show the yellow colour.

The advancing wave of suburbia was a main factor in the decision to close down the firm in 1967, and the site of the nursery is now a housing estate.

The daffodil as an Irish plant

Spain and Portugal are regarded by botanists as the main centre of the genus *Narcissus*. The flora of the Iberian peninsula has links with that of Ireland (p. 1), so perhaps that is a reason why conditions in Ireland are so favourable to the cultivation of the daffodil. Although no species of *Narcissus* is indigenous to Ireland, peculiarly Irish forms of the cultivated daffodil appear to have existed for a very long time. This was noted by F. W. Burbidge in 1889,[15] when he suggested that owing to the cool moist climate self-sown seedling variations appeared more often than in English gardens. 'If this is not so, how are we to account for varieties being discovered in Ireland which are unknown either as wild plants in Europe or in gardens elsewhere?' Burbidge lists 21 such varieties, many of which had been collected in old Irish gardens by Miss Fanny Currey of Lismore, County Waterford, and by that great individualist, W. Baylor Hartland. Burbidge pointed out that Ireland was particularly rich in those small, delicate

41: William Baylor Hartland of Cork, an early collector of
daffodils, tulips and apples.

and delightful white trumpet daffodils of the *Narcissus moschatus, N. alpestris*[16],
N. albicans groups. Their names – 'Minnie Warren', 'White Manor', 'Silver Bar',
'Robert Boyle', 'Countess of Desmond', 'Little Nell', 'Colleen Bawn', 'Leda' and
'Bishop Mann' –evoke nostalgia now. As stressed by the writers of the day, these
old kinds flourished particularly well when growing semi-naturalised in mossy,
grassy places rather than in the highly cultivated ground demanded by the
vigorous cultivars of to-day. The parents of these small white trumpet kinds
may have come in some way from Spain or Portugal just as, at a later date
(1896), Nathaniel Colgan, author of *The flora of County Dublin*, collected *N.
moschatus* in the Pyrenees and grew it successfully in his garden in Rathmines,
Dublin.[17]

When William Baylor Hartland (Fig. 41) started collecting daffodils about
1880 he was head of a firm already long established in the horticultural trade in
the south of Ireland. His grandfather had come over from the Royal Botanic
Gardens, Kew, and founded a nursery at Bellevue, Mallow, County Cork, in
1774.[18] In 1810 the business was moved to Cork city by Hartland's father, also
called William Baylor, and described by his son as 'an old time seedsman, fruit
tree and forest planter'.[19] In 1837 the firm of Hartland and Bullen sponsored a
public exhibition at their nurseries, near the Western Road, Cork, in aid of the
Cork Fever Hospital.[20]

Hartland collected with such enthusiasm that by 1883 he was able to compile his first daffodil catalogue, *A little book of daffodils nearly 100 varieties as offered and collected by W. B. Hartland*. He explored old Irish gardens for daffodils and it is evident that at that time there were many distinctly Irish types to be found, such as the large yellow trumpet 'Ard-Righ' as well as the small white trumpet daffodils already mentioned as collected by Hartland. His account of finding 'Bishop Mann' shows him at work.

> I found this daffodil years since where 'Leda' could not possibly live for such a space of time, but would have died out, viz., in an old garden at Bishopstown, near Cork, and where the border was covered over with Laurels, Ivies, Mahonias, Hypericums etc. I removed the bulbs, that had been planted for 150 years to my present residence. This garden was on the old palace grounds attached to the See of St. Finbarr's and Bishop Mann was the last resident divine, and must have been very fond of flowers. The bulbs were growing in between huge roots of beech, at least 200 years planted, and we had to use crow-bar and pick-axe to get at them and lost or mangled numbers.[21]

By 1886 the third edition of his catalogue contained over 150 kinds, Irish and otherwise. The whimsical style of this publication, *Ye original little booke of daffodils, oxlips, cowslips and primroses*, incurred the wrath of one of the leading English daffodil fanciers of the day, the Revered George H. Engleheart. In a review in *The garden* Engleheart accused Hartland of producing a pretended scientific treatise, a crude production containing incompletely digested information. The cover (Fig. 42), though quaint to our eyes, was condemned by him as an atrocity

> ... a damsel entangled in a growth of impossible daffodils, is apparently defending herself with the poker against the attacks of a flight of noxious insects; while on the opposite side a gouty of caterpillar – or is it a cornucopia? – is pouring a shower of objects like jointed dolls and cabbages down upon ancient John Parkinson and a shortsighted gentleman, whose botanical studies are much impeded by a swarm of bees hovering round his bald head.[22]

One suspects Mr Engleheart of a certain dourness of character when he advises Hartland to 'content himself with a simple catalogue until he has digested his knowledge more completely'. We can sympathise with Hartland's plea (in verse) that his critic should read the *Little booke* in the same spirit as it was written, with enthusiasm and rapture rather than 'correctly cold and regularly low'.

Hartland was indeed hurt by the attacks of Engleheart on his knowledge, on his veracity and even on his 'canine Latin'. He replied that 'the fangs of a bear and the tusks of a wild boar do not bite worse.' His sense of grievance was increased by the refusal of the editor of *The garden* to allow him to reply in full to Engleheart, so he published a leaflet, reprinting the offending review and

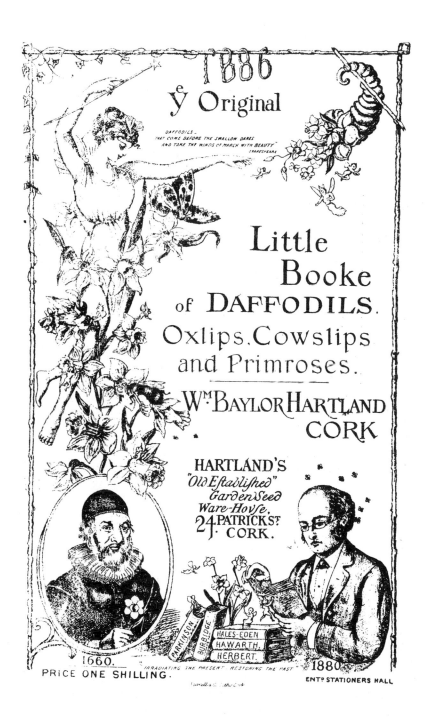

42: The cover of Hartland's 1886 catalogue so denigrated by the Rev. W. Engleheart.

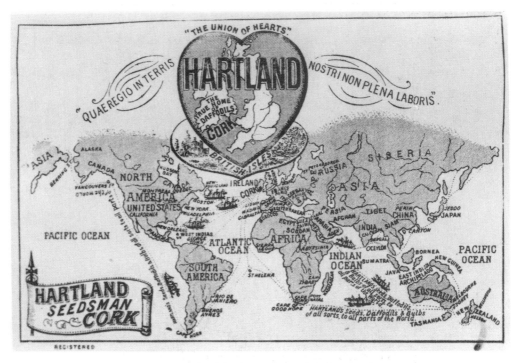

43: To Hartland Cork was the centre of the world.

adding his reply. He felt hard done by, for he had to re-write his defence from memory, since the editor had not returned his manuscript.

Hartland was right – and Engleheart wrong – in that the English lent lily is not found in Ireland. He claimed he was in good company (Parkinson, Linnaeus, Gerard, Clusius, Haworth and Herbert) in his dog Latin, and offered to send Engleheart bulbs of double Tenby daffodil to refute the claim that there was no such variety. Though the language of Hartland's defence is obscure in places, one can agree with his observation that in all cases of criticism the work and not the worker should be the object of attention.

What his later catalogues (for example, 1894) gain in accuracy they lose in charm for the general reader. By then over 200 sorts were offered in a list conventional in style. One last flourish is seen on the back, where a map shows the shipping routes of the world, all converging on Cork (Fig. 43).

Gertrude Hartland was an accurate and sensitive illustrator of her uncle's catalogues of the 1880s. In 1890 her drawings were published as Hartland's *Floral album of daffodils,* a valuable record of the flowers of the day, particularly of several of those introduced by Hartland himself and possibly still lingering in old Irish gardens. Queen Victoria's jubilee in 1897 was the occasion of an enlarged edition celebrating not only royalty but also nineteenth-century men like Watt, Stephenson, Edison and Röntgen in doggerel verse, but not without

44: Guy L. Wilson, a breeder of fine daffodils in County Antrim.

doubts about the blessings of science. The coronation of Edward VII was the occasion of another mark of loyalty by Hartland, this time with tulips. He presented 500 bulbs to Glasnevin Botanic Gardens to celebrate the event.

Hartland's other horticultural interests included double primroses, tulips and 'apples that are profitable for Irish growers from Peer to Peasant'. He collected tulips from Irish gardens and was responsible for introducing the celebrated cultivar 'Mrs Moon'. His catalogue for 1907–8 includes a list of old Irish apples headed 'Old lamps for new lamps' – 'A gathering of native Irish apples'. One of these, 'Ard Cairn Russet', named after his nursery, became a standard cultivar of the time in Britain as well as in Ireland.

Hartland's other activities included the raising of potatoes from seed. In 1908 he wrote to the paper *Irish gardening* praising his potato 'Claddagh'. In addition to the nursery he ran a shop in Patrick Street, Cork, whence he advertised orchids, stove and greenhouse plants, perpetual carnations and a floral department. A trip to Connemara resulted in his preparing a tourist guide, *Wayside Ireland,* full of poetic quotations in his usual fashion. Here, too, his pride in Cork showed in his criticism of Limerick – 'There's a want of life in the city as compared with Cork' – and of Galway – 'In every sense of the word very much behind Cork; no style about the shops'. Though the guide was to include botany, his original observations are slight. He noted mountain avens in The Burren, St. Dabeoc's heath and royal ferns (*Osmunda regalis*) in Connemara, and also saw *Fuchsia* naturalised in many places.

The *Irish daily independent* for 27 March 1893 contains an account of Hartland's bulb farm. From this we learn that he moved from Temple Hill to Ard Cairn, Ballintemple, about 1890, having decided to establish a bulb farm there, in area about ten acres. From there he was able to send baskets of flowers by the mid-day mail from Cork via Dublin and Holyhead and have them on sale at Covent Garden and other centres at 9 a.m. the next day. By this date over two tons of flowers had already been dispatched. In speed of delivery he had the advantage over the Isles of Scilly, the journey taking 18 hours as against sometimes two or three days. Daffodil and tulip bulbs were exported in barrels, mainly to America, Germany, Australia, New Zealand and even to Japan.

Hartland was an enthusiast for the improvement of rural Ireland. As Guardian of the Cork Union he instituted a scheme of prizes for cottage plots and advocated the growing of early potatoes, early vegetables and flowers along the southern seaboard, but stressed the need to start agricultural schools to back these efforts.

Baylor Hartland died at Ard Cairn in 1912, 'a gardener born and bred' in the words of the anonymous writer of his obituary in the *Royal Horticultural Society daffodil year book* for 1913. 'He has left us some excellent seedlings, 'William Baylor Hartland' and 'Countess of Southesk', one of the most lovely of all daffodils for vase decoration.' The writer compared Hartland with Peter Barr, a Scot of strong personality, and founder of the famous firm of Barr and Sugden (later Barr and Sons). Indeed, in 1884 Barr published *Ye narcissus daffodyl flowere and hys roots*, which may have been influenced by Hartland's *Little booke*.

It was Hartland's catalogue that influenced Guy Wilson (Fig. 44) while he was still a schoolboy. Guy was born at Broughshane, County Antrim, in 1886, and by the time he died in 1962 he had become famous the world over as a daffodil breeder. Even while he was at school he wrote to his mother enquiring after the progress of his daffodils.[23] When he had finished his schooling he entered the family woollen mill, though reluctantly, working at his hobby in his spare time, eventually leaving the firm to devote his whole time to his flowers.

Guy's first success came with the flowering of his seedling number 2/30, a white trumpet bred from the old cultivar 'Madame de Graaff' crossed with 'Lola'. This seedling was registered under the name 'White Dame' in 1922 and received a First Class Certificate from the Royal Horticultural Society of London. 'White Dame' was the first of many famous white daffodils raised by Wilson, his 'Kanchenjunga' and 'Cantatrice' to name but two, becoming well known wherever daffodils are grown. Though his name is so much associated with white cultivars, Wilson raised many fine seedlings in other colours also. 'Armada' and 'Home Fires' are notable red-cupped kinds. Pink daffodils, too, of Wilson's raising won awards, such as 'Irish Rose' and 'Passionale'.

Though the Reverend G. H. Engleheart did not approve of Hartland, he was more friendly towards Wilson, who had early won his approval for his

45: Lionel Richardson of Waterford, breeder of many
well-known coloured daffodils.

article 'Among my seedlings' in the *Daffodil year book* for 1915. Engleheart's comment, 'He can write English, an accomplishment not so common as supposed',[24] shows a trace of the asperity appearing in another remark of his which Wilson quoted as being in sympathy with his own views. The remark referred to the exaggerated efforts of some breeders of coloured daffodils who tried 'to make daffodils like cartwheels with large red frying pans in the middle'. Wilson said he was himself careful to guard against losing the natural grace and dignity of the daffodil, or obscuring its true character.[25]

There was a contrast between the methods of the two men. Engleheart admitted that he was very bad at keeping notes: he had few records of the exact crosses he had made and of the results, but relied largely on memory.[26] Wilson's more methodical approach and his intense interest in the pedigree of daffodils are shown in his articles on the breeding and inheritance of this flower.[27]

Guy Wilson's friendly relations with Engleheart no doubt added to the pleasures of his last years, as he could look back on the winning of the Engleheart Cup seven times. This prize is a major one, awarded for the best exhibit of twelve daffodils raised by the exhibitor himself. Though it was a sad day when ill-health forced Wilson to sell his stock and give up his life's work, he could recall great achievements, recognised in London by the bestowal of the Victoria Medal of Honour, and at home by the honorary degree of Master of Agriculture conferred by The Queen's University, Belfast. Even so, he may have recalled his words of nearly 20 years earlier, 'one might go on literally for ever exploring fresh vistas of possibilities with increasing eagerness of interest and delight, which thought makes one sigh over the brevity of a lifetime.'

In April 1974 the Guy L. Wilson Daffodil Garden at the University of Ulster, Coleraine, was declared open by Professor Fergus Wilson, Guy's nephew. Here are grown as many of Wilson's cultivars as could be collected, together with those of other well-known Irish breeders. This garden serves not only as a memorial, but also to preserve old and new cultivars, to form a gene bank, and to demonstrate the development and improvement of daffodils over the years[28].

Lionel Richardson (1890–1961) (Fig. 45) was a late starter compared with Guy Wilson, for he was 20 years old when his father bought daffodil bulbs from a local seedsman for their garden at Prospect House, Waterford.[29] Whatever kind these were, they were good enough to attract Lionel's attention. Further up the valley of the Blackwater at The Warren, Lismore, lived Fanny Currey, a pioneer in the commercial culture of daffodils.[30] Her catalogue for 1912 lists 348 different kinds, including cultivars raised by the Reverend G. H. Engleheart and other leading breeders of the day. Her exhibits won medals not only in Dublin but also in London, Edinburgh, Shrewsbury and Colchester. She encouraged Lionel's interest by gifts of bulbs, as did Sir Frederick Moore. About 1912 Lionel started crossing daffodils as a hobby, but in 1922 he started in earnest, after visits to P. D. Williams in Cornwall and The Brodie of Brodie in Inverness, two of the leading daffodil breeders of the time. He has related how Williams crossed his daffodils at random, guided only by an instinct that led him to great success. Richardson himself, after starting at random, soon settled down to keeping proper records of his crosses, though stating much of his work was trial and error. This may have been so, but after his death he was remembered as a most painstaking gardener and an earnest student of any subject relating to his work as a raiser of new kinds of daffodils.

Richardson was particularly attracted by bright coloured red and white daffodils, and would pay large sums for good seedlings from other growers for his own use as breeding stock. He was successful in raising prizewinners in virtually all classes of daffodil. When he died at the age of 71 he was considered to have been the last of the great daffodil breeders. He had won 64 gold medals and the Engleheart Cup 21 times in 26 years. During his last 15 years he won nearly 500 first prizes, 15 Class Certificates and 45 Awards of Merit for flowers of his own raising. Special awards included the Williams Memorial Medal in 1948 and the Veitch Gold Medal in 1952. All these outstanding achievements were recognised in his election as a Vice-President of the Royal Horticultural Society of London.[31]

The St Brigid and other anemones

It was on a dull November day in 1881 that Mrs Laurenson of Howth, County Dublin, brought a bunch of brightly coloured anemones to F. W. Burbidge in Trinity College Botanic Gardens. He was immediately impressed by 'the brightest and most charming anemone blooms I ever saw even in April and May'. In 1885 he wrote enthusiastically to *The Times* and it was publicity such as this that drove Mrs Laurenson to take refuge under the *nom-de-plume* of St Brigid to protect herself from the importunities of correspondents asking for seeds and roots.[32] Mrs Laurenson chose this name because she had previously lived at Kildare, the place so closely associated with St Brigid. Here she started her work with anemones, sowing seeds of French or Caen anemones (*Anemone coronaria*) and selecting only the best forms for further propagation, continuing the procedure when she moved to Howth.

By 1895 St Brigid anemones were being grown in England, for Lord Cowper obtained an Award of Merit that year for blooms from his garden in Hertfordshire.[33] Improvements, however, continued to take place in Ireland. This further development of the St Brigid anemone is credited to William Reamsbottom, of Alderborough, Geashill, County Offaly. He had married, in 1870, Mary Enraght Moony of The Doon, Ballinahown, Athlone, and the family tradition is that he found good anemones in the large walled-in garden there.[34] These he took back to his nursery and used in the production of the Alderborough strain of St Brigid anemone. He introduced his anemones commercially in 1892[35] and soon they were recognised as being of superior quality. In 1902 a correspondent of *The gardeners' chronicle* noted that Reamsbottom had exhibited his anemones at many of the leading shows in England and that

> this Irish firm has greatly improved the flower since they took in hand the St. Brigid strain of Anemones ... At that time five, or at most seven shades of colour were found in the ordinary strain; this has now been extended to some thirty ... There has been another change; the ordinary strain of St. Brigid anemone gave a large proportion of single flowers; in the case of the Alderborough strain the large percentage of the flowers are double.[36]

In the same year the Royal Horticultural Society of London gave the Reamsbottom strain an Award of Merit[37] as a strain remarkable for the 'unusually large double and semi-double flowers in rich and varied colours', and in 1903 it obtained a Gold Medal when exhibited at the Shrewsbury Show. Other growers in Ireland picked out good anemones. Of these some were single-flowered clones like 'Maconchy's Scarlet', from a garden at Raheny, not far from the anemone's original home at Howth.[38] In 1920 an Award of Merit was granted to 'Crowley's White', from S. Crowley of Tipperary. This was 'a good white form of St. Brigid anemone with large semi-double flowers of nice shape'.[39] In 1925 Mrs D. Bucknall sent to *The garden* a photograph of her strain of St Brigid anemone growing at Creagh Castle, County Cork.[40] In March of the following year yet another Award of Merit was given to St Brigid anemones, this time to the Creagh Castle strain, 'A good strain of St. Brigid anemones, ranging from white through purple and mauve shades to rose and scarlet'.[41] According to *The garden* these plants had 'much larger and more spreading flowers of a brighter and deeper colouring if that be possible'.[42] In 1930 Mrs Bucknall won a Silver Gilt Banksian Medal for her anemones, which continued to be prominent until World War II. To-day St Brigid anemones are cultivated internationally, the name being applied in England and Holland to all double or semi-double forms of the chrysanthemum-flowered type of florists' anemone.

Anemone coronaria was not the only type of anemone to be improved in Ireland. In the west at Ashford Castle, Cong, County Mayo, Mr Campbell, head gardener to Lord and Lady Ardilaun, in 1886 sowed seed he had saved from the tall white Japanese anemone (*A. hupehensis* var. *japonica*). Three seedlings were raised and he named the best of them 'Lady Ardilaun'.[43] This was put on the market in 1890, and was an important parent in the breeding of further cultivars, being an addition to the four kinds of Japanese anemone then in cultivation.[44] Messrs Lemoine, the famous French nurserymen and plant breeders, used Campbell's plant in the development of many further cultivars of diverse habit, with flowers varying in size, colour and degree of doubling.

The Ardilaun's other garden, St Anne's, near Dublin, now a public park, is commemorated by the rose 'Souvenir de St Anne's'. This, a nearly single-flowered sport from the old 'Souvenir de la Malmaison', was named and brought into general cultivation by Lady Moore.[45]

THE CHRISTMAS ROSE CONTROVERSY

Mrs Laurenson not only bred anemones but also raised improved forms of the Christmas rose (*Helleborus niger*), hybridising good varieties assembled with the aid of Burbidge and Frederick Moore.[46] In March 1883 Burbidge wrote to *The garden* describing how he had named a superior form the St Brigid's Christmas rose.[47] It was distinguished by its erect habit with leaves on straight stems remaining fresh and green at flowering time, in contrast, to the cultivar 'Maximus' with decumbent leaves which turn yellowish as the blossoms fade.

Burbidge's letter provoked an intemperate outburst from William Brockbank, of Brockhurst, Didsbury, Cheshire, a frequent contributor to *The garden*. He protested against Burbidge's proposal to call this beautiful Christmas rose after a saint.

> I, for one see no fitness whatever and charm nor beauty in the proposed name of St. Brigid's Christmas Rose and most certainly I shall never associate the flower with such a long winded and far-fetched appellation. There is no reason whatever for it beyond the fact that a few plants of it are growing on the Hill of Howth and FWB has no right to christen it that I can see.[48]

A pacific note was appended by the editor saying that he thought Brockbank had misapprehended Burbidge, and stating that the name St Brigid was applied on account of its having been found in an Irish garden, the owner of which wrote under the *nom-de-plume* of St Brigid. Despite this the battle was joined, not only over the name but also over the identity of the plant. Burbidge wrote in reply to Brockbank

> If Mr Brockbank is inclined to be just ... I think he must allow that I have equal right with himself, i.e. that I may justly claim the right to name any plant I know for a certainty to be popularly nameless and my title to do this is quite as clear as his right to protest against such a practice ... The common variety is a wretched weed in our soil as compared with St. Brigid – visitors came from all parts of England and not one of them ever saw this particular variety before.[49]

In the same issue Mrs Laurenson, 'St Brigid' herself, wrote in support of Burbidge. She described how she went to see the old lady who gave her the first root she grew. The old lady said that when she came to her home 30 years earlier the garden was famous for three things – Christmas roses, Lent lilies (*Narcissus minor*) and yellow cabbage roses. The yellow roses had disappeared but the Christmas roses and the Lent lilies were still there.

Brockbank was not appeased, but claimed that the St Brigid Christmas rose was the same as one grown by the acre in the north of England.[50] This was not accepted by Burbidge, who suggested that the English form was referable to *Helleborus niger* 'Major', the Irish one to *H. niger* 'Angustifolius'.[51] The following winter (November 1883) Brockbank transferred his attack to the columns of *The gardeners' chronicle*.[52] He went to remarkable lengths in tracing the origin of the 'true Christmas rose' (*H. niger* 'Angustifolius'), going back to Parkinson and Gerard in his efforts to prove it an English form. He conceded dryly that there was a variety 'which is well known from frequent mention of it in the columns of *The Garden* as being grown in great perfection on the Hill of Howth'. He referred to a plant received from Burbidge and Mrs Laurenson but maintained that there was no difference in the foliage characteristics from those of the plants in his own garden.

> I have never seen it flower ... If it should prove, as he states, that it is a new variety, he may with propriety give it a name, and that an Irish one, but if it should turn out to be the same old Gerard's variety, surely even St. Brigid would hesitate before giving her name to 'Christ's herbe', the true Christmas rose. Mr Barr is growing all these three varieties side by side at Tooting. The same is being done here, and we shall thus be able to compare the varieties when in bloom.

Burbidge continued to write in *The garden*:

> Mr Brockbank has tried but has utterly failed to prove that the large pale green stemmed variety of *Helleborus niger* that I call St. Brigid's Christmas Rose was known to either Gerard or Parkinson ... Mr Brockbank admits ... that there are three forms or varieties of *H. niger angustifolius* that is to say the English variety, the Scotch variety and our Irish form.[53]

Then comes the final argument, the verdict of Peter Barr, the acknowledged authority on daffodils and hellebores. 'Mr Barr tells me that the Brockhurst and the St. Brigid varieties are quite distinct in his trail beds at Tooting'. Burbidge goes on to quote from Barr's catalogue;

> This is a grand plant ... altogether removed from any variety we know ... the public are indebted to Mr Burbidge for calling attention to this fine plant. Next year we may be able to offer plants; at present we have only the specimens presented by 'St. Brigid'.[54]

The affair was wound up by an anonymous correspondent in *The garden* writing of a plant seen at Kew in 1884.

> Now that the storm raised in reference to the name of this plant has subsided, let us turn to the plant itself ... To me this plant, which bears a label upon which Mr Burbidge's name and 'St. Brigid's Rose' are conspicuously displayed, is a long way superior to what I have always seen as the Christmas Rose.

Hellebores are long-lived plants, so the true St Brigid's Christmas rose may still exist, though Brockbank may have increased the confusion he proposed to stop when he alleged that Burbidge was introducing an invalid name. It appears from Burbidge's note in *The garden*, April 25 1885, that the form described by Brockbank as plentifully cultivated around Manchester had meanwhile been distributed as St Brigid's Christmas rose.

PLANTS FROM DAISY HILL

The Daisy Hill nursery at Newry, County Down, was founded by Thomas Smith in 1887.[55] Thomas was a son of a gardener in Birmingham. After working in several English nurseries, including the famous firm of Veitch of Chelsea, he came to Newry as manager to Andrew Daly, and later Rodger, McClelland and Co (Plate 8). In 1887 he set up on his own, prospering to such a degree that his Daisy Hill nursery extended to 60 acres, stocking over 5,000 plants (see Plate 16).[56] Henri Correvon, the famous Swiss nurseryman and author visited Daisy Hill in 1911 and was greatly impressed by Smith's skill, calling him a horticulturist to the tips of his fingers.[57] Thomas Smith died in 1919, and was succeeded by his son George, an equally enthusiastic lover of plants, who kept the nursery going until about the time of the second World War.

In 1897, in a contribution to *The English flower garden*, F. W. Burbidge gave high praise to a series of *Bergenia* hybrids raised at Daisy Hill. These, with such names as 'Brilliant', 'Distinction', 'Progress' and 'Study' never seem to have become widely known, unlike that other Irish *Bergenia* 'Ballawley Hybrid' (p. 203), and may now be lost to cultivation. Another genus, *Berberis*, was improved by hybridising at Daisy Hill. Over a period of years, from about 1903 to 1933, a number of hybrids were raised between *Berberis* x *stenophylla* and *B. darwinii*. Of these 'Irwinii', 'Corallina' and 'Corallina Compacta' are still well known. In

1937 Smith introduced the intensely coloured form of *B. darwinii* called 'Firefly'.[58] *Berberis* x *antoniana* (*B. darwinii* x *buxifolia*) with flowers almost half an inch across also originated at Daisy Hill.

Apart from new kinds of *Bergenia* and *Berberis*, some other new plants came from the Newry nursery, probably more by keen observation of chance seedlings than through a planned programme. These include such diverse types as the double primrose 'Our Pat', *Laburnum alpinum* 'Newyrensis',[59] the cultivars of *Eucryphia*, *Cytisus* and *Aubrieta* called 'Daisy Hill' as well as two cultivars of *Hebe*, 'Autumn Glory' and 'Newryensis'.

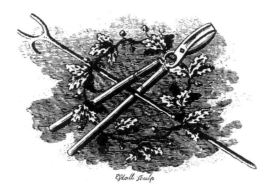

AFTER ROBINSON
THE AGE OF THE OWNER-GARDENER
ALPINE PLANTS & JAPANESE GARDENS

Though William Robinson's influence in favour of the natural style of gardening continues to the present day, the school of thought favouring the revival of an architectural style of gardening was gathering force. This was the compartmented style, in which the garden was visualised as a series of sections or compartments, one leading to another. One of the most celebrated examples is the garden at Hidcote Manor, Gloucestershire, made after the first World War. The garden there, though utilising the new plant material available from all over the world, is essentially a formal garden, each compartment with an individuality of its own. Robinson himself had admitted that his style of gardening was more suitable for the larger estates than for the smaller gardens favoured by the economic circumstances of the day. Moreover, the compartmented style was as well adapted to the small garden as to the grander surroundings of the manor. Such writers as Beverley Nichols, in *Green grows the city*, popularised the formal or semi-formal layout that could give the illusion of a larger garden by splitting up a small area so that all is not seen at once. At this time, too, the increasing number of owner-gardeners favoured the development of the alpine garden and, allied to it, the Japanese style of gardening.

This revival of the architectural influence in gardens started during Robinson's lifetime, when he was dismayed by the apparent desertion to the opposite side of his great friend Gertrude Jekyll, that other giant of the Victorian garden era. Miss Jekyll in fact kept a foot in both camps. Before her sight deteriorated she was a painter, and shared with Robinson a pictorial rather than an architectural approach to garden design. They also shared an interest in the old-fashioned plants of the cottage garden. They became close friends, visiting each other often to discuss their gardening problems, and Robinson invited her to contribute both articles and photographs to his magazine *The garden* for she was a pioneer of the art of photography. Among her contributions to his great work, *The English flower garden*, were articles on 'Colour in the flower garden' and 'Fragrance in the garden'. Their close friendship and collaboration lasted for over 50 years.

In 1889, however, Miss Jekyll was introduced to a young man named Edwin Lutyens,[1] one of a growing band of architects who rejected the pomposity of Victorian architecture and advocated, in the wake of the arts and crafts movement, a return to the traditional building craft in the more modest dwellings of the coming age. Miss Jekyll was sympathetic to these ideas, and almost immediately commissioned Lutyens to design her own house. Thus began one of the most fruitful collaborations in the history of garden design.

Two important gardens in Ireland were created by this partnership, namely Lambay Island, County Dublin, and Heywood, County Laois. Lutyens would lay out a series of architectural compartments around the house, which were then clothed with planting to Miss Jekyll's designs, but they also worked separately. Miss Jekyll was commissioned to design gardens for Mount Stewart and Drumbanagher Castle, both in County Down. Lutyens laid out the Sidney parterre at Howth Castle and the War Memorial Garden at Islandbridge, Dublin, the latter one of his most expensive and monumental designs.

It was not long before a war of words broke out between Robinson and the new generation of architectural gardeners. The first shots were fired by J. D. Sedding in his book *Garden craft old and new* (1893), in which he proposed that the ground around the house should be laid out architecturally, using the traditional crafts of the stonemason, the carpenter and the blacksmith, rather than the mass-produced ornaments of the Industrial Revolution, but that there should be a gradual transition to a wild area at the edge of the garden and on into the landscape beyond. Sedding has been credited with the lay-out of the garden at Killarney House, County Kerry, though it may have been done by the architect of the house, George Davey, under Sedding's guidance.

Sedding's ideas were not enough to draw Robinson's fire, but a later book, *The formal garden in England*, by Sir Reginald Blomfield, roused Robinson's anger. Blomfield developed Sedding's ideas of the formal area around the house, and criticised what he saw as Robinson's far-fetched notions of the wild garden, far-fetched particularly in relation to gardens of only an acre and a half in extent. He proposed, instead, what he considered a more sensible approach based on a revival of the old-fashioned English formal garden with compartments of modest dimensions and a restrained use of statuary, topiary and other ornaments. This restraint would suit the coming age, and was seen by Blomfield as a more appropriate alternative to the grandeur of the Victorian garden scene than Robinson's wild garden, which was merely a change of style but not of scale. In Blomfield's view only formal gardening was worthy of consideration and the architect of the house was the logical designer of the garden. The effect of such statements on Robinson can be imagined. In his *Garden design and architect's gardens* (1892) he reviewed these books in impolite terms, and in the next edition of *The English flower garden* he maintained that Blomfield saw the garden as 'a place for plaster images rather than living plants'. He also rounded on Sedding for his defence of the use of topiary, saying 'for him there is no art in gardening but cutting a tree in the shape of a cocked hat'. These were bitter and unfair attacks, and later that year Blomfield defended himself in the second edition of his book, maintaining that a formal garden laid out on traditional lines would be more in keeping with the home countryside. Blomfield's view was that Robinson's large scale planting of exotic plants would be out of keeping and out of scale with the surrounding countryside. This was a telling criticism of the Robinsonian style of gardening and one which augured well for the continuation of an exciting controversy, but Blomfield retired from the fray, writing that he had no wish to continue an argument in which Robinson was continuously and gratuitously insulting to his opponents. Miss Jekyll, according to a friend, followed this controversy with ironic amusement, relating that despite it all Robinson designed himself a garden all squares and Blomfield a garden with not a single straight line in it.

Blomfield, it would appear, obtained only one commission in Ireland, at Bellair, County Offaly, but from the beginning of the century the adherents of the revival of the formal garden carried out many works here. An example is the terrace at Belvedere, County Westmeath, by Brinsley Wesley. This was faithfully copied, even down to the minute details of the balustrading, from the famous old terrace garden at Haddon Hall in Derbyshire, the subject of one of the finest illustrations in *The English flower garden*. Until it was softened by the growth of vegetation it looked inappropriate in front of the Georgian mansion at Belvedere, but such was the enthusiasm for the style that this was disregarded at the time. The new Herbert Park in Dublin, too, exemplified the current taste for earlier styles. A competition for its design was won by J. Cheal and Sons of Sussex with a lay-out which included such old-fashioned features as a pergola covered walk, herbaceous borders, random rubble rather than dressed stone walls and areas of crazy-paving. At this time, too, a modest little sunken and paved garden was designed in old-fashioned style for one side of Muckross House, Killarney, by R. Wallace and Co. of Tunbridge Wells, whose landscape manager George Dillistone, published his book *The planning and planting of little gardens* in 1914. This garden was originally planted with old-fashioned flowers.

In 1910 the first major garden in the compartmented style in Ireland was begun at Ilnacullin (Garnish Island), Bantry Bay, County Cork, by Annan Bryce, a man of Scottish stock born in Belfast. It was a most unpromising site, a windswept, gorse covered island with a Martello tower. The soil is derived from Old red sandstone and shale, strongly leached by the high rainfall to a grey sandy loam deficient in organic matter and in plant nutrients. It is so shallow that it was necessary to scrape soil off the rocks to augment that which had accumulated in the hollows. Over the years this acid soil (pH 5 to 6), has been ameliorated by the addition of compost, giving a somewhat darker soil in the

46: Ilnacullin, County Cork, where many delicate plants flourish. (Reproduced by permission of the Commissioners of Public Works in Ireland).

cultivated beds. Here and there are limited pockets of peat; the lawn in front of the Italianate pavilion (Fig. 46) is one such area, but the peat has shrunk to such an extent that two extra steps had to be added to the building. Though Ilnacullin has some shelter from the wind, tucked as it is into Glengarriff Harbour, and receives some protection from Sugarloaf Mountain, the difficulties of establishing trees on the bare island are still recalled, especially as root anchorage is poor in the shallow soil. The gangs of planters had to come back and begin again in the wake of storms that tore down the barely established lines of shelter trees.[2] Ilnacullin does not owe the splendid growth of its treasures to good soil but rather to the mild climate and high rainfall, a point further illustrated by seedlings of *Griselina littoralis* growing in an epiphytic manner on *Pinus radiata*.

Bryce was interested in architecture and probably met the landscape architect Harold Peto in the south of France. Peto, who worked in an old-fashioned Italian rather than in an English style, laid out gardens on the Riviera and in England, where he created a notable garden at Ilford Manor, Wiltshire. His compartmented gardens are based on the courtyards and walled gardens of the villas of classical Rome, such as can be seen in the ruins of Pompeii, rather than on the Italian Renaissance stye. The central feature of his design for

Ilnacullin (Fig. 46) is a series of linked compartments, beginning at one end with a doubly sunk paved garden containing a pavilion and a central pool, like those in the courts of Pompeii. This was originally surrounded by a collection of antique statuary and vases to make the aura of antiquity more powerful. From this first encounter one is led through a pavilion with loggias into the second and largest enclosure, a formal lawn surrounded by shrub borders. It leads on through a gravel garden into the formal walled kitchen garden, with flower borders flanking the path and antique tablets set in the walls. At the corners of the garden are stone viewing pavilions behind which there is a break in the sequence, in the form of a piece of Robinsonian woodland gardening, before the cottage is reached, the only residence on the island. Behind it, however, the compartmented theme is taken up again as a paved rose garden with pergolas. Around this series of formal gardens the rest of the island was laid out in the compromise style advocated by Miss Jekyll, the formality at the centre leading to gradually wilder areas, and on to the open landscape. Advantage was taken of the sub-tropical climate to grow a host of interesting and tender plants. To name but a few they include such genera as *Torreya*, *Fokienia*, *Pittosporum*, *Olearia*, *Taiwania*, *Dacrydium*, *Callitris*, *Lomatia*, *Acacia*, *Agathis*, *Hakea*, *Phyllocladus* and rare species of *Rhododendron*. These collections are now well cared for, and added to by the Office of Public Works.

After the first World War the compartmented style came into its own, reaching its apogee in England with the gardens of Sissinghurst and Hidcote, both now maintained by the National Trust. In Ireland the most important post-war example was that laid around the house at Mount Stewart, County Down, by Edith, Lady Londonderry.

There was a walled-in garden with a good but old range of glasshouses and an orchard of fruit trees covered with lichen. The grounds were dotted with conifers, especially *Cupressus macrocarpa* and there were many evergreen oaks. It was fortunate that in 1921 the then Marquess came to live at Mount Stewart and that Lady Londonderry was a keen and able gardener. She has recorded how she found the place the dampest, darkest and saddest place she had ever stayed in in winter. The evergreen oaks almost touched the house and other trees had grown to block out all light and air.[3]

Lady Londonderry first commissioned Miss Jekyll to draw her a set of plans. These are now in the library of the University of California, Berkeley,[4] and are full of references to old-fashioned features. The medieval garden was recalled in a proposal for a cloister garden, and a pool garden was referred to in the same nostalgic vein as 'the tank garden'. Lady Londonderry, however, appears to have been disappointed with these plans, and proceeded to lay out the gardens herself, influenced by a number of styles, but principally in the compartmented manner. The Italian Garden contains stone work based on Italian models, but also parterres adapted from those at Dunrobin Castle in Scotland, the home of Lady Londonderry's mother. From this enclosure one steps down into the Spanish Garden, so called from the Spanish tiles on the roof of the summer house. As well as a sunken garden on two levels there are two

47: Mount Stewart, County Down, where Lady Londonderry made a garden of 'the dampest, darkest and saddest place.' (Reproduced by permission of *Country Life*).

compartments of unusual style. One is the Shamrock garden, a paved area in the shape of a shamrock, bounded by a cypress hedge. In the centre is a bed shaped in the form of the Red Hand of Ulster, planted with the red-leaved *Iresine herbstii*. On top of the hedge is cut in topiary a family hunting-party, the scene derived from the fourteenth century psalter of Queen Mary Tudor, now in the British Museum. Other topiary here includes an Irish harp cut out of yew. On the other side of the house is a stone-flagged garden with beds laid out to form a Tudor rose, and planted with blue and white flowers such as *Agapanthus*, *Crinum*, arum lilies (*Zantedechia aethiopica*) and Madonna lilies, the whole backed by a pretty dovecote. Lady Londonderry followed Miss Jekyll's ideas in employing local craftsmen to make the architectural features of the garden, such as gates, stone walls, balustrades, pillars and statues (Fig. 47). The latter are of fantastic animals rather than copies from correct classical models, as was the Victorian custom. The use of topiary was, as we have seen, one of the principal ideas of the proponents of the revival of the formal garden, and of J. D. Sedding in particular. Although the garden at Mount Stewart incorporates so many architectural features it is also full of interest for the plantsman since numerous rare plants are skilfully cultivated. The locality shares the mild and humid maritime climate enjoyed by the gardens of the south-west, but Mount Stewart

48: Herbaceous borders, Annes Grove, County Cork. (Reproduced by permission of Mr. Annesley, Annes Grove).

differs from Rossdohan and Ilnacullin in having sunnier conditions without their excessive rainfall. The trees include *Eucalyptus, Cordyline, Drimys, Davidia, Acer* species and many others. Delicate *Rhododendron* species do well, as do *Eucryphia, Feijoa, Carpenteria, Fabiana, Cassia, Clianthus, Myrtus* and other tender genera. The beautiful *Lapageria* climbs through clipped cypress; blue poppies, lilies, candelabra primroses and other rare plants too numerous to mention flourish throughout the grounds. The gardens are now safe in the care of the National Trust.[5]

One of the most admired features of the day was the herbaceous border, of which good examples are still to be seen at the National Botanic Gardens, Glasnevin, at Bealieu, County Louth, and at Annes Grove, County Cork (Fig. 48). The Victorian parterre makers had used colour in a conscious way to make their patterns, but as these were geometric they were obliged to force their flowers into many unnatural forms. Miss Jekyll and her followers worked out their colour schemes in the herbaceous border. Such borders of hardy herbaceous plants were composed of a series of tightly packed but loosely formed associations of plants. This system gave bold splashes of soft edged colour which, in the haze of a hot summer's day, were reminiscent of the loose splashes of colour with which the contemporary painters of the Impressionist school built up their pictures.

The creation of such borders came to be the particular province of ladies, for whom working in the garden became respectable as both a recreation and a profession at this time. In a standard work on the subject, *Gardening for women* (London 1908) by the Hon. Frances Wolseley, Principal of the Glynde School for Lady Gardeners in Sussex, the gardens of a number of Irish ladies are illustrated. The Hon. Emily Lawless, an Irish emigré in Surrey, Miss Jekyll's county, had a house designed for her by Lutyens and published *A garden diary* (London 1901). Mrs Norah Lindsay, born in County Galway, built up an international practice and may have advised on the gardens of her family in Ireland. Those at Castletown Cox, County Kilkenny, Palmerstown House, County Kildare and at Rathmore in the same county are in her compartmented style with many old-fashioned features. Katherine Everett, born a Herbert of Killarney and author of *Bricks and flowers* (London 1949), designed gardens at various times during her life, her most remembered achievement being her advice to her cousin Lady Ardilaun on her garden at St. Anne's, County Dublin. Lady Ardilaun, keen to work with her own hands in the garden like other ladies of her time, described the difficulties she encountered with her large gardening staff:

> Once I pulled up a weed or two, but my dear old Head [gardener] met me in the very act and looked pained and hurt, and the next day there were men and boys in every border and by-way hunting stray weeds like sleuth hounds. Another time I said I should like to learn to take cuttings, but when I saw the preparations for my lesson – bags of earth, leaf-mould and sand, pots and crocks and moss, all being carried to the garden tea-room – I felt I was wasting a lot of men's time. I was shown exactly how to do them, and I thought I had done them perfectly, though there were murmurs about making them 'firm'. When everything had been taken away I went to see where they were to be grown, but retreated quickly when, on my way to the nursery ground, I glimpsed my old friend in the potting shed, inserting one of them into a pot, while the rest lay on the bench awaiting his expert firm handling. Still, the fiction was kept up and those carnations were always called my cuttings.

Two other professional lady designers working in Ireland at this time were Mrs Solly-Flood, who had a nursery for herbaceous plants in County Kilkenny, and Katherine Levie. Mrs Solly-Flood's best remembered work is her conversion of the walled garden at Mount Juliet, County Kilkenny,[6] for Major Hugh and Lady Helen McCalmont into a series of axial walks and enclosures with sculptural focal points. Mrs Levie had served her apprenticeship in London with the firm of Milner Son and White, the firm which had descended from the practice of Edward Milner, Paxton's assistant. Mrs Levie remembers that over her desk in the office was an enormous layout for the new gardens at Muckross House, Killarney, which combined an old-fashioned pergola walk and formal walled garden with such Robinsonian features as a natural rock garden and a vast rhododendron ground. Mrs Levie's own principal surviving work is at Carrigrohane, County Cork, for Mr and Mrs J. A Wood, where she devised a raised walk and pergola to connect the house to the walled garden, a formal paved rose garden, and a geometrical lawn bounded with randomly paved edgings.

Today large herbaceous borders are often regarded as a labour-intensive form of gardening and are generally neglected in favour of more permanent plantings of trees and shrubs. Yet there are many good hardy perennial plants that do not need staking, high feeding, or frequent division as they have not been developed into highly bred florists' flowers. Instead of the typical herbaceous border of the past we may see them grown in 'island beds', as advocated by Alan Bloom of Norfolk. Such groupings do not depend on the long vistas demanded by the conventional border, and so are better adapted to the smaller gardens of today.

Though Robinson's ideas for growing plants in a natural manner were more suitable for larger areas, his *Alpine flowers for English gardens* came at a time when rock gardening was beginning to appeal to many who had only small gardens, as they could grow a diversity of beautiful plants in a limited area and develop the skills needed to cultivate the high alpines. The taste for rock gardening was further stimulated by the enthusiastic writings of Reginald Farrer, as well known in Ireland as in England. This specialised kind of gardening became very popular in the twentieth century, but the culture of alpine plants in Ireland was attempted much earlier. Walter Wade, in his enthusiasm for the Dublin Society's new botanic gardens at Glasnevin, determined to make the collections as representative of the plant kingdom as possible. Nothing came of the plan to grow seaweeds, for it was recognised that the project would be attended with much difficulty and expense but an astonishing artificial mound was thrown up for the cultivation of alpine plants, situated on the most elevated part of the garden.

> The fragments of rock for this purpose were transported from the Hill of Howth and such were selected as were already clothed with various species of mosses and lichens. These were piled together without any apparent order, so as to give the appearance of a natural rocky mound. But it is so constructed that spiral walks winding round the sides, but not visible at a distance, conduct the visitor to the summit. Here, as he ascends, he sees every grey stone clothed with its appropriate vegetation, and in every fissure of the rocks some alpine plants. When arrived at the summit of this mound, the eye is gratified with a view of the whole garden lying beneath displayed as in a map. This fantastic hill is a favourite walk, and on public days its sides and summit are usually filled with crowds of visitors.[7]

Wade's catalogue (1800) does not list the plants on this mound, but the species named in the section on herbaceous plants include many alpines. It would be a good collection today that included *Androsace chamaejasme, Primula sibirica, P. integrifolia, Gentiana pneumonanthe, Saxifraga hirculus, S. oppositifolia* and *Soldanella alpina* to pick out a few at random from those that were at the Botanic Gardens, Glasnevin, in 1800. They may not have been grown on the rock garden, for it is not likely that such species as these, requiring special skill and attention in their cultivation, would survive long under the rough conditions of the mound, which seems to have been more of a popular spectacle than a garden for delicate plants.

In a few country places rock gardens were constructed early in the nineteenth century. At Mount Shannon, County Limerick, the seat of the Earl of Clare, there was in 1839, 'a very neat piece of rock-work'.[8] At Cahir Guillamore, in the same county, advantage was taken of a natural outcrop. Here the Hon. Colonel O'Grady had made a 'handsome piece of pleasure ground, at one end of which is a beautiful rockery formed by nature, with the intent of leaving but very little for art to improve on'.[9] Nevertheless the rocks were 'tastefully enamelled with flowers of various tints and hues. These in the summer months conduce to give a most lovely and picturesque appearance'. Sculpture was not excluded, for

> the interest of this spot is increased by the circumstance of an eagle having taken up his residence here, where he sits perched upon the tallest rock, while the small birds look on him with terror and depart from his presence with precipitation, so that he answers the double purpose of use and ornament.

One may doubt whether the flowers of various tints and hues were true alpines, although such plants were being imported into Ireland by private gardeners. In the garden accounts preserved at Tullynally Castle, County Westmeath, is recorded the payment of one shilling and sixpence for *Gentiana verna* and half a crown for *G. pneumonanthe* in a list of plants bought from Messrs Lee of Hammersmith in 1831.

At Trinity College Botanic Garden, John Bain (p. 122) had a collection of alpines that impressed William Robinson in 1865 as being of the choicest kind and 'in very rare health indeed'.[10] These plants were not grown on a rock garden but in narrow borders beside the paths, and were planted in lines, one or more to each species. It might be thought that only easily cultivated kinds could be bedded out in this fashion, but Bain's collection included such comparatively delicate species as *Dianthus alpinus*, *Petrocallis pyrenaica*, *Androsace chamaejasme*, *Gentiana verna*, *Soldanella* species and numerous dwarf *Primula*. None was protected in a pot or frame, and this was proof to Robinson that if alpines are in the right soil and kept moist enough they may be grown fully exposed in the open air at all seasons. Bain laid stress on frequent division and firm planting to keep them in good condition.

It was not until the end of the nineteenth century that the construction of rock gardens and the culture of alpines became widespread, the upsurge of interest spreading from England to Ireland. This new fashion for, and understanding of, the culture of alpine plants was such that by 1910 Sir Frederick Moore was able to state that 'The rock garden is no longer a feature to be found only in large establishments or in Botanical Gardens'. He wrote this in his introduction to *Rock gardens* by L. B. Meredith, who had a notable garden at Graigueconna, Bray, County Wicklow.

In the south, at Ashbourne House, Glounthane, near Cork, Richard Beamish had a splendid garden which included a rock garden, described by W.

H. Paine[11] as one of the finest examples of modern alpine gardening in the British Isles and certainly the best in Ireland. It was landscaped on a large scale, with hills, valleys and a waterfall. Many more alpines grew well there, such as *Cyananthus incanus*, *Aethionema kotschyana*, the delicate *Lithospermum rosmarinifolium* and colonies of the hardy ladies slipper orchids *Cypripedium spectabile* and *C. macranthum*. The origin of an especially fine encrusted saxifrage, *Saxifraga callosa* 'Albertii'[12] is attributed to Asbourne House.[13] Richard Beamish cultivated Himalayan poppies (*Meconopsis*) and was the first to raise *Meconopsis* x *beamishii*, a hybrid he produced by crossing the blue *M. grandis* with the yellow *M. integrifolia*.[14] Paine's description of Ashbourne includes photographs of the rock garden and its plants, as well as some of the sub-tropical plants grown elsewhere in the garden. Though the rock garden has gone many fine trees and shrubs still grow at Ashbourne, including *Acacia*, *Camellia*, *Sciadopitys*, *Pittosporum*, *Corokia*, *Cornus*, *Osmanthus*, *Magnolia*, *Eucalyptus*, *Drimys* and a fine yew walk. Various bulbs are naturalised about the grounds.

The pages of the garden journal of the time, *Irish gardening* (1906–1922), reflected the enthusiasm then current for rock gardening, for they carried many articles on the subject, by well-known personalities. One of these was Robert Lloyd Praeger (1865–1953), so well-known as a naturalist, particularly as a botanist, that his interest in gardening might be overlooked. At this period he had a rock garden in Rathgar, Dublin, whence he wrote on the cultivation of saxifrages, *Campanula*, *Primula*, and other plants. He took particular pleasure in the many self-sown seedlings that came in his small hand weeded garden, including such choice plants as *Onosma*, *Acantholimon*, *Campanula allionii*, *Wahlenbergia* and *Romanzoffia*. His interest in the cultivation of such plants and his scientific abilities made him a particularly suitable person to write up two genera of horticultural importance, *Sempervivum* and *Sedum*.[15]

Sempervivum, the houseleeks, was in a state of confusion, no one being sure of the proper names for the cultivated plants. First Praeger collected together over 2,000 pots of house leeks from private and public gardens all over Europe. He concluded, however, that this was an impossible way of clearing up their nomenclature. Hybrids between the species were common, a source of confusion increased by the practice of distributing home-saved seed from many botanic gardens. Offsets are readily detached and can become mingled with those of other species. In any case the original descriptions are often poor and fail to demarcate species clearly: Praeger concluded that the only way to study the species was in their native haunts. He travelled to Switzerland, Austria, Italy and Bulgaria and also to Madeira and the Canary Islands, where some tender species grow. He described how he sometimes had to hook up specimens from inaccessible places by means of lengths of bamboo fitted together and ending in a hooked blade.

Praeger's other great monograph was on the genus *Sedum* or stonecrops. These, too, were in a confused state of identification in gardens. It was an easier task to unravel them as the various species are distinct botanically, but as many are rampant growers of which the smallest scrap will root even if carried some distance, they easily get mixed in cultivation. Many names in circulation proved to be invalid, and others were misapplied due to carelessness.. Hybrids, however, are rare. It was not necessary for Praeger to travel widely to examine plants in the wild, and in any case trips that he planned were stopped by the outbreak of war in 1914. However, with the co-operation of botanic and private gardens he was able to collect together and cultivate all but four of the 151 species he described in his monograph, a publication of great value, especially as it includes drawings by Miss Eileen Barnes of almost all the stonecrops he described.[16]

Another contributor to *Irish gardening* was E. B. Anderson, later to become one of the best-known growers of rare plants in England. He came to Ireland in 1909 as a research chemist, and at Sandymount, Dublin, made the second of the seven gardens he was to make during his lifetime. At first he lived in lodgings and Saturday visits to the Botanic Gardens at Glasnevin were a great solace to the laboratory worker. Frederick and Phylis Moore noticed the young man who spent so much of his spare time in the gardens and in characteristic fashion encouraged his interest by inviting him in to tea, the beginning of a life-long friendship. Bertram Anderson was soon well-known in Dublin gardening circles. From Sandymount he contributed articles ('In a small rock garden') to *Irish gardening*. Though his garden was very small, with a lawn known as 'the postage stamp', and sunless until the end of February, his skill enabled him to grow a good collection of alpines, including *Saxifraga*, *Androsace* (Plate 6), *Campanula*, *Edrianthus* and many others.

The enthusiasm for alpine culture was supported by nurseries with collections of plants of extent and variety scarcely to be found anywhere in Britain or Ireland to-day. The catalogues from Lissadell, the home of the Gore-Booths near Sligo, are illustrated with photographs of some splendid specimens growing in the gardens there. The standard of cultivation evident in the pictures of *Phyteuma comosum*, *Androsace*, saxifrages and *Primula* would be the pride of many alpine plant enthusiasts to-day, especially as the plants were grown in the open rock garden and not protected by pot culture in an alpine house. From the cultural notes it is evident that the natural soil at Lissadell was a sticky loam, but this was overcome by the free use of peat. Indeed, the use of peat became a key factor in the great success obtained with many plants. *Gentiana acaulis*, so easy to grow but so notoriously uncertain in flowering, is shown thick with flowers in a raised open bed. A garden constructed with peat blocks, the invention of Murray Hornibrook (p. 203), was described in the Lissadell catalogue for 1915:

> As far as possible the peat blocks should be laid with the heather side facing the weather, and these can be fashioned into a miniature mountain any shape you like, taking care to pack the joints between the peat blocks with loose peat. Do not let anyone imagine it will not hold together. We climbed to the top of one of Mr Hornibrook's mountains to see *Iris tectorum* in flower, and we found it absolutely solid.

No doubt it was the intervention of the war years that led to this kind of garden being forgotten until peat beds were constructed in the Royal Botanic Garden, Edinburgh, after 1920.

As examples of the remarkable range of plants offered, the 1915 Lissadell catalogue listed 20 *Androsace*, 75 *Campanula*, 70 *Dianthus* and 83 *Primula*. Several good cultivars originated there. The Lissadell *Primula* hybrids derived from *P. pulverulenta* and *P. cockburniana* became widely known and are not forgotten to-day, though selected clones like 'Aileen Aroon' (light scarlet), 'Brian Boru' (blood red), 'Red Hugh' (fiery red), and 'Maeve' (raspberry pink) are probably no longer with us. *Androsace lanuginosa* 'Lissadell Variety', *Aubrieta* 'Lissadell Pink' and *Campanula carpatica* 'Lissadell Selected White' are other plants one would like to have to-day.

The collection at Lissadell made Henri Correvon, the great Swiss lover of alpines, quite lyrical, though he was by no means impressed by Ireland as a country. He missed the alpine peaks of his own land.

> Ireland is not a country I could live in. I have travelled from the west coast to the east, and I have found the landscape on the whole dull and flat, no sharp outlines, no peaks or crags, to relieve the monotony of green plain. I must, of course, make an exception in favour of the western coast scenery, which is certainly more picturesque; and there are even some little hills which might, by a stretch of imagination be called mountains.

He did not expend much ink on his slightly erroneous description of the Botanic Gardens at Glasnevin ('Some very old yews were of special interest to me, as having been planted, probably, by our common ancestors the Celts.') Lissadell, however, remained impressed on his memory as one of the most brilliant gardens – and more especially alpine gardens – that he had ever seen

> the garden at Lissadell presents an extremely beautiful and picturesque appearance, comprising as it does all the choicest of the alpine plants. I, for one, shall never forget so brilliant a picture. Here one may find the best of the rock plants, grouped together in colonies of ten, twenty, or even in some cases a hundred plants, looking as healthy and happy as in their own natural homes.
>
> There are some very good *Eritichium nanum* and androsaces – strange to say the high alpine species do better here than the Himalayan, which latter grow at Floraire like weeds. Here may also be seen the best primulas, geraniums, campanulas and saxifrages, together with plants from the far north and Antarctic regions, all growing and flourishing in the mild, damp Sligo air. The rock garden is one of the largest I have seen, and is very well kept.[17]

Lissadell was indeed a great centre of horticultural activity in the opening decades of the twentieth century. Splendid collections of herbaceous plants were grown, as well as shrubs, roses and fruit trees. Lissadell daffodils won numerous medals at shows in Dublin, London, Birmingham, Cardiff,

Glamorgan, Shrewsbury, Brecon and Edinburgh. The many other activities on the estate included market gardening, seed potatoes, poultry, cattle, dairying ('Butter by post'), forestry and Lady Gore-Booth's School of Needlework.[18] The years between the wars saw the alpine nursery still carried on.

> Although the gardening year now drawing to a close was again a very bad one from a business point of view we have decided to persevere with our Annual list, in the hope that things must mend sometime. As mentioned in the notes in our last issue the gardens are now being got into better order again.[19]

It would seem that a new manager was in charge, for peat seems to have been forgotten in favour of leafmould. The raising of new plants continued, such as *Primula* 'Molly Malone', 'a chance seedling, very rich deep crimson, the most striking yet raised', *Geranium* 'Alannah', 'rich wine colour, almost black in centre, probably *G. traversii* x *argenteum* 'Lissadell Purple', and others.

It is saddening to think that the conditions of to-day no longer favour the maintenance of such varied activities on a private estate.

The increase in interest in the growing of alpines coincided with the fashion for the Japanese style of gardening (p. 206). Both styles use rock and water to create miniature landscapes, so inevitably there were examples of a mingling of the two kinds of garden. In a true Japanese garden the landscape is the dominant theme, using a limited range of plants to achieve an effect, but the European rock garden is a response to the availability of mountain plants from all the temperate regions of the world, and was constructed primarily to cultivate these plants, but at the same time aiming to provide them with a natural setting. Although the garden at Tully, County Kildare, was oriental in style this did not inhibit the scope of the nursery run in association with it. At the Royal Horticultural Society of Ireland's Spring Show, held at Ballsbridge in 1910, the Tully nursery showed a miniature Japanese garden which 'arranged very effectively with bridges, water, rockwork and the characteristic pygmy trees, was brilliantly gay with primulas, pillar roses and alpine plants, nicely placed in dark brown peat, which afforded a very pleasing contrast to the healthy green of the foliage'.[20] The *Primula* included *P. muscarioides*, *P. forrestii* and *P. lichiangensis*, all still scarce to-day. European primroses included Tully Garden's own form of *P. marginata*, called 'Mrs Hall-Walker'. Also shown were *Sanguinaria canadensis*, the American blood-root, saxifrages and *Androsace*.

Campanula 'W. H. Paine' is a form of *C. garganica* which originated at Tully[21] and is widely acknowledged to be one of the best. The flowers are deep violet blue, each with a strongly contrasting white eye. The name commemorates a manager of the nursery and garden, an Englishman known as 'Daddy Paine'. Whether this was derogatory or affectionate can now only be guessed at. Paine collected plants in the Pyrenees[22] and wrote a slightly inaccurate account of the plants he found on the mountains of Galway and Clare.[23] Eventually he was so affected by gout that he was wheeled about in a chair, and finally had to give up his job.

49: Murray Hornibrook (Reproduced by permission of his
niece, Mrs Rosemary Porter of Bideford, Devon).

The nursery at Tully was on an ambitious scale, covering 30 acres. Evidently markets outside Ireland were to be supplied, for there were thousands of *Morisia monantha*, saxifrages in great numbers and variety, *Aquilegia alpina*, *Shortia uniflora* and *Pyrola rotundifolia*. In 1911 Tully was visited by Henri Correvon, doyen of alpine gardeners.[24] He had never seen a completed Japanese garden before, and had regarded the idea as an absurdity. He had to admit 'now I have seen the realisation I cannot say that it is ugly or unpleasing and it is certainly both curious and characteristic'. He was much impressed by the nursery, where he saw *Daphne cneorum* much better grown that he had ever seen it before, and also a fine collection of terrestrial orchids. He wrote: 'Alpines are grown at Tully in immense quantities in pots, and they all look very healthy, even the rarest and most delicate of the gentians'.

A notable specialist alpine nursery was at Ballawley Park, Dundrum, County Dublin. This grew out of a fine garden of trees, rock and water courses created by Mrs Shaw Smith after her husband, Louis had bought the house and four and a half acres about the year 1907. Mrs Shaw Smith had never gardened before, but she became a keen plantswoman, propagating her own stock to furnish the ever expanding garden. The sale of surplus plants indicated such a demand that when her son, Desmond, wanted to retire from business she suggested he should join her in turning such sales into a commercial nursery. Ballawley Alpine Nursery lasted for about 25 years from 1929.[25] A perusal of the catalogue for 1951 shows that a wide range of plants was offered, not only for the rock garden but also for the herbaceous border. A number of good plants originated at Ballawley, such as several cultivars of *Aubrieta*, and the mossy saxifrage 'Ballawley Guardsman', well known as a free-flowering form with red flowers which did not fade quickly. Good dwarf pinks (*Dianthus*) were raised, such as 'Pinkeen', with very bright pink single flowers over a tight mat of silvered leaves, the whole only three inches high. Taller was *Dianthus caesius* 'Ballawley Variety', bearing semi-double pink flowers with dark calices on seven-inch stems. An outstanding herbaceous plant, still much appreciated, is *Bergenia* 'Ballawley',[26] created by crossing *B. beesiana* with *B. delavayi*. The dark stems rise to two feet, carrying heads of deep fuchsia-purple flowers. At one time Ballawley had a fine collection of the old double primroses, especially the pink 'Rose du Barri'. Large drifts of the *Primula juliae* hybrids grew in the private garden, and in a small greenhouse in the nursery contained a superbly grown batch of *Primula edgeworthii* and its white form, then new to cultivation and still rare to-day.

The nursery did not long survive the retirement in 1954 of Desmond and his wife Cynthia. To-day there is no nursery in the Republic of Ireland specialising in alpines on the scale of Lissadell or Ballawley, though enthusiasts keep the culture of alpines alive. There are flourishing branches of the Alpine Garden Society centred on Belfast and on Dublin with shows of a standard highly regarded by the parent society in England.

The cult of rock gardening encouraged the growing of dwarf conifers. The great authority on these small trees was Murray Hornibrook (Fig. 49), who lived in Ireland for nearly 20 years, settling down at Knapton, Abbeyleix, about the time of his marriage in 1906. There he built up a fine collection of dwarf conifers, wrote a book that is still a standard work on the subject, but his death went unrecorded in the horticultural press. Until recently the details of his life have been virtually unknown, even to those who value his book, *Dwarf and slow growing conifers*, first published in 1923, the second edition in 1938.

Murray was born at Hampstead, London, in 1875, the seventh of a family of eight children. He was tall and delicate when young, so often ill that he was backward at school, which led to so much bullying and caning that he ran away from his preparatory school. As he refused to return he was sent to a day school instead. In 1887 began his association with Ireland, a country he came to love. In that year he went to stay at Schull, County Cork, with Canon Abbott, a connection on his father's side. His life was still not happy, for his mother, to whom he was devoted, died at the early age of 40 and he did not enjoy working in London, in the office of his elder brother's distillery. His solace was music, for he shared the musical talents of his family. He took a course at the Guildhall School of Music and played the violoncello at many amateur concerts. Then came a turn in his fortunes. It may have been Canon Abbott's interest in the boy that led his family to think he was a late developer and that with good coaching might get into a university, for he was sent to the canon's brother at Leighlin, County Carlow. There began a period he later described as one of the happiest of his life. He learned to ride and to fish, and developed his first recorded interest in gardening, the culture of roses. Though Canon Abbott wanted him to study at Trinity College, Dublin, Murray preferred to go to Cambridge. He was studying for the church, in accordance with the wishes of his father, but as his studies progressed he felt less and less fitted for such a career. While on holidays at Kilkee, County Clare, he met John Atkinson, a barrister and later Attorney-General, who invited him to become his secretary. This entry into politics led eventually to his becoming resident magistrate for an area that included Abbeyleix.

Murray leased Knapton, Abbeyleix, about the time of his marriage to Gladys, daughter of Sir William Thompson. There they made the garden, for both were keen gardeners, and he built up the collection of dwarf conifers which was to be the basis of his published work. He purchased and propagated all the kinds he could find in nurseries and gardens, as well as finding naturally occurring variants of spruces and junipers, which he brought into cultivation.

Though the name of Murray Hornibrook[27] will always be linked with his exhaustive studies on dwarf conifers, he was interested in many other kinds of plants. He experimented with moraines, hybridised dwarf *Campanula*, specialised in saxifrages and was the inventor of the peat garden, as described in 1915 (p. 199). Rare plants grew very well in these peat blocks; for example Hornibrook was able to give Glasnevin a 'yard wide block of peat packed tight with sprouting shoots of *Shortia galacifolia* in full flower'. Seeds of rare plants were sent to him by an aunt in British Colombia and he acknowledged the generosity of Sir Frederick Moore.

During his years at Knapton, Hornibrook contributed a number of articles on alpines to *Irish gardening*, but his horticultural activities there came to an end in 1922, for with the change of administration he was retired compulsorily. He presented a collection of dwarf conifers and many choice alpine plants to the National Botanic Gardens, Glasnevin,[28] before moving to England, first to Rhyde House, Ripley, Surrey, whence he wrote to *The gardeners' chronicle* on some recently discovered dwarf conifers. However, he never made another collection of these plants, though contributing an occasional article on them to *The garden* and to the *Journal of The Royal Horticultural Society*. The *Report of the conifer conference* (London, 1931) included a paper by him on dwarf conifers in cultivation.

The Hornibrooks spent much time every winter in the south of France, where Murray took a great interest in the wild forms of *Iris* and *Narcissus*, and in Italy. By 1933 they had bought a house in Normandy, the Villa Medova, Entretat, Seine Inferieure. Here the garden was a series of slopes and terraces, with shrubs mostly on the slopes and herbaceous plants on the terraces. He collected irises and several hundred roses, including species, hybrid teas, old-fashioned roses and climbers.

50 & 51: Japanese Garden, Tully, County Kildare.

In 1940 the Hornibrooks had to leave hurriedly, just ahead of the German forces, escaping to England in an old cargo boat. The war years were spent in Cornwall, where they did all they could to help the French resistance movement. Murray is remembered at this period as an excellent cook, a craftsman who could make a lovely doll's house for his daughter, filled with copies of the family furniture, and as an affectionate and generous father and uncle, witty and humorous. He was interested in old prints and wrote a book on the subject in collaboration with a French friend.

When the war was over the Hornibrooks returned to the Villa Mendova, to find the garden largely wrecked and overgrown with brambles after occupation in turn by the Germans and the Americans. A great many of the roses had survived, the old-fashioned kinds flowering more freely than when they had been hard-pruned annually. Murray set to work and cleared the garden of the invading undergrowth, but lived to enjoy it for only a short time, dying in 1949. No obituary appeared in the horticultural papers, but his monument is his book on dwarf conifers, in which he describes about 500 different forms. It is still quoted as the standard work, and is regarded as a testimony of his skill in tracing old cultivars as well as discovering new ones and introducing them to cultivation.[29]

To-day nothing is left of Knapton. It was an attractive small Georgian house, built by the first Viscount de Vesci for his brother during the latter half of the eighteenth century, with a splendid lean-to curvilinear glasshouse by Richard Turner attached.[30] As no one lived there after the Hornibrooks left, the house gradually fell into decay and was finally demolished between 1955 and 1959. Some yew trees, a tall Lawson cypress and the remains of a walled kitchen garden with the Turner glasshouse (which was dismantled and removed in the late 1980s) are the only signs that this was once an important garden.

As already mentioned, the interest in rock gardens and dwarf conifers occurred about the time that the Japanese style of gardening was introduced. On 12 January 1905 was signed the Anglo-Japanese alliance and this led to an upsurge of interest in Japanese culture, including gardening. At the Japan-British Exhibition of 1910 in London, Japanese gardens, plants, stone lanterns, and 2,000 pigmy trees were featured. In Ireland, at Tully House, Kildare, Colonel William Hall-Walker (later Baron Wavertree of Delamer) who had often visited Japan, became so enthusiastic that in 1906 he imported a Japanese landscape gardener to lay out his garden. Thus a whole family came to Kildare and lived there for four years – Tassa Eida, his wife and two sons, Minoru and Kaji – as strange an interlude, in those days, for Kildare as for the family so far from home. The Eida family's stay in Kildare was determined by the time it took 40 labourers to build the garden.

That relations were not always happy is suggested by legends still persisting in the locality. At the entrance to the gardens is a large bowl on a pedestal, the last detail to be completed. A dinner was given, to which the neighbouring landowners were invited. Naturally Eida was there. During the meal conversation turned, not unexpectedly, to the subject of oriental wisdom.

Eida, pressed to give an example of paternal precept, told that his mother had given him a piece of advice: "Beware of three things – the heels of a mule, the horns of a bull and the smiling face of an Englishman."[31] One can imagine the consternation of the party as Eida rose from his seat and left the room, packed up and left Ireland, never to return.

Perhaps Eida needed more oriental wisdom, or perhaps he wisely integrated with local society during his stay in Kildare, for when he came he did not drink, gamble or back horses. Before he left he did all three, and departed a poor man, collecting on his way five shillings from Colonel Hall-Walker, the result of a wager that two Chusan palms, *Trachycarpus fortunei*, would not survive in that locality. They still thrive.

Memories still current of the great undertaking tell how semi-mature Scots pines were transplanted from near Dunmurray, on one occasion arriving too late in the town square to go further in the short winter day. The tree was left overnight on its big float, with one Matthew Lynch on guard with a lantern to prevent traffic running into it. Hundreds of tons of rock were transported from Ballyknockan, perhaps a three-day round journey. The men received a shilling a day subsistence, out of which sixpence went on bed and breakfast, leaving sufficient for three pints of stout. In summertime sleeping out of doors left more for the 'extras'.

The garden at Tully is a combination of five types of Japanese garden styles (Figs 50 & 51) – walking, viewing, symbolic, contemplative and a garden for taking tea. These are all combined in a symbolic story of the life of Man from the Gate of Oblivion and the Cave of Birth to the Gateway to Eternity. Childhood and learning, decisions in life, matrimony, ambition, the gaining of wisdom, and then the peace and contentment of old age unfold as the visitor traces his way through the garden. There was another section also laid out by Eida, now in the grounds of the National Stud, with artificial lakes and islands, planted with willows, dogwood, pines and bamboos to make a water and island type of Japanese garden, so that Colonel Hall-Walker could enjoy a mile long walk through the tea garden and round the lakes.

In 1915 Colonel Hall-Walker gave over Tully to be the British National Stud, which it remained until 1944, when it became the property of the Irish government, and has been maintained since by the Irish National Stud Co. Today Tully is the only great Japanese garden surviving in Ireland. The other great example was at Hollybrook House, Skibereen, County Cork. This was in a different style – a water-and-island garden for strolling or for boating. Here the theme was one of peace and tranquillity as one drifted over placid waters, passing stone lanterns on arching pedestals, perhaps disembarking at a landing stage to meditate in an arbour. This garden, covering about four acres, was created by Mrs Mary Morgan, who in the first decade of the present century voyaged to Japan in her steam yacht *Boadicea* (437 tons) and brought back two Japanese gardeners, together with fine stone lanterns and other garden furniture. In the house itself there was a room decorated in Japanese style. The gardens are too large and elaborate to be maintained by private enterprise in the economic circumstances of today.

EPILOGUE

The Garden Scene in Ireland Today

We have seen how Irish gardens have gone through many changes down the centuries, in each era adapting to the conditions of the day. When the second World War ended in 1945 great changes were found in the social scene which had their impact on gardens also. The profession of head gardener was rapidly approaching extinction, and instead of the often autocratic individuals such as suffered by Lady Ardilaun (p. 195), a new kind of college trained horticulturist appeared on the scene, orientated towards a career in one of the public services on terms and prospects of promotion with which the private garden owner could not compete. Now we are in the age of the owner-gardener, cultivating with his own hands small areas comparable in size to those which started it all in the monastery enclosures long ago. This could be said to be a reflection of the do-it-yourself aspect of much of today's social scene.

Yet Ireland is still known abroad for its great gardens, mainly Robinsonian in style, attracting visitors by their wealth of species growing luxuriantly in our oceanic climate, and by the beauty of their setting. Gardens well cared for by the families that created then have an elusive quality hard to define and difficult to perpetuate under public ownership, just as great houses lose something of their aura when no longer lived in as family homes. Kilruddery, County Wicklow, is fortunate in this respect. It is the oldest formal garden still surviving in Ireland, and was landscaped in the late seventeenth century in the style of Le Notre, with canals, clipped hedges of lime, hornbeam, beech and yew, set off with statues and fountains. Not far away the magnificent formal gardens and arboretum at Powerscourt are now maintained by the Slazenger family despite the tragic loss of the mansion by fire.

Most of the larger gardens that survive, however, are in the natural Robinsonian style. Mount Usher, created on the banks of the River Vartry by

52: Samuel Heard, creator of Rossdohan, County Kerry.

four generations of the Walpole family, has changed hands, and under the care of Mrs Madeleine Jay a host of rare trees including *Eucalyptus*, *Magnolia*, conifers, *Eucryphia* and *Rhododendron* and other shrubs and plants continue to flourish in this sheltered valley. In County Cork that other great river garden, Annes Grove, has been well maintained and developed by the son and grandson of Richard Grove Annesley, the creator. Here the visitor may enjoy a unique visit looking from the woodland garden down steeply to the River Blackwater, where grow moisture loving *Primula*, foliage plants and graceful bamboos. Annes Grove is a garden within a garden, for inside walls is a smaller landscape, with rocks and water clothed with rare plants.

In the far south-west, in County Kerry, Rossdohan, created by Samuel Heard (Fig. 52), and Derreen are famous for their tree ferns. The former, rescued from near dereliction by the Walker family, is furnished with large trees, notably *Acacia* and an undergrowth formed of a rich collection of tender shrubs from the southern hemisphere. Derreen was planted a century ago by Lord Landsdowne and is still in the family. As at Rossdohan, vistas open to wonderful views of the Kerry coastline. Further inland, at Dunloe Castle Hotel, Killarney, rare conifers in fine condition flourish in a remarkable arboretum. Near Dublin, too, Mrs Sally Walker maintains the family home at Fernhill, with noble trees, fine rhododendrons, shrubs, rock and water plants.

Not all the great gardens surviving in private hands are situated in mild areas. The demesne at Birr Castle, County Offaly, has a particular fascination in offering a microcosm of the changes in garden style through the years. From the steps of the castle is seen an eighteenth century landscape park with a distant view of a bridge and woodland beyond. The walled garden, placed in typical fashion at a distance from the house, shows Victorian features, including a *Rhododendron* garden on a bed of imported peat. Here is the formal baroque garden laid out by the sixth Earl and Countess of Rosse. The Camcor River, flowing past the castle, has been made into a Robinsonian style river garden, leading to the lake and arboretum. The late Lord Rosse was an ardent collector of rare plants, trees and shrubs, and many of the specimens at Birr are important as raised from seed sent home by plant collectors. The garden there, unlike most well known Irish gardens, is on limestone as also is Tullynally, County Westmeath, another midland demesne which has gone through changes during the centuries. Nothing remains now of the elaborate eighteenth century canals and water garden, these being swept away when the natural style of landscaping came in. Today the visitor can enjoy the lakes, one curved to imitate a river, woodland walks through the wild garden with fine trees and shrubs, both those long established and those recently planted by the Hon. Thomas Pakenham, the present owner. The walled garden, once the site of an elaborate Victorian garden, still contains a fascinating 'weeping pillar' from that era, a type of fountain dripping into a lily pond, a fine central walk of Irish yews, and a terrace planted with shrubs and herbaceous plants. Abbeyleix, the former home of the Viscounts de Vesci, is another finely wooded demesne in the midlands, with a famous bluebell wood and some rare trees. Though Headfort, County Meath, now houses a school, the trees and shrubs survive, especially many unusual *Rhododendron* and the remarkable collection of conifers. An old midland estate revived is at Emo Court, County Laois, where Mr C. D. Cholmeley-Harrison restored the house to the demesne, clearing undergrowth, cleaning the lake and planting up the vistas with choice shrubs and trees to supplement the fine old specimens surviving from the times when it was the seat of the earls of Portarlington. Emo Court is now under the management of The Office of Public Works. At Kildangan, County Kildare, the tradition of arboreta was continued by the late Roderick More O'Ferrall. The conditions imposed by a cold climate and a limy soil are reflected in his choice of such genera as *Prunus*, *Sorbus*, *Cotoneaster*, *Malus* and other flowering trees and shrubs to supplement the existing mature trees round the house.

It is now widely recognised that such gardens and demesnes are part of our national heritage, although hitherto, especially in the Republic of Ireland their owners received little official help to maintain them so that they might be enjoyed by future generations. Sympathetic interest has been shown by Bord Failté (the Tourist Board), which assists in promoting the tourist potential of those gardens open to the public, and by An Taisce (the Irish National Trust) through its Heritage Gardens Committee which sought ways and means to support the owners. That committee guided the cataloguing of the plants growing in leading Irish gardens. An Taisce, however, is a voluntary body with no funds to acquire or maintain gardens. Meanwhile the owners face rising costs which are not covered by admission charges. Most carry on through their personal involvement in the day to day management of their properties, adopting all advances in labour saving techniques such as ground cover planting and the use of herbicides. It is fortunate that the natural style of gardening so suited to the Irish scene is one well adapted to such methods.

A few of the great gardens that have come down to us have come under the care of public agencies and have a secure future. A number of such agencies are involved, and though some might consider this an illogical arrangement it has an advantage in that it encourages diversity of ideas in the management of the gardens. In this respect, though, some exciting developments are in hand. The National Botanic Gardens are to be central in a co-ordinated system linking many of the gardens in public ownership. This opens up the prospect of exploiting even more the varied resources of the Irish soils and climate by locating parts of the plants collections in different gardens.[1] Ilnacullin, County Cork (p. 191) is excellently maintained by the Office of Public Works, which has also taken responsibility for Heywood, County Laois (p. 189), The War Memorial at Islandbridge in Dublin (p. 189), both designed by Sir Edwin Lutyens, and Glenveagh Castle, County Donegal, where many interesting plants grow in the gardens round the romantically situated castle. The beautiful Muckross demesne at Killarney, County Kerry, has been in state care for many years. Fota, County Cork, where the planting of splendid trees and shrubs by the Barrymore family goes back almost 200 years, is about to become the latest garden to come under the management of the Office of Public Work. Fota was saved to take on a new lease of life as the property of University College, Cork, thanks largely to the initiative of Professor Thomas Raftery. However after the College authorities decided they could no longer justify continued ownership, Fota was sold and several years of great uncertainty ensued.

The John F. Kennedy Park, County Wexford, was developed by the Forest and Wildlife Service, and was transferred in 1994 to the Office of Public Works. This arboretum, founded with the help of American friends to commemorate President Kennedy, was officially opened in 1968.

Among local authorities, Dublin County Council has been to the fore in maintaining the landscape at Marley, County Dublin, and the distinctive plant collections at Malahide Castle, in the same county, with their emphasis on plants of the southern hemisphere. The gardens at Malahide Castle were the creation, during the latter part of his life, of Milo, Baron Talbot de Malahide (Fig. 53), sponsor of the splendidly illustrated, six-volume *Endemic flora of Tasmania*, publication of the final volumes being seen to by the Hon. Rose Talbot after the death of her brother.

53: Milo, Lord Talbot de Malahide, creator of one of the last
great gardens of Ireland.

In Northern Ireland three great gardens, Castlewellan, Mount Stewart and
Rowallane, all in County Down, happily have a secure future in public care,
though Sir John Ross-of-Bladensburg's garden at Rostrevor has gone.
Castlewellan, created by successive Annesleys since the eighteenth century
(Plate 11), was purchased by the Northern Ireland government in 1967 and is
now designated as the National Arboretum under the care of the Northern
Ireland Forest Service. A glance at the plant catalogue shows how rich is the
collection of conifers, trees and shrubs. The gardens at Mount Stewart were
started by Lady Londonderry in 1921 (p. 193) and skilfully developed into a
series of compartmented gardens. In 1956 she handed over the property to the
National Trust. Rowallane, a name familiar on account of the *Primula*, the
Japanese quince, the *Hypericum* and the *Viburnum* that originated there, is
another National Trust property, the creation of Hugh Arymtage Moore who
had a particular flair for developing this beautiful garden around the natural
features of the site, and in doing so assembled a collection of plants of
exceptional interest.

Though Ireland has lost so many of the great gardens made during the last
150 years, dedicated individuals have created some new ones, even during

recent decades.[2] Malahide and Glenveagh have already been mentioned, and in the south-east, at Mount Congreve, Waterford, Mr Ambrose Congreve has made a garden on a large scale, with massed plantings of such genera as *Magnolia*, *Camellia*, *Rhododendron* and *Embothrium*, among them specimens of many rare trees and shrubs. *Camellia* are a feature also at Kilmokea in the adjacent County Wexford. Here the late Colonel Price and Mrs Price blended the formal and informal to make a fascinating garden round the house, and bravely extended it into a water and woodland garden. At Ardsallagh, County Tipperary, Mrs Betty Farquhar, also started from scratch, growing rare trees, shrubs and plants of great diversity in surroundings now sheltered where once were open fields. In the same county, at Clogheen, is Glenleigh, a garden initially made by Mrs Burkhardt and then extended by Mr and Mrs Calder-Potts. With the backdrop of the Knockmealdown Mountains and within a fringe of picturesque trees are sweeping lawns traversed by a stream. This is the axis of a garden of moisture loving plants, with groups of shrubs, the whole bordered by a small river along which is being developed a woodland garden. Killiney, County Dublin, is a mild spot where the late Mr and Mrs Sidney Maskell grew a wealth of plants in a medium sized garden which appeared larger because of its varied design.

More recently, a number of international designers have laid out gardens in Ireland which combine both formality and informality of design. The first of these, Aughentaine, County Tyrone, consists of a series of paved terraces descending to an informal glade of trees and shrubs and was designed by Percy Cane (1881–1976) in 1956. A different combination of naturalism and formality characterises the design of Sir Geoffrey Jellicoe for the grounds of the Church of Ireland Cathedral at Armagh, and the layout of John Codrington for the public park at Adare, County Limerick, for Nancy, Countess of Dunraven. Formal settings have been provided for two pavilion-like houses, one by Codrington for a new house at Slevyre, County Tipperary, and the other by Russell Page (1906–1985) for the eighteenth century villa designed by the great architect, James Gandon, at Emsworth, Malahide, County Dublin. A more naturalistic approach to design and planting is taken by Lanning Roper (1912–1983) in his designs for various gardens in Ireland, the principal ones being those at Trinity College, Dublin,[3] Glenveagh Castle and Marble Hill, County Donegal. Some of the more notable design features at Glenveagh Castle were the work of the garden architect, James Russell, however, including the dramatic unbroken flight of steps which ascends the hillside and which is almost Aztec-like in appearance. A similarly exotic feature is the Chinese Moon Garden at Drenagh, County Londonderry, devised by the Canadian landscape gardener, Frances Rhoades.

The combination in the one garden design of formality of layout next to the house with increasing naturalness of design as the garden reaches out into the surrounding landscape, together with an occasional note of exoticism, appears to epitomise contemporary garden design.

It is encouraging to reflect that these efforts can be taken as examples of gardens up and down the country, perhaps small in the context of those of former days, but evincing a very personal care and understanding of the great wealth of plant species available to us today The acme of such skilled culture is seen in the growing of alpine plants from the high mountains of the world. We have seen how some large rock gardens were made in Ireland in the past. Today rock gardens are small. Since this type of garden is especially vulnerable, depending heavily on the owner-creator, the activities of the Alpine Garden Society (p. **XX**) are important in encouraging newcomers and in maintaining rare plants in cultivation. Of the gardens that come to mind it will have to suffice to mention in the Republic, Beech Park, County Dublin, where the late David Shackleton cultivated a celebrated collection of alpines in addition to no less remarkable borders of herbaceous plants maintained until very recently by his son and daughter-in-law. In Northern Ireland the late Dr Molly Sanderson's garden at Ishlan, Ballymoney, County Antrim, had an air of maturity despite the ever increasing collection of rare plants of all types. As one more example, Robert Gordon's garden at Tyanee in County Londonderry, not far from the town of Portglenone, also shows this skill and care in developing the beauties of the individual plant, a kind of gardening so different from the sweeping efforts of the landscapers, but just as important to the human spirit. Though for historical reasons there was no development of a distinctive Irish cottage garden, the modern dwellings clustered today round every town and village need pleasant gardens round them, a desire aided by the ready availability of container grown plants in garden centres throughout the country and encouraged by the National Gardens Competition, organised by Bord Failté over the last 30 years. The Royal Horticultural Society of Ireland has more members every year, and local societies have been founded or revived in many places in town and country. Though it is harder now to stage shows with large exhibits than in the days when such events were a day off and a source of professional pride for head gardeners, new classes are popular, notably those for flower arrangements. Excursions to see gardens in Ireland and abroad are well attended.

Along with the interest in preserving our heritage gardens has come the realisation that many good plants are being lost to cultivation. No longer can we rely on nurseries to maintain large collections of cultivars. It is good, therefore, that the Irish Garden Plant Society is, in co-operation with its British counterparts under the umbrella of the National Council for the Conservation of Plants and Gardens (NCCPG), seeking to preserve plants, particularly cultivars, that are in danger of being lost. This society has successfully launched a journal named *Moorea* in commemoration of the Moores of Glasnevin. The Landscape Association of Ireland is a body of professionals concerned with maintaining and improving the appearance of our parks, gardens and our countryside in general, holding conferences to discuss effective action. Responsibility for the landscape as a whole has become fragmented; though the setting of a few industrial and many private dwellings has been good, too many are isolated efforts not always blending happily with their surroundings and not sufficient to ensure a trend towards a generally pleasing landscape. This can only come about when there is close cooperation between all bodies, public and large and small, in a common effort to provide an integrated landscape setting for the future.

Whatever social changes may come, Ireland shares with Britain one of the most favourable climates in the world for gardening, and the love of plants is so much part of human nature that there will always be gardens as long as the world endures. Nevertheless, to glance back to the past helps us to appreciate the distinctiveness of Irish gardens and to realise what we do to carry forward this heritage to the future.

Chapter 1

1   Lhuyd, E. 1712. *Philosophical transactions* 27: 524.
2   Lloyd he had reverted to the old spelling of his name.
3   Mitchell, F. 1976. *The Irish landscape*. London.
4   McEntee, M. A. 1978. *Irish journal of agricultural research* 17: 168169.
5   Talbot de Malahide, M. 1965. *Journal of the Royal Horticultural Society* 90: 207-17, 245-50.
6   Mitchell, F. 1986. *The Shell guide to the Irish landscape*. p. 79. Dublin.
7   Mitchell, F. 1986. p. 99.
8   Richey, A. G. 1879. *Ancient laws of Ireland*. Vol. 4. Dublin.
9   Graves, R. 1961. *The white goddess*. London. p. 202.
10   Kelly, F. 1976. The old Irish tree-list. *Celtica* 11: 107-124. Nelson, E. C. & Walsh, W. F. 1993. *The trees of Ireland*. Dublin. pp. 14-16.
11   Forsyth. W. 1810. *A treatise on the culture and management of fruit trees*. 5th edition. London. p. 455.
12   MacCana, P. 1970. *Celtic mythology*. London. p. 50.
13   Plummer, C. (editor). 1922. *The lives of the Irish saints*. Vol. 2. Oxford.
14   Reeves, W. (editor). 1894. *The life of St Columban by Adamnan*. Vol. 3, p. 10. Oxford.
15   Joyce, P. W. 1903. *A social history of Ancient Ireland*. London. p.5.
16   Murphy, G. 1958. *Early Irish lyrics*. Oxford. p. 8.
17   Murphy, T. (editor) *Annals of Clonmacnoise*.
18   Bede. *A history of the English church and people*. Book I, chapter 1.
19   Reeves, W. 1894. p. 206.
20   de Suse, J. 1905. *Ionae Vitae Sanctorum Columbani*. Vol. 2, 25, p. 292. Hanover & Leipzig.
21   Hore, P.H. 1900. *A history of the town and county of Wexford*. Vol. 1, pp. 10-41. London.
22   Meyer, K. 1913. *Ancient Irish poetry*. London.
23   Moloney, M. F. 1919. *Irish ethno-botany*. Dublin. p. 59.
24   Sweetman, H. S. (editor) 1877. *Calendar of documents relating to Ireland (1252-1284)*. London. p. 81.
25   Curtis, E. (editor) 1932. *Calendar of Ormonde deeds (11721350)*. Dublin. p. 150.
26   Sweetman, H. S. 1877. p. 81.
27   Harbison, P. 1970. *A guide to the national monuments of Ireland*. Dublin. p. 51.
28   Curtis, E. 1932.
29   Sweetman, H. S. 1886. *Calendar of documents relating to Ireland (1302-7)*. London. p. 86.
30   Meskimmin, S. 1811. *Carrickfergus*. Belfast. p. 116.
31   *Irish farmers' journal & weekly intelligencer* 3 (24 December 1814): 130.
32   Trinity College, Dublin. Ms Journal of Louisa Beaufort (1807), f. 2.
33   Harris, W. 1744. *The antient and present state of the County of Down*. Dublin. p. 55.
34   Young, A. 1780. *A tour in Ireland*. Vol 2, p. 95. Dublin.
35   Sweetman, H. S. (editor). 1875. *Calendar of documents relating to Ireland (1171-1251)*. London. p. 77.
36   Ball, F. E. 1905. *A history of the County of Dublin*. Vol. 3, p. 81. Dublin.
37   de Breffny B. & ffolliott, R. 1975. *The houses of Ireland*. London. p. 15.
38   de Breffny, B. 1977. *The castles of Ireland*. London. p. 34.
39   Salisbury Ms. Grounde Plot of the Castle of Caire', 1599.
40   *Journal of the Royal Society of Antiquaries of Ireland*, 10 (ser. 5): 403.
41   *Irish farmer's gazette* (June 1851).
42   Moloney, M. F. 1919. p. 59.
43   O'Donnell, T. J. (editor). 1960. *Selections from the Zoilomastic of Philip O'Sullivan Beare*. Dublin. Appendix A.
44   Lombard, P. 1632. *De Regno Hiberniae*. Louvain.
45   Cecil, E. 1910. *A history of gardening in England*. London. p. 87.
46   Hamilton, H. C. (editor). *Calendar of state papers relating to Ireland, (1586-88)*. London. p. 240.
47   Salaman, R. N. 1949. *The history and social influence of the potato*. Cambridge.
48   Lewis, S. 1837. *A topographical dictionary of Ireland*. Vol. 1, p. 10. London.
49   Hennessy, P. *Life of Sir Walter Raleigh*, quoted by Salaman, R.N. 1949.
50   Trinity College, Dublin. Ms. 1209/67.
51   Nelson, E. C. 1991. 'Reserved to the Fellows': four centuries of gardens at Trinity College Dublin, in Holland, C. H. (editor). *Trinity College Dublin and the idea of a university*. Dublin. pp. 185-222.
52   Salisbury Ms.: see Fig. 42 in Holland, C. H. 1991.
53   Collier, J. P. (editor) 1891. *The poetical works of Edmund Spenser*. London. p. 187.
54   Grossart, A. (editor) 1868. *The Lismore papers*. Vol. I, (1613) p. 50, (1615) p. 98, (1617) p. 146.
55   Grossart, A. 1868. Vol. I, p. 243.
56   Dinely, T. 1870. *A voyage through the kingdom of Ireland*. Dublin. p. 74.
57   *Quarterly bulletin of the Irish Georgian Society* 20 (January-June 1977).
58   Benn, G. 1823. *A history of the town of Belfast*. Belfast. p. 242.
59   *Anthologia Hibernica* 1 (1634): 195.
60   Craig, M. 1976. *Portumna Castle*. Dublin.
61   Trinity College Dublin. Ms. 1209 (32).
62   Russell, C. W. (editor) 1877. *The calendar of state papers of Ireland (1611-4)*. London. p. 127.
63   Grossart, A. 1868. Vol. 4, p. 185.
64   Grossart, A. 1868. Vol. 4, p. 218.

65   Grossart, A. 1868. Vol. 4, p. 219.
66   Grossart, A. 1868. Vol. 4, p. 206.
67   Grossart, A. 1868. Vol. 4, p. 121.
68   Trinity College Dublin. Ms.
69   Bodleian Library, Oxford. Carte Ms. 110, f 1102.
70   Falkiner, C. L. 1911. *Calendar of Ormonde manuscripts*. Vol. 6, p. 282. London.
71   *Kilkenny Archaeological Society journal* 4 (new series) (1862): 105.
72   Falkiner, C. L. 1911.
73   Falkiner, C. L. 1911. pp. 150, 169, 183.
74   Falkiner, C. L. 1911. p. 280.
75   Falkiner, C. L. 1911. p. 465.
761   651, published in English in 1670.
77   *Quarterly bulletin of the Irish Georgian Society* 18 (April-September 1975).
78   *Country life* 162 (1977): 78-81, 146-149.
79   Boedlein Library, Oxford. Petty Mss.
80   *The Dublin intelligencer* (17 April 1711).
81   Grove White, J. 1913. *Historical and geographical notes of Buttevant etc.* Vol. 3, p. 20. Cork.
82   Singer, S. W. (editor) 1828. *State letters of Henry, 2nd Earl of Clarendon.* Vol. 1, pp. 237, 407. London.
83   Public Records Office of Northern Ireland, Belfast. Ms. Map of Limavady.
84   Ball, F. E. 1902. *A history of the county of Dublin.* Dublin.
85   National Archives, Dublin. Ms. Minute books, Board of Governors, Royal Hospital, Kilmainham.
86   National Archives, Dublin. Ms. Minute books, Board of Governors, Royal Hospital, Kilmainham.
87   Cecil, E. 1910. pp. 189, 210.
88   National Library of Ireland, Dublin. Phillips Ms. 6682. M. Dowdall, 'A description of County Longford'.
89   Nelson, E. C. 1983. Sir Arthur Rawdon (1662-1695) of Moira: his life and letters, family and friends and his Jamaican plants. *Proceedings of the Belfast Natural History and Philosophical Society* 10: 30-52.
90   Harris, W. 1744. p. 103; Nelson, E. C. 1983.
91   Mahaffey, R. P. (editor) 1907. *Calendar of the state papers of Ireland, 1663-1665.* London. pp. 589, 636, 637.
92   Mahaffey, R. P. (editor) 1907. *Calendar of the state papers of Ireland, 1647-1660.* London. p. 621.
93   Mahaffey, R. P. (editor) 1907. *Calendar of the state papers of Ireland, 1663-1665.* London. p. 440.
94   Mahaffey, R. P. (editor) 1908. *Calendar of the state papers of Ireland, 1666-1669.* London. p. 38
95   Mahaffey, R. P. 1908. p. 558.
96   Mahaffey, R. P. 1908. p. 693.
97   Mahaffey, R. P. 1908. p. 530.
98   Mahaffey, R. P. 1908. pp. 382, 392, 440.
99   *Ulster journal of archaeology* 3 (1885): 56-57.
100   Royal Irish Academy, Dublin. Ms. minute book of the Florists' Club. Nelson, E. C. 1982. The Dublin Florists' Club in the mid-eighteenth century. Garden history 10: 142-148.

101   *The flying post, Dublin* (28 December 1711).
102   Green, D. 1956. *Gardener to Queen Anne.* Oxford. Plate 21.
103   Chart, D. A. (editor). 1913. *Historic Manuscripts Commission report on various collections.* Vol. 8, p. 242. London.
104   Chart, D. A. 1913. p. 261.
105   Chart, D. A. 1913. p. 267.
106   Ainsworth, J. 1961. *The Inchiquin manuscripts.* Dublin. p. 109.
107   Ainsworth, J. 1961. p. 116.
108   National Library of Ireland, Dublin. Ms. 2791.
109   Switzer, S. 1718. *Iconographica rustica.* London.
110   MacLysaght, E. 1942. *The Kenmare manuscripts.* Dublin. p. 121.
111   McCracken, E. 1979. Irish nurseries and nurseryman, in Nelson, E. C. & Brady, A. (editors). *Irish gardening and horticulture.* Dublin. p. 180.
112   *Country life* 162 (14 July 1977): 80.
113   Colvin, H. & Craig, M. 1964. *The architectural drawings in the library of Elton Hall.* Oxford. Plate 74.
114   Malins, E. & The Knight of Glin. 1976. *Lost demesnes.* London. p. 13.
115   Malins, E. & The Knight of Glin. 1976. p. 9.
116   Malins, E. & The Knight of Glin. 1976. p. 28.
117   *Journal of the Kildare Archaeological Society* 2 (1898), no. 5.
118   Guinness, D. & Ryan, W. 1971. *Irish houses and castles.* London. p. 200.
119   Guinness, D. & Ryan, W. 1971. p. 127.

Chapter 2

1   The claim that Addison lived at Glasnevin is a myth - Nelson, E. C. & McCracken, E. M. 1987. *'The brightest jewel': a history of the National Botanic Gardens, Glasnevin, Dublin.* Kilkenny. pp. 40-41.
2   Malins, E. & The Knight of Glin. 1976. *Lost demesnes.* London. p. 37.
3   Strickland, W. The Chetwodes of Woodbrook, Queen's County. *Journal of the Kildare Archaeological Society* 9: 213.
4   Hussey, C. 1967. *English gardens and landscape 1700-1750.* London. p. 81.
5   Williams, H. *The poems of Jonathan Swift.* Vol. 2, p. 374.
6   Nelson, E. C. & McCracken, E. M. 1987.
7   Malins, E. & The Knight of Glin. 1976. p. 34.
8   National Gallery of Ireland, Dublin.
9   Malins E. & The Knight of Glin. 1976. p. 43.
10   Malins E. & The Knight of Glin. 1976. p. 91.
11   Dalton, J. 1838. *The history of the county of Dublin.*
12   McParland, E. 1976. The buildings of Trinity College, Dublin. *Country life* 159: 2.
13   *Walker's Hibernian magazine* (1786): 593.
14   Malins, E. & The Knight of Glin. 1976. p. 61.

15   *Faulkiner's Dublin journal* (11 October 1746).

16   *Walker's Hibernian magazine* (November 1794): 437.

17   Rankin, P. 1972. *Irish building ventures of the Earl Bishop of Derry.* Belfast.

18   Public Records Office of Northern Ireland, Belfast. The Shannon Papers: Ms letter from Robert Pratt to the Earl of Shannon, 2 December 1760.

19   *Journal of the Kildare Archaeological Society* 9: 219.

20   Nelson, E. C. & Colvin, C. 1988. 'Building castles of flowers' — Maria Edgeworth as gardener. *Garden history* 16: 5870.

21   National Library of Ireland, Dublin. Tighe Papers: Mss 88025.

22   Fitzgerald, B. (editor) 1953. *The correspondence of Emily Duchess of Leinster (1731-1814).* Dublin. p. 36.

23   Nelson, E. C. 1995. Patrick Browne and the flowers of Mayo: a biographical essay, in Nelson E. C. & Walsh, W. F. 1995. *Flowers of Mayo. Dr Patrick Browne's Fasciculus Plantarum Hibernië 1788.* Dublin: Edmund Burke Publ.

24   Nelson, E. C. & Walsh, W. F. 1995. *Flowers of Mayo. Dr Patrick Browne's Fasciculus Plantarum Hibernië 1788.* Dublin: Edmund Burke Publ.

25   Nelson E. C. & Walsh, W. F. 1995. Appendix I.

26   Linnean Society, London. P. Browne Mss.

27   Pim, S. 1979. The history of gardening in Ireland, in Nelson E. C. & Brady, A. (editors) *Irish gardening and horticulture.* Dublin. p. 49. Duthie, R. 1987. Introduction of plants to Britain in the 16th and 17th centuries by strangers and refugees. *Proceedings of the Huguenot Society* 24: 403-420. Duthie, R. 1988. Some pre-1800 illustrations of auriculas and the information they provide about the plant in former times. *National Auricula and Primula Society (Southern Section) Yearbook:* 37-46.

28   Kilruddery Mss. Household accounts E/2/I (with acknowledgement to The Knight of Glin).

29   Nelson, E. C. 1982. The Dublin Florists' Club in the mid-eighteenth century. Garden history 10: 142-148.

30   Parkinson, J. 1629. *Paradisus in sole paradisi terrestris.* London.

31   Longfield, A. K. 1975. Samuel Dixon. *Bulletin of the Irish Georgian Society* 18: 109-136.

32   Temple, W. 1685. *Upon the gardens of Epicurus.* London.

33   Malins, E. & The Knight of Glin. 1976. p. 68.

34   *A statistical survey of the county of Cavan.* Dublin. (1802).

35   Nelson, E. C. 1987. Joseph Spence's plans for an Irish garden. *Garden history* 15: 1218.

36   Stroud, D. 1975. *Capability Brown.* London. p. 61.

37   Fitzgerald, B. 1953. Vol 1, p. 129.

38   Stroud, D. 1975. p. 246.

39   Malins E. & The Knight of Glin. 1976. p. 102.

40   Malins, E. & The Knight of Glin. 1975. p. 71.

41   Trinity College, Dublin. Daniel Beaufort Ms. diary, p. 75.

42   Trinity College, Dublin. Daniel Beaufort Ms. diary, p. 75.

43   National Library of Ireland, Dublin. Ms 3275.

44   Coote, C. 1801. *A general view of the Queen's County.* Dublin. p. 66.

45   Dutton, H. 1824. *A statistical survey of the county of Galway.* Dublin.

46   Dionizy, L. M. M. 1986. *Oxford companion to gardens.* Oxford. p. 374.

47   Neale, J. P. 1823. *Views of the seats of noblemen and gentlemen.* London.

48   Neale, J. P. 1823.

49   Dutton H. 1802. *Observations on Mr Archer's Statistical survey of Dublin.* Dublin.

50   Dutton, H. 1802.

51   Dutton, H. 1824.

52   Rankin, P. 1972.

53   Belmore Mss.

54   Belmore Mss.

55   [Hayes, S.] 1794. *A practical treatise on planting.* Dublin. p. 106.

56   Ferrar, J. 1796. *A view of ancient and modern Dublin.* Dublin.

57   Dutton, H. 1824.

58   Fitzgerald, B. 1953. Vol. 1, p. 150.

59   Fitzgerald, B. 1953. Vol. 3, p. 214.

60   Dutton, H. 1824. p. 440.

61   Coote, C. 1803. *A statistical survey of the County Armagh.* Dublin. p. 361.

62   *Falkiner's Dublin journal* (24 July 1787).

63   *Falkiner's Dublin journal* (24 July 1787).

64   Public Records Office of Northern Ireland, Belfast. Annesley Mss.

65   National Library of Ireland, Dublin. Ms minute book of the Commissioners of Mountjoy Square.

66   National Gallery of Ireland, Dublin.

67   Public Records Office of Northern Ireland, Belfast. Caledon Mss. Estate ledger 1790-1809 (D 2433/39/3); Journal 1790-1809 (D 2433/33/3).

68   Public Records Office of Northern Ireland, Belfast. Caledon Mss. Estate ledger 1790-1809 (D 2433/39/3); Journal 1790-1809 (D 2433/33/3).

69   National Library of Ireland, Dublin. Ms 3275.

70   Public Records Office of Northern Ireland, Belfast. Ms. D 1470/3.

71   Dutton, H. 1824. p. 56.

72   Brewer, H. & Neale, J. P. 1825. *The beauties of Ireland.* London.

73   Brewer, H. & Neale, J. P. 1825.

74   Brewer, H. & Neale, J. P. 1825.

75   Coote, C. 1801.

76   *Journal of Irish agriculture and practical horticulture* (1819).

77   *Journal of Irish agriculture and practical horticulture* (1826).

78 Longford/Westmeath Public Library, Mullingar. Ms.

79 Hussy Ms., Donard, County Wicklow.

80 *Irish farmer's and gardener's magazine* 1 (1834): 660.

81 *The gardener's magazine* 2 (1827): 149.

82 Murphy, E. 1834. Statistical notices Mountshannon. *Irish farmer's and gardener's magazine* 1 (1833-1834): 647.

83 *Irish farmer's journal and weekly intelligencer* (22 October 1819): 44.

84 Dutton, H. 1808. *A statistical survey of the county of Clare.* Dublin. Preface.

85 Dutton, H. 1808.

86 Dutton, H. 1802. *Observations on Mr Archer's statistical survey of the county of Dublin.*

87 Dutton, H. 1808. p. 161.

88 Dutton, H. 1808. p. 161.

89 *Irish farmer's journal and weekly intelligencer* (18 September 1813): 17.

90 *Irish farmer's journal and weekly intelligencer* (1818).

91 Dutton, H. 1824.

92 Dutton, H. 1824.

93 Dutton, H. 1824.

94 Dutton, H. 1824. p. 441.

95 Dutton, H. 1824. p. 435.

96 Neale, J. P. 1823.

97 Puckler-Muskau, H. 1832. *A tour of England, Ireland ...* London. p. 359.

98 *Irish farmer's journal and weekly intelligencer* (1813)

99 Dutton H. 1808.

100 *Irish farmer's journal and weekly intelligencer* (16 December 1815).

101 Dutton, H. 1802.

102 Dutton, H. 1802.

103 *Irish farmer's and gardener's magazine* 1 (1833): 235.

104 *The gardener's magazine* (June 1828).

105 *Irish farmer's and gardener's magazine* (1842): 201.

106 *Dictionary of national biography.* Vol. 3, p. 1264. (1908). London.

107 *Dictionary of national biography.* Vol. 3, p. 1264. (1908). London.

108 Gilpin, W. S. 1832. *Practical hints upon landscape gardening.* London. p. 45.

109 Slane Castle Mss.

Chapter 3

1 Loudon, J. C. 1850. *The villa gardener.* London. p. 3.

2 Loudon, J. C. 1822. *An encyclopaedia of gardening.* London. p. 80.

3 Bence-Jones, M. 1978. *Burke's guide to country houses, volume 1, Ireland.* London. p. 107.

4 Malins, E., & The Knight of Glin. 1976. *Lost demesnes.* London. p. 139.

5 Malins, E. & The Knight of Glin. 1976. p. 63.

6 Loudon, J. C. 1844. *Arboretum et fruticetum Britannicum.* London. p. 108.

7 Young, A. 1790. *A tour of Ireland.* Dublin.

8 Nelson, E. C. & McCracken, E. M. 1987. 'The brightest jewel': a history of the National Botanic Gardens, Glasnevin, Dublin.* Kilkenny. p. 25.

9 Linnean Society, London. Ellis Mss. J. Foster to J. Ellis 15 October 1770 (quoted by Nelson, E. C. & McCracken, 1987. p. 27.)

10 Nelson, E. C. (editor) & McKinley, D. L. 1991. *Aphrodite's mousetrap. A biography of Venus's Flytrap with facsimiles of an original pamphlet and the manuscripts of John Ellis, F.R.S.* Aberystwyth.

11 Linnean Society, London. Ellis Mss. J. Foster to J. Ellis 12 October 1768.

12 Bean, W. J. 1976. *Trees and shrubs hardy in the British Isles.* (8th edition) Vol. 3, p. 479. London.

13 Bean W. J. 1976. Vol. 3, p. 479.

14 Loudon, J. C. 1844. p. 109.

15 Loudon J. C. 1844. p. 1952.

16 Loudon, J. C. 1844. p. 109.

17 Loudon, J. C. 1844. p. 109. Nelson, E. C. & Colvin, C. 1988. Building castles of flowers' - Maria Edgeworth as gardener. *Garden history* 16: 58-70.

18 Loudon, J. C. 1844. p. 109.

19 Bean, W. J. 1976. Vol 3, p. 498.

20 McCracken E. M. 1979. Nurseries and seedshops, in Nelson, E. C. & Brady, A. (editors) 1979. *Irish gardening and horticulture.* Dublin. p. 182. Nelson, E. C. & McCracken, E. M. 1987.

21 Wakefield, E. 1812. *An account of Ireland, statistical and political.* London. p. 562.

22 Public Records Office of Northern Ireland, Belfast. Foster/Massereene Papers.

23 Wakefield, E. 1812. p. 562.

24 Malins E. & The Knight of Glin. 1976, p.119.

25 Loudon, J. C. 1844. p. 110.

26 Anonymous. [not dated]. *Guide to Tullynally.*

27 Nelson E. C. & Colvin, C. 1988.

28 Loudon J. C. 1844. p. 110.

29 Loudon J. C. 1844. p. 2120.

30 *Irish farmer's and gardener's magazine* 1 (1834): 101, 264, 564.

31 *The gardener's magazine* 13 (1837).

32 *Magazine of natural history* 1: 403-406. *Magazine of natural history* 2: 305-310.

33 Trinity College Dublin. Louisa Beaufort Mss. Diary 1807, p. 24. *Irish farmer's journal* (9 September 1815). *Transactions of the Royal Irish Academy.*

34 *Magazine of natural history* 1: 403-406. *Magazine of natural history* 2: 305-310.

35 Bean W. J. 1976. Vol. 3, p. 510.

36 Nelson, E. C. & Andrews, S., 1992. The origin of *Ilex x altaclerensis* (Loudon) Dallimore Lawsoniana' and a confusion of Hodginses. *Glasra* 1 (n.s.): 111-114.

37   National Library of Ireland, Dublin.
38   Loudon, J. C. 1838. p. 269.
39   *Dublin penny journal* 1 (1832): 41-42.
40   Ferrar, J. 1807. *A view of antient and modern Dublin*. Dublin.
41   Loudon, J. C. 1822. p.125.
42   Loudon J. C. 1838. Vol. 1, pp. 113, 129.
43   Loudon, J. C. 1822. p. 115.
44   Loudon J.C. 1822. p. 112.
45   Loudon J. C. 1822. p. 125.
46   Loudon J. C. 1822. p. 81.
47   *The gardener's magazine* (1818).
48   Malins E. & Bowe P. 1980. *Irish gardens and demesnes from 1830*. London. p. 20.
49   Malins, E. & Bowe, P. 1980. p. 20.
50   Trinity College, Dublin. Mss.
51   Loudon, J. C. 1838. p. 1095.
52   *The gardener's magazine* 2 (1826): 14.
53   *The gardener's magazine* 5 (1829): 112.

Chapter 4

1   William Molyneux to his brother Thomas, quoted by Nelson, E. C. & McCracken, E. C. 1987. *'The brightest jewel': a history of the National Botanic Gardens, Glasnevin, Dublin*. Kilkenny. p. 8.
2   Kirkpatrick T. P. C 1912. *History of medical teaching in Trinity College, Dublin*. Dublin. p. 204. Nelson, E. C. 1982. The influence of Leiden on botany in Dublin in the early eighteenth century. *Huntia* 4: 133-146. Nelson, E. C. 1991. 'Reserved to the Fellows': four centuries of gardens at Trinity College, Dublin, In Holland C. (editor). *Trinity College Dublin and the idea of a university*. Dublin. pp. 185-222. Nelson, E. C. 1993. Botany and medicine; Dublin and Leiden. *Journal of the Irish Colleges of Physicians and Surgeons 22:* 133-136.
3   Botany Library, The Natural History Museum, London, quoted by Nelson, E. C. & McCracken, E. M. 1987; Nelson, E. C. 1991.
4   Nelson, E. C. 1987. Botany, medicine and politics in eighteenth century Dublin and the origin of Irish botanical gardens. *Moorea* 6: 33-44. Nelson, E. C. 1991.
5   *Transactions of the Dublin Society* 4 (1804): 215-221.
6   Colgan, N. 1904. *Flora of County Dublin*. Dublin. p. xxiii.
7   Dublin Society. Ms minute book 1793.
8   Warburton, J., Whitelaw J., & Walsh R., 1818. *History of the city of Dublin*. Dublin.
9   Warburton, J., Whitelaw J., & Walsh R., 1818. p. 130.
10   Nelson E. C. 1981. A select annotated bibliography of the National Botanic Gardens, Glasnevin, Dublin. *Glasra* 5: 1-20.
11   Colgan, N. 1904. p.xxxv.
12   *Proceedings of the Dublin Society* (1819-1820).
13   *Proceedings of the Dublin Society* (27 April 1820).
14   *Quarterly journal of forestry 63* (1969): 242-251. Nelson, E. C. & McCracken, E. M. 1987.
15   Nelson, E. C. 1987.
16   *Notes from the Botanical School of Trinity College, Dublin* 1 (1896): 1-14. Nelson, E. C. 1991.
17   *The gardener's magazine* 7 (1831): 229.
18   *The gardener's magazine* 7 (1831): 230.
19   *Irish farmer's and gardener's magazine* 1 (1834): 468.
20   Nelson, E. C. & Probert, A. 1994. *A man who can speak of plants: Dr Thomas Coulter (1793-1843) of Dundalk in Ireland, Mexico and Alta California*. Dublin.
21   Moore, D. 1850. *Handbook for the Botanic Gardens of the Royal Dublin Society, Glasnevin*. Dublin.
22   Nelson, E. C. 1992. William Henry Harvey as Colonial Treasurer at the Cape of Good Hope: a case of depression and bowdlerized history. *Archives of natural history 19:* 171-180.
23   Nelson, E. C. & McCracken, E. M. 1987.
24   *The Irish naturalist* 27 (1918): 162-163.
25   *The gardeners' chronicle* (1866): 537-538.
26   *Blumea* 2 (1962): 427-493.
27   *Journal of the Cork Historical & Archaeological Society* 46 (2nd series) (1941).
28   Nelson, E. C. 1990. James and Thomas Drummond, as curators in Irish botanic gardens. *Archives of natural history 17:* 4965.
29   Power, T. 1845. *Botanist's guide to the county of Cork*. London & Cork.
30   Power, T. 1845.
31   *Journal of the Cork Historical and Historical Society* 62 (1957): 77-94. McCracken, E. M. 1980. The Cork Botanic Garden. *Garden history* 8: 41-45.
32   Power, T. 1845.
33   *The gardener's magazine* 4 (1828): 164.
34   Stewart, S. A, & Corry, T. H. 1888. *Flora of the north east of Ireland* Cambridge. p. xix.
35   McCracken, E. M. 1970. *The palm house and Botanic Garden, Belfast*. Belfast.
36   *The gardener's chronicle* 3 (new series) (1875): 817.
37   McCracken, E. M. 1970. *The Palm House*. Belfast: Belfast Parks. (not dated, c. 1980)
38   Maxwell, R. 1991. The pride of M'Kimm. *The Garden* 116: 118-121.
39   *The gardener's chronicle* 23 (1897): 50-53.
40   *The gardener's chronicle* 36 (1904): 417-418.
41   *Irish farmer's and gardener's magazine* 1(1834): 420.
42   Fitzgerald, P. & M'Gregor J. J. 1827. *History, topography and antiquities of the county and city of Limerick*. Dublin. p. 614.
43   Lenehan, M. 1866. *Limerick: its history and antiquities*. Dublin.

Chapter 5

1   *Irish farmer's and gardener's magazine* 1 (1834): 658.

2 Nelson, E. C. 1979. To protect and promote the science of horticulture' - the origins and early history of the Royal Horticultural Society of Ireland 1816-1830. *Garden history 6 (3)*: 65-71. See also *Irish farmer's journal and weekly intelligencer* (15 March 1817); Faulkiner's journal (10 April 1817).

3 *Irish farmer's and gardener's magazine* (1840): 378.

4 *Irish farmer's and gardener's magazine* (1836): 233.

5 *The gardener's chronicle* (1849): 71.

6 *The gardener's chronicle* (1848): 688.

7 *The gardener's chronicle* (1848): 703.

8 *The gardener's chronicle* (1848): 315.

9 *The gardener's chronicle* (1848): 365.

10 *The gardener's chronicle* (1848): 419.

11 *The gardener's chronicle* (1848): 452.

12 *The gardener's chronicle* (1848): 731.

13 *The gardener's chronicle* (1848): 651.

14 *The gardener's chronicle* (1848): 703.

15 *The gardener's chronicle* (1848): 795.

16 *The gardener's chronicle* (1848): 813.

17 *The gardener's chronicle* (1848): 615.

18 *The gardener's chronicle* (1849): 19-20.

19 *The gardener's chronicle* (1849): 278-279.

20 *The gardener's chronicle* (1849): 275.

21 *Irish farmer's gazette* 8 (1849): 237-238.

22 *Irish farmer's gazette* 8 (1849): 237-238.

23 *Irish farmer's gazette* 8 (1849): 370.

24 *Irish farmer's gazette* 8 (1849): 394.

25 *The gardener's chronicle* 19 (1854): 303.

26 *Irish farmer's and gardener's magazine* 7 (1840): 376-380.

27 *Irish farmer's and gardener's magazine* 4 (1837): 223.

28 *Irish farmer's and gardener's magazine* 7 (1840): 189.

29 *Irish farmer's and gardener's magazine* 6 (1839): 237.

30 *Irish farmer's and gardener's magazine* 1 (1833-1834): 51, 103, 420, 574.

31 *Irish farmer's and gardener's magazine* 3 (1836): 502.

32 *The gardener's magazine* 6 (1830): 26-27.

33 *The gardener's magazine* (1829).

34 Nelson, E. C. (editor). 1983. *John Lyons and his orchid manual*. Kilkenny: Boethius Press. Facsimile of Lyons' book (1843) with modern introduction.

35 County Library, Mullingar.

Chapter 6

1 Watkin, D. 1974. *The life and works of C. R. Cockerell*. London. p. 167.

2 Colvin, H. 1954. *A biographical dictionary of English architects 1660-1840*. London. p. 505.

3 Colvin, H. 1954. p. 505.

4 Kilruddery Mss.

5 Powerscourt Mss. Powerscourt plans, vol. 1, p. 39.

6 Colvin, H. 1954. p. 50.

7 Bence-Jones M. 1978. *Burke's guide to country houses Vol. 1. Ireland*. London. p. 211.

8 Bence-Jones M. 1978. p. 116.

9 Colvin, H. 1954. p. 50.

10 Flora and sylva 1 (1903): 95.

11 *The gardener's magazine* 1 (1825): 10-14; *The gardener's magazine* 2 (1826): 146-152.

12 *The gardener's magazine* 5 (1829): 84.

13 Fraser, J. 1844. *Handbook for travellers in Ireland*. Dublin .

14 Fraser, J. 1844.

15 Belmore Mss.

16 Weight Mss.

17 *Irish farmer's gazette* (1863): 250.

18 Loudon J. C. 1840. The landscape gardening of Humphrey Repton. London. p. 525.

19 *Irish farmer's gazette* (1863): 250.

20 *Irish farmer's gazette* (1863): 250.

21 Fraser, J. 1843. *Handbook for travellers in Ireland*. Dublin.

22 *Irish farmer's gazette* (1862): 389.

23 *Irish farmer's gazette* (1863): 250.

24 Niven, N. 1839. *A prospectus of the proposed public gardens at Monkstown Castle, Dublin*. Dublin.

25 *The garden* 7 (1875): xi-xii. Nelson, E. C. & McCracken, E. M. 1987. *'The brightest jewel': a history of the National Botanic Gardens, Glasnevin, Dublin*. Kilkenny

26 *The cottage gardener and journal of practical horticulture* (1856): 157.

27 *Irish farmer's and gardener's magazine* 1 (1833-1834): 6-8.

28 *Irish farmer's and gardener's magazine* 1 (1833-1834): 144.

29 *Irish farmer's and gardener's magazine* 1 (1833-1834): 517-520.

30 *Irish farmer's and gardener's magazine* 1 (1833-1834): 517-520.

31 *Irish farmer's and gardener's magazine* 1 (1833-1834): 517-520.

32 *Irish farmer's and gardener's magazine* 1 (1833-1834): 517-520.

33 Nelson, E. C. & McCracken, E. M. 1987.

34 Niven, N. 1838. *Visitor's companion to the Botanic Garden, Glasnevin*. Dublin.

35 Niven, N. 1838.

36 *Irish farmer's gazette* (1849).

37 *The gardeners' chronicle* (1864): 1226-1227.

38 *The cottage gardener and journal of practical horticulture* (1856): 90.

39 Niven N. 1839.

40 Niven N. 1839.

41 *Irish farmer's gazette* (1862): 243.

42 National Library of Ireland, Dublin. Ormonde Mss.

43 *The gardeners chronicle* (1864): 1179.

44 Abercorn Mss, Baronscourt.

45 National Library of Ireland, Dublin. Domville Mss.

46   National Library of Ireland, Dublin. Domville Mss.

47   Niven, N. 1863. An ornamental plan for the arrangement of the Dublin Crystal Palace Garden. *Irish farmer's gazette* (1863): 405.

48   The style of this garden, though undocumented, is similar to that at the adjoining estate of Killakee.

49   For a full account of the history of the Irish yew see Nelson E. C. 1981. The nomenclature and history in cultivation of the Irish yew *Taxus baccata* 'Fastigiata'. *Glasra* 5: 33-44. Nelson, E. C. 1981. The Irish yew. *The Garden* 106: 429-431.

50   Praeger, R. L. 1934. *The botanist in Ireland.* Dublin. p. 191.

51   *The gardeners' chronicle* (1863-1865).

52   *The cottage gardener and journal of practical horticulture* (1861): 131

53   *The cottage gardener and journal of practical horticulture* (1861): 142.

54   McCullen, J. 1992. A landscape history of The Phoenix Park, Dublin. *Glasra* 2 (new series): 83-126.

55   *The cottage gardener and journal of practical horticulture* (1861): 62.

56   *The Irish farmers' gazette* (1866): 117.

57   Niven, N. 1869. *Redemption thoughts.* Dublin.

58   *The gardeners' chronicle* (1871): no. 73, 793. Nelson, E. C. & McCracken, E. M. 1987.

59   National Botanic Gardens, Glasnevin.

60   Colby, T. 1837. *Ordnance Survey of the county of Londonderry.* Vol. 1. Dublin.

61   Moore, D. & More, A.G. 1866. *Cybele Hibernica.* Dublin.

62   *The gardeners' magazine* (1835): 117.

63   Colby, T. 1837.

64   Moore D. 1835. *Companion to the Botanical magazine.* p. 303.

65   Praeger, R. L. 1934. p. 78.

66   *Proceedings of the Royal Dublin Society* 100: iv-vi (Report for 1863).

67   *Proceedings of the Royal Dublin Society* 100: iv-vi (Report for 1863).

68   Morley B. 1972. Edward Madden. *Journal of the Royal Horticultural Society* 97: 203-206.

69   *Freeman's journal* (1839). Nelson, E. C. & McCracken, E. M. 1987.

70   Cecil, E. 1910. *A history of gardening in England.* (3rd edition) London. p. 272.

71   Nelson, E. C. 1987. *Sarracenia* hybrids raised at Glasnevin Botanic Gardens, Ireland: nomenclature and typification. *Taxon* 35: 574-578. Nelson, E. C. & McCracken, E. M. 1987.

72   *The gardeners' chronicle* (1879): 765-767; *The garden* 5 (1889): 35; *The gardeners' chronicle* (1903): 299-300; *Proceedings of the Linnean Society of London* 1902: 26-27.

73   *The gardeners' chronicle* 6 (1889): 212.

74   *The garden* 69 (1906): 18.

75   *The garden* 66 (1904): iv.

76   Nelson, E. C. 1991. The waxing of a glorious rajah. *Kew magazine* 8: 8189.

77   *The garden* 47 (1895): 306.

78   *The gardeners' chronicle* 38 (1905): 460.

79   Nelson, E. C. 1987. Who was Veronica of *The garden? Newsletter of the Garden History Society* 20: 34

80   McCracken, E. M. 1971. *The palm house and Botanic Garden, Belfast.* Belfast. p. 17.

81   Chadwick, T. C. *Sir Joseph Paxton.* London.

82   Chatsworth Mss. Letters of Joseph Paxton, 8 November 1840.

83   Chatsworth Mss. Letters of Joseph Paxton, 11 January 1858.

84   Chatsworth Mss. Letters of Joseph Paxton, p. 108

85   Chatsworth Mss. Letters of Joseph Paxton, 1 November 1840.

86   Chatsworth Mss. Letters of Joseph Paxton, 8 November 1840.

87   Chatsworth Mss. Letters of Joseph Paxton,

88   Chatsworth Mss. Letters of Joseph Paxton, 8 November 1840.

89   *Irish farmer's and gardener's magazine* 6 (1839): 87.

90   Chatsworth Mss. Letters of Joseph Paxton, 6 August 1844.

91   Chatsworth Mss. Letters of Joseph Paxton, November 1858.

92   Chatsworth Mss. Letters of Joseph Paxton, 25 September 1862.

93   Milner, H. E. 1890. *The art and practice of landscape gardening.* London.

94   Powerscourt, Viscount. 1903. *A description and history of Powerscourt.*

95   *The gardeners' chronicle* (1884): 4507.

96   *The gardeners' chronicle* (1863): 167.

97   Lyrath Mss. We are indebted to Dr E.C. Nelson for drawing this unpublished information to our attention. Nelson, E. C. 1985. A Nesfield plan for Lyrath, County Kilkenny. *Garden History* 13: 156-159

98   Temple House, County Sligo. Percival Mss.

99   Powerscourt Mss. Powerscourt plans, vol. 1, notes.

100 Powerscourt Mss. Powerscourt plans, vol. 1, notes.

101 Personal communication from Angus MacLaren Esq., a descendant of Mr Thomas.

102 Powerscourt Mss. Powerscourt plans, vol. 1, notes.

103 Powerscourt Mss. Powerscourt plans, vol. 1, notes.

104 Abercorn Mss. Baronscourt.

105 *Souvenir of the opening of St Stephen's Green as a people's park.* (1880). Dublin.

106 *The gardeners' chronicle* (1898): 510.

107 *The gardeners' chronicle* (1898): 510.

108 *The gardeners' chronicle* (1884): 510.

109 *The gardeners' chronicle* (1912): 399.

110 *The gardeners' chronicle* (1876): 107.

111 Gillman Mss. Quotation for the supply of hothouses at Powerscourt, County Wicklow.
112 *Irish gardening* (October 1911): viii.
113 *Irish gardening* (October 1916): x.
114 *The gardeners' chronicle* (1905): 512. *The Irish farmer's gazette* (1870): 266.
115 *Irish gardening* (October 1911): viii.
116 Diestelkamp, E. J. & Nelson E.C. 1979. Richard Turner's legacy. *Taisce journal* 3 (1): 4-5. Nelson, E. C. & McCracken, E. M. 1987.
117 McCracken, E. M. 1971.
118 *Catalogue of the Great Exhibition, London.* (1851). Vol. 1, p. 310.
119 Diestelkamp E. J. 1981. Richard Turner (c. 1798-1881) and his glasshouses. *Glasra* 5: 51-53.
120 Diestelkamp E. J. 1981.
121 W. Malcolmson (personal communication).
122 Malins, E. & Bowe, P. 1980. p. 39.
123 Malins, E. & Bowe, P. 1980. p. 39.
124 *The gardener's record* (8 October 1870): 472.
125 *Ordnance Survey of Ireland, King's County.* (1857). Dublin.
126 Hemphill, W. D. 1860. *Stereoscopic illustrations of Clonmel.* Dublin. p. 50.
127 Such seats, stamped with Mallet's name, are to be seen frequently in Irish gardens.
128 *The Irish farmer's gazette* (1862): 243.
129 *The Irish builder* (1 March 1880): 221.
130 The names of the manufacturers are stamped on the statuary in the garden.
131 Lady Waterford (personal communication).
132 Powerscourt, Viscount. 1903.

Chapter 7

1 Robinson, W. 1899. *The English flower garden.* (7th edition). London. p. viii.
2 Robinson, W. 1899. p.vii.
3 Taylor, G. 1954, p. 160 in Hadfield, M. (editor) *Gardener's album,* quoted in Duthie, R. E. 1974. Some notes on William Robinson. *Garden history* 2 (3): 12-21.
4 Duthie, R. E. 1974.
5 *Gardening illustrated* 57 (1935): 202.
6 *Gardening illustrated* 57 (1935): 202.
7 Taylor, G. 1951. *Some nineteenth century gardeners.* London. p. 68.
8 Taylor, G. 1951. p. 6.
9 Taylor, G. 1951. p. 69.
10 Taylor, G. 1951. p. 70.
11 *The gardeners' chronicle* (1864); *The gardeners' chronicle* (1865).
12 Robinson, W. 1868. *Gleanings from French gardens.* London. p. v.
13 Robinson, W. 1870. *Alpine flowers for English gardens.* London.
14 *The garden* 15 (1879): 298; *The garden* 1 (1872): 528.
15 Robinson W. 1883. *The English flower garden.* (1st edition) London.
16 Robinson, W. 1897. *The English flower garden.* (?? edition) London. p. 741.
17 Robinson, W. 1897. p. 2.
18 Morley B. D. & Nelson E. C. 1979. Irish horticulturists II: William Edward Gumbleton (1840-1911) connoisseur and bibliophile. *Garden history* 7 (3): 5365.
19 *The gardeners' chronicle* 49 (3rd series) (1911): 205.
20 *The gardeners' chronicle* 20 (1896): 506-507
21 *The gardeners' chronicle* 49 (3rd series) (1911): 255.
22 *The gardeners' chronicle* 49 (3rd series) 1911: 255.
23 *The gardeners' chronicle* 101 (1937): 164-165.
24 *The gardeners' chronicle* 101 (1937): 164-165.
25 Nelson, E. C. 1979. *Magnolia campbellii* in County Cork. *The garden* 104: 495-496.
26 Lieut. Commander A. Crosbie (Cobh; personal communication).
27 Lieut. Commander A. Crosbie (Cobh; personal communication).
28 Crawford, T. & Nelson, E. C. 1979. Irish horticulturists I: W. H. Crawford. *Garden history* 7 (2): 23-26.
29 Bean, W. J. 1973. *Trees and shrubs hardy in the British Isles.* (8th edition). Vol. 2, p. 644.
30 Crawford, T. & Nelson, E. C. 1979.
31 Adair, J. 1878. *Hints on the culture of ornamental plants in Ireland.* (3rd edition) Dublin.
32 Walsh, W. F. & Nelson, E. C. 1987. *An Irish florilegium II.* London.
33 *The garden* 9 (1876): 48.
34 *The gardeners' chronicle* 4 (3rd series) (1888): 485.
35 *The garden* 34 (1888): 403.
36 40. Crawford, T. & Nelson E. C. 1979.
37 *The gardeners' chronicle* 4 (3rd series) (1888): 485.
38 *The garden* 41 (1892): 163.
39 Willis, D. 1978. The daffodil map of Ireland. *Daffodils in Ireland.* Bangor. p. 12.
40 *The garden* 61 (1902): iv.
41 *Gardening illustrated* 57 (1935): 202.
42 *Gardening illustrated* 57 (1935): 202.
43 Nelson, E. C. & Elliott, B. 1988. The strange death of William Robinson. *Garden History Society Newsletter Autumn 1986*: 11-12.
44 7. Pim, S. 1984. *The wood and the trees. A biography of Augustine Henry.* (2nd edition) Kilkenny. Morley B. D. 1979. Augustine Henry: his botanical activities in China, 1882-1890. *Glasra* 3: 21-81.
45 Nelson, E. C. 1984. The garden history of Augustine Henry's plants, in Pim, S. 1984. pp. 217-236.
46 *New flora and silva* 12 (1940): 180-187.
47 *New flora and silva* 12 (1940): 180-187.
48 Nelson, E. C. & McCracken, E. M. 1987. 'The brightest jewel'. *a history of the National Botanic Gardens, Glasnevin, Dublin.* Kilkenny.
49 *The gardeners' chronicle* 71 (1922): 252.
50 *The gardeners' chronicle* 27 (1902): xxviii; *The gardeners' chronicle* 46 (1909): 329; Nelson, E. C. & McCracken, E. M. 1987.

51 *Irish gardening* 1 (1906): 1; *Irish gardening* 5 (1911): 1; *Irish gardening* 10 (1915): 1.

52 *Irish gardening* 10 (1915): 1; Nelson, E. C. & McCracken, E. M. 1987.

53 *The gardeners' chronicle* 51 (1912): 252-253.

54 *The gardeners' chronicle* 51 (1912): 274-275.

55 Nelson, E. C. & McCracken, E. M. 1987; Walsh, W. F., Ross, R. I. & Nelson, E. C. 1983. *An Irish florilegium.* London.

56 *The gardeners' chronicle* 116, 1944 p. 124.

57 *New flora and silva* 2 (1930): 171-179, 230-238

58 *Journal of the Royal Horticultural Society* 74: 473-475.

59 Thomas, G. S. 1984. Lady Moore. *Moorea* 3: 51-54.

60 Cabot, F. 1984. 'As it was in the beginning'. *Bulletin of the American Rock Garden Society* 42: 22-48.

Chapter 8

1 P. Dickson (personal communication, 1978)

2 *The gardeners' chronicle* 125 (1949): 204.

3 *Rose Society of Northern Ireland annual* (1969): 45-49.

4 Nelson, E. C. & Deane, E. 1993. *Glory of Donard.A history of the Slieve Donard Nursery, Newcastle, County Down.* Belfast. pp. 1-5.

5 Nelson, E. C. 1993, in Nelson, E. C. & Deane, E., pp. 44-57.

6 Nelson, E. C. 1993, in Nelson, E. C. & Deane, E.

7 Slinger, L., quoted in Nelson, E. C. & Deane, E. 1993. p. 60.

8 Nelson, E. C. & Deane, E. 1993.

9 G. Watson (personal communication, 1978.)

10 *Irish gardening* 7 (1912): 27.

11 *Irish gardening* 5 (1910): 72

12 G. Watson (personal communication, 1978.)

13 G. Watson (personal communication, 1978.)

14 Walsh, W. F. & Nelson, E. C. 1987. *An Irish florilegium II.* London.

15 *The garden* 35 (1889): 391.

16 Both these daffodils are now classified as *N. pseudonarcissus* subsp. *moschatus.* (*Flora Europaea* vol. 5 (1980).

17 *The garden* 50 (1896): 257.

18 *The gardeners' chronicle* 30 (1901): 328.

19 W.B . Hartland & Sons [no date] *Concise list of fruit trees.* Cork.

20 *Irish farmer's and gardener's magazine* (1837): 428; Morris, M. 1985. Irradiating the present: restoring the past - the Hartlands of Cork. *Moorea* 4: 27-41.

21 *The garden* 30 (1886): 385

22 *The garden* 30 (1886): 323.

23 Willis D. 1978. *Daffodils in Ireland.* Bangor. This contains an account of Wilson's daffodil breeding.

24 *The garden* 79 (1915): 531.

25 *Daffodil year book* (1939).

26 *Daffodil year book* (1937): 34-35.

27 *Daffodil year book* (1935); *Daffodil year book* (1938).

28 Willis, D. (1978). The Guy L. Wilson daffodil garden, in *Daffodils in Ireland.* Bangor.

29 *Journal of the Royal Horticultural Society* 86 (1961): 532.

30 *Journal of the Royal Horticultural Society* 86 (1961): 532.

31 *Journal of the Royal Horticultural Society* 86 (1961): 533-534.

32 *Journal of horticulture and cottage gardener* (7 December 1893).

33 *Journal of the Royal Horticultural Society* 54 (1895)

34 R. Enraght-Moony (personal communi-cation, 1980)

35 *Proceedings of 16th International Horticultural Congress.*

36 *The gardeners' chronicle* 32 (3rd series) 1902: 3-4; Walsh, W. F. & Nelson, E. C. 1987. *An Irish florilegium II.*

37 *Journal of the Royal Horticultural Society* 27 (1902): xxxvi.

38 May Crosbie (personal communication).

39 *Journal of the Royal Horticultural Society* 48.

40 *The garden* 89 (1925): 210.

41 *Journal of the Royal Horticultural Society* 52 (1927).

42 *The garden* 89 (1925): 94.

43 *The garden* 42 (1892): 356.

44 *Journal of the Royal Horticultural Society* 72 (1947): 306-308.

45 Thomas G. S. 1971. *The old shrub roses* (4th edition) London. pp. 23, 199.

46 *Gardening illustrated* 59 (1937)

47 *The garden* 23 (1883): 276-277.

48 *The garden* 23 (1883): 281-283.

49 *The garden* 23 (1883): 317.

50 *The garden* 23 (1883): 333.

51 *The garden* 23 (1883): 362.

52 *The gardeners' chronicle* 20 (1883): 591-592.

53 *The garden* 24 (1883): 459-460.

54 *The garden* 24 (1883): 459-460.

55 *The garden* 25 (1884): 6; Grills, A. 1993. A famous Irish nursery: Daisy Hill Nurseries, Newry. *Moorea* 10: 3-10.

56 *The gardeners' chronicle* 65 (1919): 287.

57 *The gardeners' chronicle* 50 (1911): 351.

58 *Journal of the Royal Horticultural Society* 74 (1949): 36-40.

59 Nelson, E. C. 1984. *An Irish flower garden.* Kilkenny.

Chapter 9

1 *Lutyens exhibition catalogue.* London. 1981. p. 69.

2 Murdo Mackenzie (personal communi-cation).

3 Londonderry, Marchioness of. 1956. *Guide to Mount Stewart.* p. 5.

4 Tooley, M. 1985. Gertrude Jekyll at Mount Stewart. *Moorea* 5: 53-60.

5   *The gardeners' chronicle* (1959): 318.

6   *Irish homes and gardens* (c. 1910).

7   *Transactions of the Dublin Society* 1 (1799, 1800). Nelson, E. C. & McCracken, 1987. *'The brightest jewel': a history of the National Botanic Gardens, Glasnevin, Dublin.* Kilkenny,

8   *Irish farmers' and gardeners' magazine* 6 (1839): 87.

9   *Irish farmers' and gardeners' magazine* 6 (1839): 87.

10 *The gardeners' chronicle* (1865).

11 *The gardeners' chronicle* (1911): 315, 322.

12 Formerly called *Saxifraga lingulata* 'Albertii', also known at *Saxifraga lingulata* 'Albida' - Keith Index hortensis gives these as separate plants.

13 Ingwersen, W. [c. 1949]. *Handbook No. 1.* East Grinstead.

14 Taylor, G. 1934. *An account of the genus Meconopsis.* London. p. 71.

15 Nelson, E. C. 1994. Robert Lloyd Praeger's Crassulaceae: a commentary on possible type specimens in the National Botanic Gardens, Dublin, and on illustrations in the Royal Irish Academy, Dublin. *Bradleya* 11: 91-106.

16 Nelson, E.C. 1994.

17 *The gardeners' chronicle* (1911).

18 *Lissadell catalogue* (1915).

19 *Lissadell catalogue* (1931-1932).

20 *Irish gardening* 5 (1910): 72.

21 *Irish gardening* 9 (1914): 113.

22 *Irish gardening* 6 (1911): 81.

23 *Irish gardening* 6 (1911): 97.

24 *Gardening illustrated* (29 October 1911); *Gardening illustrated* (18 November 1911).

25 Mrs C. Shaw Smith (personal communication).

26 Walsh, W. F. & Nelson, E. C. 1987. *An Irish florilegium II.* London.

27 Lamb, J. G. D. 1994. Murray Hornibrook: a mystery resolved. *The new plantsman* 1: 76-77.

28 McNally, D. 1990. Murray Hornibrook (fl. 1905-1942): the father of dwarf conifers. *Moorea* 8: 23-29. Nelson, E. C. & McCracken, E. M. 1987.

29 We are indebted to Mrs Rosemary Porter, Devonshire, for many details of her uncle, Murray Hornibrook.

30 Dr E. C. Nelson (personal communication).

31 J. Colleran, personal communication.

Epilogue

1   [Brady, A.] 1992. *National Botanic Gardens, Management plan.* Dublin.

2   For descriptions of some present-day Irish gardens see George M. & Bowe, P. 1986. *The gardens of Ireland.* London; Connolly, S. & Dillon, H. 1986. *In an Irish garden.* London.

3   Nelson, E. C. 1991. Reserved to the Fellows': four centuries of gardens at Trinity College, Dublin, in Holland, C. (editor). *Trinity College Dublin and the idea of a university.* Dublin. pp. 185-222

Editorial note.

In September 1995 the statutory powers and functions of the Commissioners of Public Works with regard to heritage matters were transferred to the Minister of Arts, Culture and the Gaeltacht. Thus all the state-owned gardens in the Republic of Ireland hitherto taken care of by the Office of Public Works are now managed by the Department of Arts, Culture and the Gaeltacht.
